HEART *of* IRON

HEART
of IRON

MY JOURNEY FROM TRANSPLANT PATIENT

TO IRONMAN TRIATHLETE

KYLE GARLETT

GCLS/MULLICA HILL BRANCH
389 WOLFERT STATION ROAD
MULLICA HILL, NJ 08062

CHICAGO
REVIEW
PRESS

Library of Congress Cataloging-in-Publication Data

Garlett, Kyle.

Heart of iron : my journey from transplant patient to ironman triathlete / Kyle Garlett.
p. cm.

Summary: "Throughout his life, there was nothing Kyle Garlett hated more than losing, and he knew early on that four diagnoses of cancer could not match his spirit of competition. His appetite for victory and success and his love of life pushed him past his health hurdles-including a bone marrow transplant, hip replacement, and a heart transplant-and into the greatest challenge of his life: the Ironman Triathlon World Championship. Kyle tells his amazing life story, beginning with his diagnosis of lymphoma and continuing through years of chemotherapy that destroyed his joints and weakened his heart, leading up to his journey to the Ironman Triathlon, in which he competed not once but twice. His miraculous recovery and athleticism are recounted, along with his becoming an Olympic torch bearer, a Leukemia and Lymphoma Society spokesperson, and a motivational speaker"— Provided by publisher.

ISBN 978-1-61374-005-7 (hardback)
1. Garlett, Kyle. 2. Track and field athletes—United States—Biography.
3. Cancer—Patients—United States—Biography. 4. Heart—Transplantation—
Patients—United States—Biography. 5. Ironman triathlons—United States. I. Title.

GV697.G37G37 2011
796.42092—dc23
[B]

2011019704

Interior design: Jonathan Hahn
All interior images from the author's collection unless otherwise noted.

Copyright © 2011 by Kyle Garlett
All rights reserved
First edition
Published by Chicago Review Press, Incorporated
814 North Franklin Street
Chicago, Illinois 60610
ISBN 978-1-61374-005-7
Printed in the United States of America
5 4 3 2 1

For my wife, Carrie, the bravest woman I know
For my parents, who taught me how to love life
For my doctors and nurses, who gave me that life to love

For all newly diagnosed cancer patients, please believe
For everyone waiting for an organ, your call will come

For all organ donors and their families,
"Thank you" hardly scratches the surface

CONTENTS

PROLOGUE

OCTOBER 10, 2009

It was the moment I was dreading most: just floating, waiting, anticipating.

I really had no idea what to expect from myself in those last few minutes of countdown. How does anyone know? How does anyone truly prepare for a moment like this?

The moments and minutes to follow, sure. That path was mostly set. You could spend a small fortune and fill a small library buying all the books that tell you how to prepare for the day that follows. But the final minutes that ticked toward 7 AM remained an individualized agonizing mystery.

Which is why I was so surprised to find myself treading water, unexpectedly calm and relaxed. Instead of the churning stomach and racing mind that I had anticipated, I was actually enjoying the moment. The water was warm and clear and beautiful. Kailua-Kona Bay is thousands of miles from the place where Ferdinand Magellan first gazed upon the world's largest ocean, bestowing upon it the Latin name *Mare Pacificum*. But on this morning, in this very special place where the earth is still being made anew by active lava flows on Kilauea, the Pacific was indeed a peaceful sea.

The morning sun dazzled, breaking over Mauna Loa and illuminating the shifting kaleidoscope of colors dotting the ocean floor. The crowd, numbering beyond twenty thousand, was spirited and enthusiastic.

Regardless of personal acquaintance, your day's mission was theirs. Simply put, the energy of the moment was transcendent and sublime, and I could have floated in it forever.

But then, with a cannon shot marking the start of the seven o'clock hour, we were off headlong into the boil of thrashing arms and kicking legs.

I've heard it said that the start of an Ironman triathlon is like swimming inside a washing machine set on heavy duty. It's the full-contact portion of the sport, and it's no stranger to the occasional busted nose or blackened eye. When nearly two thousand people are all trying to swim along the same buoy-directed path, there isn't often a more expedient avenue to get around slower swimmers than to go right over them. And that quite often leads to a stiff kick to the face. It's no way to start a 2.4-mile swim or an entire day that will require you to cover 140.6 self-powered miles by the stroke of midnight.

As one of those "slower" swimmers and as someone who didn't feel the need to taste his own blood to begin the longest day of his life, I seeded myself appropriately. My pre-cannon-fire float was done on the fringes of the main pack, safely away from the soon-to-be-exploding ocean.

This was, of course, a race. And the shortest and quickest distance between two points has always been a straight line. So by strategically choosing discretion over definitude, I was adding a minute or more to my swim time. But a 2.4-mile swim was already going to take me close to two hours. What was a handful of seconds really going to matter?

As we began the swim, the remaining prerace jitters quickly transferred into powering kinetic energy, and I felt great. I settled into the solid rhythm of my training, a good pace and breathing pattern that would take me 1.2 miles out to sea, then back.

In the water or out, I will never be mistaken for Michael Phelps. Or, for that matter, someone who swam competitively for his high school junior-varsity team. I am five foot eight on my particularly tall days and barrel chested with a matching set of hips. While the long and lean swimmers cut through the water like an America's Cup racing yacht, I look like the tugboat sent to retrieve those yachts if they ever snap a mast.

Don't get me wrong. A tugboat is plenty seaworthy and more than capable of swimming 2.4 miles. It's just not very efficient or aesthetically pleasing when doing so. And it will never become a model for those looking to illustrate the perfect gliding swim stroke.

Which, I suppose, only adds to the irony of having so many spotters on surfboards and TV cameras in boats following my progress. You can rest assured, however, that none of that tape has found its way into an Ironman instructional video.

For those of you who don't know, an Ironman follows up the 2.4-mile swim with a 112-mile bike ride. Since this wasn't just any Ironman, but *the* Ironman—the Ford Ironman World Championship in Kona, Hawaii— after getting out of the water, I would be looking at 112 miles on my bike over blistering hot lava flats and against race-famous head winds.

On a bike or off, I will never be mistaken for Lance Armstrong (although out of the saddle, we actually do have several similarities and bear many of the same scars, both inside and out). For me, 112 miles is long and torturous. Throw in air temperatures in the upper nineties, lava fields that add another twenty degrees of reflected heat, and winds that turn your downhills into climbs up the Pyrenees, and the 2.4-mile swim becomes just an amuse-bouche on Chef Ironman's plate of delights.

"Swimming within yourself"—that is, keeping your focus, sticking to the plan, recognizing your strengths and weaknesses but not pushing beyond them to where it might hurt you miles down the road—becomes paramount. Conservation of energy is key. The swim is just the prologue of the book to be written that day. To burn through it too quickly, at least for an athlete like me, is to burn out too soon. The tank can't be empty until mile 140, the final mile of the full marathon that follows the 112-mile bike.

So as I swam that morning, I focused on staying steady. Reaching up and pulling down. Climbing the ladder in the water. Moving steadily along the row of buoys that formed the out-and-back course.

As I reached the right-hand 180-degree turn at the furthest buoy out to sea, I got my first real sense of just how far out I had gone. During the first 1.2 miles, there was nothing to reference but orange marker buoys contrasted against the never-ending blue of the Pacific Ocean. The horizon was completely empty. But now, as I raced back toward the coast of Hawaii, the Big Island didn't seem so big. Or at all close.

At the sight of being so far away from safe land, I felt a brief flow of panic attempting to surface. And if it wasn't for the person on the surfboard directly to my right, who I could see each time I turned my head to breathe, it no doubt would have. But with him and his board in sight and my other senses detecting several other volunteers in my general vicinity, I kept it together. I tried to stay in the moment and remain focused on my stroke.

By this time, the crowd of competing swimmers around me had thinned to a trickle. This was expected, of course. As I already mentioned, this wasn't just any Ironman race. This was the World Championship. This was a field of the finest athletes in the world. It consisted of men and women who, unlike me, very well could be mistaken for Michael Phelps or Lance Armstrong.

As a sportswriter for years, I had covered and written about groups of athletes such as these—the kind of athlete who seems superheroesque in his or her ability to push the physical body beyond all logical human boundaries. I'd just never pictured myself among them, even if it was only for the start of the race and I possessed no actual hope of keeping pace with them.

I wasn't a complete fish out of water (no pun intended) trying to finish an Ironman that day. Sure, there were the physical limitations of genetics, as well as other issues. But mentally, I felt capable. I had advantages and experiences that many of the great athletes tackling the course that day didn't. And they were experiences I planned to lean on when the road eventually got rocky, as it was guaranteed to do.

With no one and nothing to look at and the metronome of my swim stroke (reach, pull, repeat) droning on in my head, my thoughts began to wander.

I am doing the Ironman! Unbelievable! Twenty years ago this was the furthest thing from mind. Forget twenty years—try two years. Not only am I at the Super Bowl, I'm actually on the field!

Not to be repetitive or show a lack of vocabulary within the recesses of my inner thoughts: *Really! Unbelievable!*

THERE ARE ESSENTIALLY three ways to get into the Ford Ironman World Championship in Kona. You can qualify, which basically means that, in your age group, you are one of the world's elite long-distance triathletes. Nearly 90 percent of the athletes who race in Kona each year get there by qualifying—which would also explain why, by the swim turnaround, I was swimming largely by myself.

Ironman also holds a lottery for two hundred additional race slots. But since this is a worldwide event that serves as a beckoning mecca for even the most casual of triathletes, each year there are several thousand applicants willing to spend forty dollars for a chance at one of those cherished slots. For the lottery winners, it truly is winning the lottery. The chance to race in Kona is likely a once-in-a-lifetime occurrence for them.

And finally, there are the special-interest athletes, those with stories. There is the inspirational Jon Blais, who completed the Ironman in 2005, five months after he was diagnosed with amyotrophic lateral sclerosis (ALS), or Lou Gehrig's disease. There are perhaps the most famous Ironman competitors never to win the race, Rick and Dick Hoyt, better known as Team Hoyt. Rick is a quadriplegic with cerebral palsy; Dick is his father. Together they have completed the Ironman six times.

Then there is me. I didn't qualify for Ironman. I never will. And when it comes to beating the odds of chance and fitting into a very small and positive percentage of the population (for example, winning the Kona lottery), historically I haven't fared well.

I was at Ironman as a special-interest athlete. Like Jon Blais and Rick and Dick Hoyt before me, I have a story.

HEART of IRON

1

1989

Twenty years before I found myself swimming in the Pacific Ocean with the best triathletes on Planet Earth, I was your typical teenager growing up in Wichita, Kansas. For those of you who didn't maturate in a mild-mannered Midwestern "almost-city" like Wichita, "typical" for a teenager in his final year of high school meant working on his college résumé on weekdays and driving up and down Douglas Boulevard or parking at the neighborhood fast-food restaurant on the weekends.

Once upon a time, when there were regular cattle drives up the Great Plains, Wichita was an important way station for cowboys, their cows, and the businesses of ill repute that served them. And because of whom that crowd drew to town—including a young Billy the Kid, among others—it was also the former home of legendary lawmen Wyatt Earp and Bat Masterson. The section of town known as Delano, where the majority of the gambling, drinking, philandering, and gunfighting took place, made the Atlantic City of the 1920s, as seen in *Boardwalk Empire*, seem like a sleepy and virtuous Victorian village.

By 1977, when my college professor parents, Fred and Marti Garlett, were hired to teach at Friends University in Wichita, public carousing and uncontrolled gunplay had become a thing of the past. The cows of the nineteenth century had been replaced by twentieth-century airplane manufacturing. And the neighborhood of Delano featured more than fifteen churches and a minor-league baseball stadium. Any mixed-use commercial developments that combined saloons with brothels were noticeably absent.

From kindergarten through twelfth grade, I called the west side of Wichita home. It was suburban, with large neighborhoods, old trees, and quiet residential streets. The combination of the time, the 1970s and '80s, and place made the neighbors friendly and the safety and security of children playing in yards and streets a given. Bikes were ridden, but never with a helmet. Walks home from friends' houses after dark were made without second thoughts. And there was a sense of understanding that Saturday was for soccer, or whatever sport was in season, and Sunday was for church and family gatherings. It wasn't quite *Leave It to Beaver*—in our world, June Cleaver had a job and rarely did housework while wearing pearls—but it wasn't *The Sopranos* either.

Initially my father, born and raised in Kansas City, was the band director at the college where my parents taught. He'd been a musician all his life and was a killer on the trumpet, leading off Wichita's annual Fourth of July fireworks display with the playing of "Taps." He'd led a jazz band, a marching band, and a concert band, and many nights of my youth had been spent watching him conduct. I'm a lot like my father, both in looks and in even temperament, and no doubt some of that similarity consciously comes from idolization and my feeling as a child that he was the coolest guy I knew. Imagine, a job where you get to perform onstage wearing a blue tuxedo with ruffles. (Remember, this was the late 1970s and early '80s. Ruffles were hot.)

By the time my Wichita school days were winding down, my dad had left behind his baton and trumpet and moved from the music department to continuing and adult education. He was working on his doctorate at Columbia University—light-years away from Wichita and Friends University—and the part-time program at Columbia took him to New York a few days each month.

My mother was a Chicagoan who came to Kansas for college, where she met and married my dad. She'd taught kindergarten through third grade before our move to Wichita, but she became a teacher of teachers—

a professor of elementary education—at Friends. There she extended her influence on children's education from just one classroom to literally hundreds.

Where my dad and I can be seen as quiet and closed on occasion, my mother is not. She enjoys talking about almost anything, including emotions and feelings (imagine that). I have heard the phrase "A penny for your thoughts" more times than I care to remember. For my thoughts, a penny has always felt like a woefully cheap offer. In the case of my mom, you'd be overpaying. Just wait five seconds, and she's sure to voice those thoughts without the need of a one-cent bribe.

The driving personality of the family, my mom had an unapologetic openness that also made her the perfect selection for her second but most noteworthy job in Wichita: that of *Romper Room* teacher. She landed the most visible television role for children in the entire state when I was still in kindergarten, which instantly made me the most well-known kid in school.

Miss Marti, as she was known in the *Romper Room* world, was a genuine celebrity. During dinners out, she was often approached for autographs. One year, with a much older and larger me by her side as Do Bee, the giant bee that came on the show to pass along lessons and tips to the children, she blew the whistle to start the opening parade at the Ringling Bros. and Barnum & Bailey Circus. We also made a yearly tour through the ALCO retail stores that dotted the plains of western Kansas for fan autographs and pictures with Do Bee (me).

For nearly a decade, my mom juggled the two jobs—that of college professor and children's television host—and two personalities. But by the time my dad was making his frequent trips to New York and I was beginning my final year of high school, she'd moved on from both and was working as an administrator for the Wichita public school district.

As I began my senior year in high school, I was looking to the years beyond it by continuing to add to my résumé. I'd been in debate for two years, I'd been in choir since the beginning of high school (my dad's instrumental instincts weren't passed on to me), and just a couple months earlier, I'd won the job of senior class president. I played team sports carlier in my high school days, which would have made me typical on many a college application. But due to a lethal mix of speed and agility that pushed me into playing the positions of baseball catcher, football nose guard, and soccer goalie, my confining levels of athleticism landed me on the sidelines by the time I was a senior. Sadly, the desire to be Major League Baseball's next George Brett is in itself not enough to actually make it happen.

By early August 1989, I had long given up my dream of playing professional sports; I'd since switched my focus to talking about them. The University of Missouri was my targeted college of choice, and I planned to major in broadcast journalism. My long-term goal was to be a sports anchor in a major television market or the play-by-play voice of a professional team by the time I turned thirty. I was seventeen years old, and thirty was about as long-term as my brain could comprehend. Anything older, and I would become my parents.

Columbia, Missouri, was still a year away. Until that future came, there was a fall of Friday night football and postgame parties to attend. (Just because I wasn't on the team didn't mean I couldn't hang out with them.) There were girls to chase, and hopefully date. There was a cakewalk of a class schedule that was the envy of everyone exhibiting the early symptoms of senioritis. With early admission to Mizzou locked in and most of the academic heavy lifting done the previous two semesters, I flanked my AP English and calculus classes with two hours of music, an hour of debate, and a pair of honor study halls—which made for a mockery of the word "honor."

A couple of weeks before classes started, I went shoe shopping with my mother. The pre-school-year new-shoes shopping trip is also very typical of Midwestern life, as I'm sure it is elsewhere. The habitually humdrum nature of the end-of-summer ceremony also makes it infinitely forgettable. I'd been on nearly a dozen other such excursions with my parents over the years. Or least I assume I have. I had shoes as a kid, shoes I didn't pay for. And the parental units seem to be the most likely suspects. But I don't remember any of those outings.

Except this time.

The reduced rumble of the passing mall traffic was unremarkable in its banality. This was 1989, but since I didn't purchase a pair of the newly released Reebok Pumps—I left those to Dominique Wilkins and Spud Webb—there was nothing memorable about the shoes that I left the store with that afternoon. The sneaker peddler, clad in a referee's uniform, looked just as ridiculous and unfit to pass official judgment on any level of sporting event as all the rest before him.

The nuts and bolts of our afternoon at the mall were as equally commonplace as all the rest. And I'm sure my attitude—that of a seventeen-year-old who was slightly disagreeable at the notion of spending a Saturday afternoon with Mom at the mall, but very agreeable to the use of her credit card—was consistently teenage. What did stand out, however, was the lump that I felt along the right side of my neck, just under the jaw.

It was fairly large, about half the size of a golf ball. It was also hard like a golf ball. But it was absent any pain or discomfort when I pushed and probed it with my fingers, which I found myself unable to stop doing. It was probably this lack of associated pain that kept it from detection until that moment.

I sized it up with fingers, trying to use my somewhat limited knowledge of the human body to figure out what it was. When that didn't jog loose any ingrained anatomical instruction, I turned to my mother. Despite two graduate degrees and an adult lifetime of teaching college students, she was just as puzzled. We sat there on the wood-slatted bench, the two of us, waiting for my senior year's tennis shoes to be brought from the back room, but now with a very obvious cloud of nervous energy hanging over our heads.

In dealing with my parents, my modus operandi was usually silence and secrecy. I don't have any children of my own. But I imagine that the closed-mouth, keep-your-feelings-to-yourself policy that I largely lived by is pretty typical for a teenager, especially a teenage boy. Although as I get older, and allegedly wiser, I also recognize that a part of that policy was born of my own personality.

This unofficial adaptation of this approach frustrated my mom. She prefers open books, while I really like how they look on the shelf with neatly organized spines all reading in the same direction. I have since slowly opened the doors of expressing myself and sharing those secrets and thoughts (writing a tell-all book should qualify), but her frustration still exists. I'll never get to where she is, and she'll never fully accept that I can't be coaxed along further.

The bottom line is, I hate big deals. They're hassles. So if something I'm thinking or feeling might lead to a big deal (that is, the worried declarations of a mother that her son needs to see a doctor, and quickly), I usually stay silent. But that time in 1989, I didn't. I did the exact opposite of stay silent.

Later that day and into the next, as I analyzed my surprisingly open and communicative response, the truth landed hard. I was open because I was honestly scared.

It was probably nothing, I told myself. My knowledge of the human body was limited, but it wasn't a vacuum of ignorance either. Common sense gleaned from the minimal knowledge that had been imparted to me by the Kansas public school system (no offense, I like Kansas, but let's be honest—it's not exactly thought of as the bellwether of scientific enlightenment) also told me in a fairly authoritative voice that it was probably nothing. There are a hundred reasons why a neck gland would swell.

But within that hundred or so nothings, there were also a few somethings. And that's what I couldn't shake.

Earlier in the summer of 1989, I traveled abroad pretty extensively. The year before, my family hosted an exchange student from Cancún, Mexico, so it only seemed polite to have his seventeen-year-old American brother spend the month of June with him on the Mexican Riviera. It was a good time had by all, especially me, but according to my doctor, it was also a possible source of an infection.

Lump suspect number one.

After June had passed and I'd returned home to the States very uncharacteristically tan, I quickly repacked for a trip to Europe with my high school choir. July 14, 1989, was the French bicentennial, and we were lucky enough to be one of several American choirs that had been invited to Paris to perform at the Eiffel Tower. For two weeks, we bused around western Europe, being American high school kids, taking in the sights and sounds and occasionally singing. Westminster Abbey and St. Paul's Cathedral in London also highlighted the performance itinerary.

I'm all about experiencing another culture when traveling internationally. For example, when my German class took a spring-break trip to Germany, Austria, and Switzerland a year earlier, I drank beer. It would have been rude not to. But in France, I was never able to give myself over to the customary local cuisine. *Tête de veau*, also known as calf's head, never made it past my lips. I am proud to say that *boudin noir*, or black blood sausage, is something that I have never eaten. And this Kraft Macaroni & Cheese kid will never consider escargot, bulots, or any other shell-dwelling, slug-type creature to be food.

My doctor, however, not trusting that I'd stuck solely to Parisian Burger Kings, considered the European travels to be lump suspect number two.

Thinking it was probably an infection of some kind, likely picked up in one of the five countries where I'd spent my summer, the doctor prescribed an antibiotic. Two weeks of pills and all should be well.

It wasn't.

The days passed, classes started, I turned eighteen, the prescription ran its course, and the lump refused to respond. So back to the doctor I went.

This didn't particularly worry me. Just because it wasn't an easy fix didn't mean it wasn't fixable. And as far as I could tell, my parents weren't particularly worried either. When you hear hooves, you think horses. And we were still very much in that phase of discovery. Thoughts about zebras were still a long way off.

The doctor's diagnosis and suggested course of treatment at my second visit was more of the same, just a little more intense. His thought—and to this day I have no reason to think that he was practicing anything but sound and solid medicine—was that I was still suffering from an infection. An antibiotic, just one with a little more oomph, remained the most likely cure.

That is, until two more weeks passed, the prescription again ran its course, and not only did the lump remain, but two new, slightly smaller lumps on the other side of my neck had appeared. As before, there was no pain or tenderness with these new lumps. I could move them a little, each like a small marble attached to a short tether. Every time I'd finish exploring their limited range of real estate, the two fresh protuberances would pop back into place.

The mystery deepened, as did my doctor's concern. He never told me what he thought the ultimate diagnosis might be at that point. It would have been speculation, and that's not what he'd been trained or paid to do. But no doubt he had an educated guess. Instead I was referred to an ear, nose, and throat doctor, who could presumably unlock the riddle definitively.

My level of anxiety grew, as did my parents'. But there was still no talk of worst-case scenarios when we sat around the dinner table. Physically, I felt just fine. And other than making trips to the doctor's office, our busy lives continued along uninterrupted. I've always been good at compartmentalizing potential issues from actual problems. When you feel healthy and life's other realities demand your full attention, it becomes fairly easy to do. The upcoming visit to the ENT was just one more thing to place on my after-school plate.

It's NOT EVERY day that you have a monumentally significant, life-halting, life-altering conversation with your doctor. I've been so blessed to have no less than five of these conversations, the first coming on September 14, 1989.

I remember the exact date because it also happens to be my mother's birthday. She and I went together to see the ENT, who, as luck would have it, turned out to be the husband of a pediatrician whom my mother frequently scheduled for informational spots on *Romper Room*. It was good to have that connection, making him a friendly face by proxy. But the words that came out of his mouth when we first arrived were anything but welcome.

"Biopsy." "Lymphoma." "Cancer."

In an effort to slow down the rising blood pressures in the room, he stated quite flatly, and without a hint of irony (which is how the following statement should always be delivered), "If you're going to get cancer, this is the one to have."

I was a newly turned eighteen-year-old in the first month of my senior year. Doc, for the sake of argument, let's say I'm not going to get cancer. What might it be then?

There was no other possible outcome given. I was still a day away from the biopsy and more than a week away from any final pathologist's report; yet here I was getting the "cancer pep talk" before a malignancy had even been diagnosed. I appreciated the efforts of the friendly face. I believed him when he said that lymphoma was the kind of cancer you wanted. But I didn't want any kind of cancer, good, bad, terminal, curable, or otherwise. In that very moment, I even promised to sever all ties with friends born between June 22 and July 23. That's how dedicated I was to being cancer free.

My internal protests and self-declarations to stuff my face full of antioxidant-rich berries the moment I left the building couldn't slow the chain of unfolding events. Surgery and a biopsy were scheduled for the very next morning.

IN THE BRILLIANT 1987 Coen brothers' film, *Raising Arizona* (which to this day remains in my top-five movies of all time), H. I. McDunnough has a dream about the "lone biker of the apocalypse . . . a man with all the powers of hell at his command." The biker leaves a path of destruction as he blazes across the empty desert, shooting lizards with shotguns and blowing up bunnies with hand grenades. Even the desert flowers burst into flames in the wake of his passing motorcycle.

The visual of the scene plays out on a lonely desert road with nothing around but the passing asphalt and painted centerline. As my mother and I made the predawn drive on the largely empty interstate to the east side of Wichita and the hospital that awaited me, I couldn't help but think of that scene—the gathering storm, the helplessness to stop it, and the desolation of the drive that ends with damnation.

In the movie, H.I.'s unsure if the biker is a dream or a vision. But "The Fury"—as he describes Florence Arizona's reaction to the discovery of her missing baby—is all too real. It's also the thing that unleashes the biker of the apocalypse.

My situation that morning wasn't nearly so dramatic. In fact, if I hadn't been driving across town on a lonely highway with the centerline ominously illuminated by our headlights, or if I didn't love the movie so much, the parallels most likely would have never entered my head. But who can account for the thoughts, conscious and otherwise, that stream through the brain at five in the morning?

Maybe it was the earliness of the hour or that I'd moved further along into the film and was now silently replaying the best chase scene in the history of Hollywood ("Son, you got a panty on your head"). But the thirty-minute drive across town to the hospital saw no more than five words pass between my mother and me. I was not trying to reclaim my role as the silent and secretive one. There was simply nothing to say. We weren't just thinking zebras; we were expecting them. And the expectations behind that reality left us both mute.

As surgeries go, this was really nothing more than a change-the-oil operation. A small incision would be made along the side of my neck (I realized that "small" was a relative term to future procedures), allowing the removal of one of my swollen lymph nodes. With premeds, surgical prep, the actual procedure, and the closing sutures, the entire thing lasted less than an hour.

My doctor was great and quite chatty for such an early morning. He talked and walked me through everything that he was doing. Of course, since it was happening less than two inches from my left ear, I could also hear everything: the snipping and cutting, the sizzle of the cauterization, and the final tugging and clipping of the stitching. But the steady explanations coming from the man with the scalpel kept me mostly at ease—well, him, and a significant assist from his two very talented partners, Valium and Demerol.

Back in recovery, I sat with my mother, still not saying much. The fog of my meds slowly lifted. As they did, the haziness that had me comparing the skills of my surgical team to that of pioneers like Starzl, Barnard, and DeBakey was slowly replaced by the crushing enormity of what I'd just gone through.

It was no liver or heart transplant. I wasn't having a brain tumor removed or one of my appendages amputated. And I knew that at the end of the day, my worst-case scenario was the diagnosis of a very treatable cancer.

But that word—"cancer"—can't be prettied up with chocolate sprinkles of curability. With much respect to disparaged women everywhere, cancer is the mother of all *c* words. The shared imagery that all human beings have when presented with the word "cancer" is one of horrific pain and a stolen life. One can argue the complete accuracy of these images and the phrase "stolen life," as I often do now more than two decades later. But for the inexperienced teenager living in the 1980s, cancer was as bad as it got.

But I was still several uncertain days away from the definitive diagnosis. My doctor came into the recovery room to see me before I left. He explained the biopsy to my mother and told us that before anything could be determined with certainty, a pathologist needed to spend some quality time with my lymph node. And just how many days that might take was also an uncertainty.

"Having just seen the lymph node, what do you think?" I said.

He started to answer me, then sputtered, and eventually stopped. "Let's just wait to see what the pathologist says."

And that, with his eyes and his tone, said it all.

ELEVEN DAYS LATER on September 26, I knew the results were coming. A few days after my biopsy, word had come down from my doctor that the lymph node and the pathologist's report were on their way to Yale. A diagnosis had been made, but very talented Ivy League doctors were needed for confirmation. Although I also knew that shipping off part of me to New Haven, Connecticut, was unlikely to be triggered by a benign tumor. No one gets a second opinion when they're handed a favorable diagnosis.

As I pulled into our driveway on the twenty-sixth and opened the automatic garage door, I was confronted by the usual suspects that make up your typical Midwestern garage: the lawn mower, snowblower, various tools (varying widely in their levels of use), garbage cans, paint cans, cans filled with cans, a homemade model train set that had traveled to homes in three states because my father couldn't bear to part with it, and both of my parents' cars.

It was 3:15 on a Tuesday afternoon. My parents both had busy workdays that stretched well beyond my day in school. I certainly didn't know what their class or meeting schedules were for the day, or any day, but I knew it was highly unusual for both of them to be home at 3:15 on a Tuesday. It wouldn't take both of them to tell me, "No cancer, no problem."

I entered the house through the garage and into the laundry room, punching the automatic garage-door opener behind me as I passed. I made my way past the adjoining kitchen and into the living room, wading through the heaviness of the air. There were almost no lights on. Even though it was still midafternoon, the layout of that portion of the house had east-facing windows and almost always required lights. And there, in the darkening gloom of the living room, eyes fixed on me, sat my parents.

My dad, back in town after his September trip to Columbia, was the first to break the silence. "Why don't you sit down? We need to talk to you."

He'd missed the biopsy, which I'm sure weighed heavily on him. My dad is old school when it comes to his family. It's his job to protect those whom he loves. He is the oldest of three children, and his father, my grandfather—another Fred to whom I looked strikingly similar—spent his entire adult life severely disabled. Many of the male burdens of his 1950s household fell on his shoulders at a very early age. Now, as my father several decades later, he preferred to shoulder the load. It's who he is.

I slid silently into the chair between my parents, waiting for more.

My mom spoke next, getting straight to the point. "You have lymphoma."

My mom is a published author three times over and takes great pride in her use of the English language. Before I'd arrived home from school, she'd been living with my diagnosis for a couple of hours and had played every conceivable version of verbal disclosure in her head. But there is no gentle way to break that news. The prettiest rhetorical pillows do not soften the blow. So instead, she ripped off the Band-Aid and cut to the chase.

I stayed silent.

There were no passionate denials, bargainings with God, or spontaneous utterances of grief. Only quiet acceptance.

It was exactly what I had expected to hear since even before the biopsy. I'd become resigned to this specific diagnosis some days ago. But still, I hadn't quite been prepared for the finality of those three words: "You have lymphoma."

IN THE FOURTH grade, everyone in my class got to pick a topic for an independent study project. I chose to study the Titanic.

My healthy interest in the infamous ship and subsequent disaster turned into a bit of a nerd's fascination with the subject. I bought a detailed model of the Titanic, which my father and I painstakingly worked on for at least an hour each evening over the course of three months. With my model complete and my fascination only growing, I joined the Titanic Historical Society, becoming the youngest member in its Wichita chapter. I attended the annual banquet held every April 15 to commemorate the day of its sinking. (My model sat proudly on the head table, next to the president of the chapter and the mayor of Wichita.)

I even went on local television, with model in tow, as a "Titanic expert." (I had pretty solid connections with the host of a particular kids' show on Wichita's ABC affiliate.)

But at the moment I found out I had cancer and heard those three words, "You have lymphoma," my life, cruising along at top speed without a care in the world, in need of no lifeboat drills, had struck its own iceberg.

Like the ship in those initial moments after impact, I had no idea just how disastrous the collision would ultimately be. Most of the iceberg, and my future life as a cancer patient, remained hidden beneath the dark and moonless surface.

2

STAGING

I wouldn't necessarily say that I crave the spotlight and look for attention, but I don't shy away from it either. When there is attention on me, either through being on a stage, on camera, or just being a person of interest, I remain comfortable. And it's always been like this.

As previously mentioned, my mother had been the *Romper Room* teacher for the state of Kansas and on television every weekday morning for a number of years, starting when I was in kindergarten. Because of her TV chops and my willingness to work for free, I landed a couple of local commercials as a kid. I was also selected to play one of the leads in my first-grade class's production of *Santarella*—a Christmas version of *Cinderella*.

One would assume, of course, having seen the cover of this book, that the lead role I was given was that of Prince Charming. Well, you would be wrong. I auditioned for and was unanimously selected by the class of six- and seven-year-olds to play Cinderella's evil stepmother. (I didn't take the landslide vote to be a mandate of my skills as a thespian, so much as a classroom of kids finding delight in watching a boy pretend to be an old woman.)

Throughout my school days, I'd appeared in more plays and musicals, shown up on television a few more times, taken up debate, and even run for and won the job of senior class president in the final weeks of my junior year. So maybe I craved the spotlight a little. I wasn't exactly an eighties version of a Kardashian, but I wasn't a wallflower either.

So there was a part of me, I have to admit, that enjoyed some of the attention that came along with being the guy in school who had cancer. It was a small part. As I began the staging process of the disease and began to find out just what it meant to be a cancer patient, that part shrank faster than a souvenir T-shirt bought on Venice Beach. But initially there was a little pride in being the guy who was going to take on this challenge.

It was most likely an idiotic combination of cockiness and naïveté, but a part of me actually saw the diagnosis as a challenge. *OK, so this is going to change things a little bit, but I can beat it. And think about it; how cool will it be to begin college as Kyle, cancer survivor?*

Not to worry. The coolness factor was stripped away rather decisively the first time I met with my brand-new oncologist.

FOR PEOPLE NOT from Wichita, it can sound like the end of the earth, like Dorothy's lone way station on the road to Oz, filled with tumbleweeds, wheat fields, and the occasional gun-rack-adorned pickup truck. The image of the city was only further denigrated when John Hughes decided to make Wichita the ever-so-awful landing site of Steve Martin and John Candy's weather-diverted flight to Chicago in his 1987 film *Planes, Trains, and Automobiles.*

The sneering disgust with which Steve Martin's character, Neal Page, said, "I could be stuck in Wichita?" sent a shockwave of funk throughout the city, which would only lift a year later when hometown hero Barry Sanders won the Heisman Trophy.

The reality of Wichita is that it's a city of high-tech manufacturing. Cessna, Beechcraft, and Learjet (now a part of Bombardier) all maintain their headquarters in Wichita, and Boeing and Airbus maintain a manufacturing presence in the city nicknamed "Air Capital of the World."

Many great entrepreneurial and entertainment minds hale from Wichita. In 1958, Dan and Frank Carney, graduates of the University of Wichita (now Wichita State), borrowed six hundred dollars from their mother to open the first Pizza Hut. There are now some thirty-four thousand Pizza Huts around the world. Koch Industries, the nation's second-largest privately owned company, was founded and is headquartered in Wichita. If you've ever enjoyed a television episode or film version of *Star Trek*, you can thank a Wichita native, actress Laurel Goodwin. Before there was James T. Kirk, Leonard "Bones" McCoy, or Montgomery "Scott" Scotty, there was Yeoman J. M. Colt, as portrayed by Goodwin in the 1965 rarely seen original pilot episode of *Star Trek*. On the back of her eight lines of dialogue (four of which constituted "Yes, sir," "Yes, ma'am," or "Captain?"), a franchise was launched, and a fringe genre was made mainstream.

If you find yourself unimpressed with the influence that Laurel Goodwin has had on American history and culture, Wichita also boasts hometown connections to Robert Ballard, the oceanographer and explorer who discovered the wreck of the Titanic; decorated journalist Jim Lehrer; multiple-platinum-selling musician Joe Walsh; and the best reality-TV host working today, Jeff Probst.

Wichita also has some really great doctors. At least that's my experience, in hindsight. But the very first day spent with my very first oncologist left me more than a little guarded.

When I first met with my oncologist, I was naturally scared. I'd long since graduated from the fire-truck exam tables and lollipop bribes of my pediatrician. But when you're eighteen, it's hard not to think of an oncologist as an "adult" doctor. People go to see him when they're old and dying. I was young and living. My biggest health challenge should have been trying to stay pimple free for my senior pictures. Instead, I was talking with the man who would hopefully get me cancer free in time for the rest of my life.

He was all business when he first came into the cold and colorless exam room. Very few pleasantries, even fewer explanations. Not exactly a people person. We got right down to business with the first order of the day, a bone marrow biopsy.

Those three words, "bone marrow biopsy," danced in the air for a moment before penetrating my head.

"Does that hurt?" I naïvely asked.

"Not usually," he lied.

Over the next ten minutes, I found out just how egregious his breach of trust was. To call his casual assurance a "lie" is akin to saying that Mrs. O'Leary's cow started a campfire. In no universe is there a being who would describe the taking of one's bone marrow as anything other than agonizing.

The procedure, which is all part of the process to see just how far advanced the disease is (referred to as staging), starts innocently enough, minus a touch of dignity. After you drop your pants to expose the hips, the skin above your pelvic crest (known as the *ilium*, for those of you playing the Latinized, medical-school version of Operation at home) is numbed with a shot, and a small incision is made to expose the bone. The hip is the physician's preferred target because of its nearness to the surface and relative thick density. But the numbing medication can only go so far. After you run through flesh and work down to the bone, Lidocaine loses its usefulness.

At this point, the doctor takes what can best be described as a miniature apple corer and shoves it into the bone as far it will go. Bone is . . . well, *bone*, so you can imagine how smoothly the shoving-it-in process goes. On the scale of dissection tranquility, it's somewhere between a knife through warm butter and a claw hammer on granite, cheating toward the latter.

But after shoving, twisting, and finally getting it into the bone, the doctor's battle has just begun. He now needs to tug out the ensnared chunk of bone, allowing access to the marrow underneath. And sadly, the only way to do that is for him to literally pull as hard as he can while two or three nurses hold the patient on the table. It's a game of bone tug-of-war that would make Spanish Inquisitor General Tomás de Torquemada proud.

I'll concede the possibility that my bones are particularly tough. I do like cheese in all its many forms. I've joined the rest of the fat-conscious world in my adult years, but back when I was growing up in Kansas, whole milk, and lots of it, was the preferred choice. And no one has ever accused me of having the hips of the V-shaped male physique so desired by the female of the species. But even someone with advanced osteoporosis and the waistline of a ballerina would find this battle of the bone filled with pain. For thick-boned me, it was excruciating.

He pulled and tugged while I gripped the table with all of my rapidly vanishing strength. He was sweating and cursing calcium. I was sweating and groaning—my deep guttural groans were those of someone encountering the complex combination of physical agony and mental anguish on an extreme scale previously unimaginable.

I wasn't just having my bone broken in the prolonged slow motion of frame-by-frame advance. My spirit and eighteen-year-old sense of invulnerability were being crushed. The sliver of pride that I envisioned for myself on the other side of cancer was gone. But the suffering that lay ahead was omnipresent. If this was what it was like to be a cancer patient, I wanted no part of it.

As I lay there on the table, struggling to maintain my tough and impenetrable exterior, I noticed a quiet whimpering coming from the corner of the room. Because of the nonchalant nature of the doctor's manner in explaining what was happening, he'd had my parents stay for the procedure. We didn't know any better. It wasn't supposed to hurt, right?

I managed to break the "deer in headlights" spell that had frozen all three of us in a catatonic state, and I called over to my dad to take my mom out to the waiting room. He did so immediately without any protest from her, leaving me to finish the fight alone.

Mercifully, it did eventually end. The bone, about the size of a pencil lead, was removed, and a needle was inserted to extract the marrow. Lying on my side, hands still frozen into their locked clamp on the table, feeling broken, I began to cry. The pain of the procedure had passed, but a long and seemingly endless highway of misery stretched out before me. The weight of that reality was too much for my tears to hold. They broke under the uncontainable load and streamed forth down my face.

I'D SEEN MY share of doctors and emergency rooms as a kid. At the age of two, I fell down a couple of concrete steps in our garage and fractured my skull. Other incidents that occurred when I was a toddler included a near drowning in the pond behind our Hillsboro, Kansas, house and a fall on my face that resulted in one of my bottom baby teeth punching a gaping hole clean through the skin below my lip.

Later, when I was old enough to play sports, I continued to suffer the bumps, bruises, breaks, and scrapes of a rough-and-tumble, adventurous boy. Some might think my list of career injuries indicates a certain amount of clumsiness on my part, but nothing could be further from the truth. When it came to uncontrolled, rapid descents into unyielding terra firma, I simply had no fear. Coordination never entered into it, I swear.

But even with a fractured skull in my diverse boo-boo biography, my most serious incident of touch-and-go trauma came when a dog bit me at the age of ten.

I was lucky enough to know the dog in question. He was a neighborhood cocker spaniel named Barney, so it was easy to check his rabies records. And there were some extenuating circumstances surrounding the incident that spared him the label of "community menace" and his owner the shame of a BEWARE OF DOG sign adorning his property: he was an invited guest into our backyard to mate with our cockapoo, Cricket.

I was playing outside with one of my friends when my mom called us in for dinner. We climbed the six-foot-tall back fence (further evidence of my fearlessness) and made our way across the yard to the house's rear door, blissfully focused on the food that would soon fill our bellies. What I didn't realize at the time—I was only ten—but have since become wise to was the perfect storm of amorous angst that my presence in the yard was antagonizing.

It was dusk—mood lighting for Barney, but also a cloak of darkness that hid him from easy view. It was the end of a long day of attempted courting by Barney. As any man will tell you, the best chance for successful coupling comes after you've worn down the woman's defenses with the persistence of a swamp mosquito. And it's been nearly thirty years now, so my memory might be a little fuzzy, but I swear I heard Barry White playing in the background.

The circumstances were perfect for what was at that point probably a very worked-up pooch. He'd put in the time and set the mood perfectly, and then I came stumbling along and caused *canis copulatis interruptus.*

It happened fast, but what I do remember was bending over to reach down and pet Barney, then him lunging at my face, quickly biting, then letting go, perhaps because he'd recognized me as his friendly neighbor belonging to that backyard.

The flow of blood was immediate. When I first pulled my hands away from my face, they were sticky and covered. Letting out a scream, I made for the back door as quickly as my little legs would take me, the sobs beginning to roll uncontrollably.

Walking into the house where my mother was, I really got scared. She let out a scream louder and more terrified than mine. *Oh my God,* I thought. *What must I look like to elicit a shriek just one decibel shy of glass shattering?* I began to cry harder.

I never saw it, but I've been told that it looked like I'd just had my face ripped off with a hacksaw. Barney's teeth had entered my skin on either side of my nose, narrowly missing my right eye. I also had a tooth puncture above the right eye that caused a cascading stream of blood that completely engulfed that side of my face. Short of an encounter with Leatherface of *Texas Chainsaw Massacre* fame, I couldn't have looked much worse.

The reality of my condition, however, was far more superficial. There was plenty of blood, but only three puncture wounds. Once the mess was cleaned up with what I hope were fairly cheap towels, the punctures stopped bleeding altogether.

About forty-eight hours later, an infection developed, and I did have to be hospitalized for several days to receive IV antibiotics. Since it was the face, and the brain is only a short hop, skip, and jump away, the doctors didn't want to take any chances. But when it was all said and done, physically I wasn't much worse for the wear. I did, however, come away with a couple of very valuable lessons learned.

Number one: Under no circumstances should you interrupt, accidentally or otherwise, a male dog engaged in the delicate art of seduction.

And number two: Always maintain your game face. Never let on to the actual or perceived seriousness of a situation when said knowledge will do nothing to alleviate it and will instead quite probably exacerbate it.

So as I left the oncology exam room a few minutes later, minus a small amount of bone and marrow but completely drained of morale, I kept a brave face. How could life ever be the same? How could I get through this? How could I let on to the people who cared most about me just how scared and defeated I felt?

The faux bravery that I displayed in front of my parents carried me through the rest of the evening and took me to the house where our senior-class homecoming float was being built. Everyone knew what was happening with me, so even though as class president I was responsible for its completion, others had assumed (with my deep appreciation) the task of design and construction.

I showed up just an hour after having my hip excavated, knowing that I'd get both sympathetic words and the touch of normalcy that I craved. I sat on a lawn chair quite gingerly, watching the work and speaking very little. I suddenly felt very isolated, as if these people, whom I'd known since we were taking naps and eating cupcakes in kindergarten together, were now total strangers.

The shared experiences that had provided the solid bonds of our collective community had taken suddenly divergent paths. Would they still want me as a peer? Would I become Mr. Melancholy, the guy you would never want to invite to your "It's Saturday night and Mom and Dad are out of town, so let's get crazy" high school blowout? Could we even hang out at lunch on a Tuesday? Me, the cancer boy, and them, the class of 1990, a group that had the rest of their limitless lives to imagine.

My friends were predominantly a driven and ambitious bunch. College was in many of their futures, and plans for law school and medical school lay in futures beyond that. (We were also prone to commit mischief and pranks—placing a dozen or more FOR SALE signs in front yards or going on 2 AM golf-ball hunts—as long as no one got hurt.) Because of my own floating status between the football team, music, debate, and now student government, the social cliques where I found my friends spanned the spectrum of late teenage years. I'd attended two of the elementary schools that eventually fed into my high school, giving me broad foundations of friendship to build from. I'd been in the same general neighborhood for all of my Wichita years, and our family attended the same church for the thirteen years we lived there.

I was lucky to have such a wide-ranging collection of friends. And many of my close relationships could be traced back to our kindergarten years. There is a special quality to friendships that can be traced along a timeline that begins with afternoon naps and snack time and then makes continuing stops at "first day of junior high," "first day of driver's ed," and "the last day of childhood."

My friends were a loyal group. We'd tear each other down at times, because that's what teenagers do. But if an outsider tried to join in on the tearing, my friends and I would defend each other to the end. If my greatest threat had been external, there would have been no less than thirty people that would have rallied instantly to my aid. But "cancer," just that word alone, can change everything. My friends were attempting to build their own lives. They were focused on the roads ahead that would shape their own futures. Would they have room to help save mine? Where would I fall if these roles had been reversed? I left the laughing and float building behind after no more than a half hour.

I'd done pretty well immediately following the diagnosis. A friend of mine showed up at my house less than ten minutes after my parents broke the diagnosis news. He had been looking ahead to a college soccer scholarship but had recently blown out his knee while playing, which gave him his own mess to work through. Yet he was a life preserver, rescuing me from the heaviness of that moment in the way that only friends who care enough to rib and mock you can. He started calling me Chemo. I called him Gimp. And for the rest of that afternoon, we rounded up our closest circle of friends and actually found the energy to laugh.

Those few hours with Shawn and Jim and Chris gave me hope and confidence that not only could I beat cancer, but I could also do it with little to no disturbance to the year ahead. It was the beginning of my take-no-prisoners-in-the-war-on-cancer attitude. But the night following the bone marrow biopsy, that same resolve, which had seemed so certain, now lay shredded at my feet. I was ready to raise the white flag.

However, the staging process had just begun. This was only day one of three. Tomorrow it was on to the lymphangiogram.

THE ONCOLOGIST WHO'D preformed my bone marrow biopsy and taken the lead on my staging came with quality credentials. Everyone said that when it comes to treating cancer, in Wichita he was one of the best. But as I discovered in day one of my life as a patient, there is a big difference between treating cancer and treating a person. Bedside manner was not his bread and butter.

But the kindly old radiologist who was charged with performing my lymphangiogram oozed compassion and reassurance. His manner and presence immediately put me at ease, which was decidedly unexpected, considering that the basement room I'd been ushered into looked like a concrete bunker built by the German army along the bluffs of Normandy in 1944. It probably also helped that he didn't speak like Colonel Klink or say things like, "We have ways of making you talk!"

We were down in the basement because a lymphangiogram is essentially a specialized full-body X-ray of your entire lymphatic system. A radioisotope is injected into the system through the top of the feet, and it lights up all of the lymphatic pathways like a giant roadmap of the human body. Where the radioisotopic dye bunches up into pockets of light on the map, you have malignancies. (It's not quite that simple. I'm sure the large number of radiologists who just read my description could write an entire chapter of corrections and additions. But since most of you have never operated a fluoroscope or laced a tiny plastic catheter into a node the size of pinhead, it's close enough.) The only complicated part is finding those pinhead-sized nodes and getting the catheter attached. It was explained to me by Dr. Not Colonel Klink that typically a blue dye is injected into the feet between each toe (yikes), making the nodes easier to see. But he was old school, both in how he practiced medicine and for how long he'd been a member of AARP. He didn't need no stinking dye!

My toes gave him a thank-you low five.

Once he found and threaded the lymph nodes by eyesight only—an incredibly intricate piece of surgical precision that was pulled off in no more than fifteen minutes—the rest of the day was pretty slow and uneventful. Unless you consider the introduction of radioactive particles into your body—particles that will stay in there for up to two years—an "event." After the yesterday that I'd just had, I did not.

Truly, I just had to lie there motionless while the radioisotopes did their thing. They weren't particularly fast or energetic radioactive particles. When something goes into your bloodstream, it races to the far reaches of your body in an instant. Getting dye to run through the lymph system is more like sucking a really thick and icy milkshake through the narrow end of a silly straw. There is no payoff without patience and persistence.

I'm not sure how much patience I really had that morning, but I had come to the realization that any day without someone merrily mining your bone for marrow was a day that, at a minimum, deserved a gold star of glee. Admittedly, my good/bad barometer had been pitched off its axis and was in serious need of recalibration.

The hours passed, the dye charted its course, and the fluoroscope took its photos. Other than a couple of stitches in the top of each foot—the second and third new holes hollowed into my flesh in the previous twenty-four hours—I escaped the hospital with minimal damage.

Not unlike momentum in sports, which ebbs and flows and extends for durations that far exceed the moment in time causing the original shift, confidence in yourself to overcome the obstacles that you face operates within the same dynamic. I was floundering after my bone marrow biopsy and facing the plank that I was about to walk like a condemned man. But after the lymphangiogram, the task at hand felt doable. There would be no easy battles in my war on cancer—which I had learned was called Hodgkin's disease—but I had the sense that each battle would be winnable.

At home, that attitude was evident in my parents as well. We'd all rees-tablished an equilibrium following the blow of the diagnosis and the horrible first impression that cancer had made with my bone marrow and me. The skies overhead hadn't suddenly gone blue, but they were no longer filled with marching tornadoes of doom. Like much of what unwantedly invades our lives, it became just one more thing in life. For me, there was school. For my parents, it was work. There were our relationships and personal lives as well. And now we had cancer. It was a big and important thing that would consume the others if we let it. But in reality, my best chance at survival, and sanity, was to treat it like "one more thing."

My parents did as much as they could to make life feel normal. Dinner conversations involved school, the future, my friends, and the closing baseball season. When cancer was mentioned, it was done in a very matter-of-fact manner. Some people change tone, drop their volume, or adopt a "poor, poor you" look on their face when the topic of cancer is touched on. Or they simply don't mention it all, preferring instead to dance around it. That wasn't the way we handled it. We actually chose to handle it.

My mother and father are the products of Depression-era parents. Because of my dad's father's disability, back when the world was far less accommodating to such conditions, he'd witnessed a number of hardships. My mother's father, Jim Watson, worked on the railroad during World War II and later had his own farm in northern Illinois. My mom too had been steeled by the conditions of her childhood and the lessons passed down by her parents.

They were tougher than I thought. Not that my expectation was for them to become puddles of self-pity at having a son with cancer. But their quick adaptation to the life that had been thrust upon us surprised me. It also helped shape my own responses and reactions. We were realistic. We hadn't become ostriches with buried heads that were unable to see the chore that needed to be completed. But we were positive, upbeat, and going about our daily lives with just a slightly heavier plate than a week before.

PART THREE OF the staging process—on day three of my introduction to all things Hodgkin's lymphoma—was a full-body CT scan. Technically it's a "noninvasive" procedure, which leads one to naturally drop his or her defenses. But technically speaking, Justin Bieber is a platinum-selling recording artist who was the youngest solo male act to top the Billboard charts since Stevie Wonder in 1963. Sometimes technicalities smell an awful lot like the miles of cattle ranches that line the highways of western Kansas.

There is no cutting or drilling required for a CT scan. Other than the mark left by a simple IV, the skin is spared any further blemishes. But once you've had your first barium sulfate contrast shake, the word "non-invasive" loses all meaning.

Have you ever driven by one of those cattle ranches? Remember the smell? Now, let's pretend that those odor particles weren't microscopic and floating through the air but were instead concentrated into a thick, condensed, milky liquid just a few gradations below gelatinous. Think milk that's about a week past its expiration date, then remove any specks of good flavor that might remain. (I'm not certain, but that may be the exact process of diffusion that leads to barium sulfate contrast.) Now pretend you are forced to drink this concoction.

The CT scans of 1989 are not the CT scans of today. Back then, it took more than four hours for a full-body scan. That's four hours strapped to a table that moves, inch by imaging inch, through a spinning doughnut the size of a John Deere tractor tire. That's four hours of hearing, "Take a breath. Hold it." Pause for image. "Breathe. OK. Take a breath. Hold it." Pause for image. "Breathe. OK. . . ."

Meanwhile, the barium is settling nicely into the stomach, which you were forbidden to fill with food or water since the previous midnight, and the IV is intermittently releasing iodine contrast into the blood stream, which leaves you with an oddly soothing yet simultaneously troubling warm sensation spreading throughout your groin.

Noninvasive? Sure. But on my list of ways to spend a day, it's somewhere in the neighborhood of setting up a Justin Bieber fan site.

Once the staging tests were complete, it was time to meet again with my oncologist, who looked a lot less scary without an apple corer in his hand and with me wearing my pants. He had the results that would determine the course of therapy I'd undergo.

He started off the meeting with the obligatory "We want to catch it early" speech, which in my opinion did seem a bit ill timed. We caught it when we caught it, and I felt that was pretty early. I was an eighteen-year-old with a swollen lymph node. When my original doctor heard hooves, he thought horses, not zebras. To focus on the fact that it did indeed turn out to be a pack of zebras felt like Monday-morning quarterbacking.

Hodgkin's lymphoma, it was explained, is staged by four body quadrants—left side, right side, above the diaphragm, and below the diaphragm—and by whether or not you're symptomatic (chills, night sweats, and weight loss are among the symptoms). Since I had the disease on both sides of my neck (and in my left armpit, as revealed by the lymphangiogram), had nothing below the diaphragm, and was asymptomatic, I was officially staged a 2A.

What did being a stage 2A really mean? Was there any significance to the end result of the last seventy-two hours of torture? Yes. It was decided that since I was an eighteen-year-old 2A with a whole life still to live, chemotherapy would be taken off the table. The catchy nickname given to me by my friend just an hour after diagnosis no longer fit.

My upcoming treatment would only consist of radiation to my neck, chest, and, in place of a splenectomy, my abdomen. It was great news, worthy of celebrating, which we did. It also meant that I would be moving on to yet another doctor, this one a radiation oncologist.

3

RADIATION

In the 1983 television film *The Day After*, the cities of Kansas City, Missouri, and Lawrence, Kansas, are the setting for the aftermath of a nuclear exchange between the United States and the Soviet Union. I remember watching it with the morbid fascination of a kid who lived among the very same Kansas missile silos depicted in the film and who was familiar with the neighborhoods and landmarks that were destroyed in its fictitious nuclear war.

Ronald Reagan wrote in his diary that the film "was very effective and left me greatly depressed." It's also been suggested by some historians that it affected him to the extent that his attitudes on nuclear policy changed and that it was a factor in the Intermediate-Range Nuclear Forces Treaty that he agreed to with Mikhail Gorbachev three years later in Reykjavik, Iceland.

Whatever its effects truly were on the attitude coming out of the White House, for the twelve-year-old kid living in my house, it fashioned the image in my head of what it was like to have radiation poisoning. If there was one thing that could be said about the film's star, Steve Guttenberg, it was that in the early 1980s he had a great head of hair. Watching him lose it around the crown like a poor man's Friar Tuck was alarming. In terms of traumatic turns in front of the camera for Mr. Guttenberg, its only rival is *Police Academy 4: Citizens on Patrol*.

Truth be told, I had no idea what to expect when I first met with Dr. Richard Baumann, my radiation oncologist. I remembered the clumps of lost hair and skin lesions from *The Day After* and other Hollywood depictions of radiation. Near my dad's office at the university where he taught, there was a fallout shelter, complete with signs that had the nuclear symbol on them, no doubt built in the early 1960s. Just that year I'd lost a very special uncle to a brain tumor, and I'd seen the destructive effects of radiation therapy on him.

My ease with Dr. Baumann was immediate. He was professorial in manner with the male pattern baldness to match. He could have just as easily been lecturing about the evolution of English literature from Chaucer to Tennyson, but instead he was explaining to me fractionated rads and the different acute and cumulative side effects that I could expect. We also mapped out a daily treatment plan that would begin that first week of October and run through most of February.

The first areas of treatment would be my neck and chest—where we knew the cancer to be present. But since there are also areas of the neck and chest that needed to be safeguarded—like the lungs and thyroid—protective lead blocks had to be cast before any radiation could start.

But using those blocks, and making sure they'd line up with the tissues they were meant to preserve, would be far more difficult than the simple X-ray that it took to make them. For that I had to choose between one of two external marking devices—tattoos, or temporary iodine lines.

It sounds like an easy choice. I had no desire for permanent body art of any kind (other than a full-color tattoo of Yosemite Sam swilling a stein of frothy beer or one that simply read I'M ON STUPID). But there was one very large caveat that had to be considered. The process of iodine marking was a detailed one that involved lying underneath a fluoroscope while a technician traced ever so carefully around my lungs. A mark outside the lines would have consequences well beyond a messy sketch. It was a process that no one wanted to do more than once. And, oh, by the way, iodine isn't waterproof.

See where this is going?

If I opted out of the tattoo and in favor of the iodine, I'd also be opting out of all showers for the foreseeable future. As I previously mentioned, homecoming was right around the corner, and I was a teenage boy. Once I hit dating age, I adopted a strict shower-a-day policy—a policy that I took seriously and was not quick to break.

I was stuck between your classic rock and a stinky place.

In the end, the permanence of purple marks on my neck, chest, and stomach were too much to accept. Call it the last innocent hope of the hopelessly naïve, but at that point I was still convinced that I could come out on the other end of February with no permanent reminders of what I planned to be just a passing brush with cancer. I didn't want a keepsake. And I was also fond of the fairer sex, who down the road might not care for purple tattoos and the answers to the questions they were sure to beg.

At that time there were two primary girls on my radar—Angie, an incredibly sweet and pretty cheerleader, who'd been a high school–esque on-again, off-again girlfriend since my sophomore year. I'll never forget the look of heartbreak on her face when she first found out about the diagnosis. And there was Valerie, a year younger than I was and the sister of a good friend; our complicated relationship could best be described as an intense friendship peppered with a couple attempts at romance. She'd been my date to prom the year before and would be again later that spring. But those proms, and my wishes, never resulted in her elevation to girlfriend status. She ultimately resisted my wiles, much to the relief of her brother.

Looking ahead to radiation, I didn't question my ability to juggle classes with treatments. My chronic case of senioritis ensured that my level of evening studies would remain at a mild and manageable level. But my responsibilities for the extracurricular activities that I had taken on might be in jeopardy. As would, possibly, my desires to be a social member of the senior class. That included dating, of course. But mostly it involved simple acceptance. Other than cancer, nothing else about me had changed.

I understand saying that is a little like the old joke, "Other than that, Mrs. Lincoln, how was the play?" But it was true. And as a teenage cancer patient, it was a paramount concern. You spend much of your high school days trying not to stand out and apart from your classmates. But now I did. And all I wanted was just to be normal Kyle.

Nine years earlier I'd attended a summer church camp about thirty minutes into the Kansas countryside with a girl named Misty. From what I remember, she looked bright and fun, was usually smiling, and was almost always swimming at the pool during afternoon activities time. We weren't really friends; you could best describe us as friendly. But she is more memorable to me than anyone else that attended camp that August. She was the girl with leukemia, swimming with the bald head.

My conversations with Misty were always short and never frequent. Perhaps she had some really good friends, but they didn't come from my circle of camp cohorts. To be blunt and honest, we simply didn't know how to act with or talk to a girl who was dying. How does any eight- or nine-year-old know?

Misty was largely alone during camp, mostly isolated from the kids her own age, and shamefully I'd done nothing to try and include her. It wasn't calculated cruelty on my part. I wasn't being mean to Misty in any direct way. But I'm sure the isolation hurt her just the same.

The adult me, more than thirty years later, can forgive the ignorance of a kid. I can look back and understand my actions, or lack thereof. Ignorance leads to fear, which results in a sort of willful blindness, which in this case led to dismissal. That the dismissal was that of a girl in need of nothing more than normalcy and friendship never occurred to the nine-year-old me. Or, if it did, the blindness crowded it out. And because of that, the nine-year-old me has never quite forgiven himself.

The next spring, on her birthday, Misty was buried. I attended the funeral, my first for someone who wasn't both very old and a member of my family. It was the first time I experienced a funeral that was not for the mourning of the life that had passed but for the mourning of the life that never would be. The most haunting moment, one I will never forget, came when we sang happy birthday to this little girl, a girl who would never live her life, a girl who no doubt left the world a poorer place by her absence, a girl who just wanted to be normal. She just wanted to do normal things like a normal kid her age.

To this day, I still regret never taking the time to get to know Misty, to find out what her likes were, what she most disliked, and where she'd have liked her life to end up, if not for the leukemia. But I never found those things out. She passed into and out of my life without my knowing her. But nine years later I did understand her. Quite well. I had become her. The one who was different.

A YEAR AND a half earlier, when I was a sophomore, I was blessed with a spring-break trip with my German class to visit West Germany (Germany was still divided in March 1988), Austria, and Switzerland. A number of my former teammates from when I played football as a freshman and sophomore were in the class, and we all were successful in talking our parents into forking over the dollars to make the "cultural experience" happen. And by "cultural experience," I of course mean beers at the Hof-bräuhaus in Munich.

We were all good kids and, for the most part, responsible. And it should be noted that drinking as sixteen- and seventeen-year-olds broke no German laws. And it should be doubly noted that when a bunch of teenagers wandering around Munich run into an American serviceman stationed in Germany who offers to take them around the city during his evening off, and said evening just so happens to coincide with one of the more than two hundred beer festivals that dot the civic calendar, it's bad form for those teenagers to say no. Also, German beer is really, really good.

So there we were, a group of American teenagers taking trips to see the Glockenspiel and Neuschwanstein Castle, the inspiration for Disneyland's Sleeping Beauty Castle, while spending our free time in the evening practicing our German.

"*Ein bier. Danke.*" Glug, glug. "*Sehr gut!*"

Then, on day three of our trip, we all boarded buses that would drive us the forty-five minutes from our hotel just outside Munich to the concentration camp at Dachau.

It was a beautiful if slightly chilling morning. Not a cloud was in the sky, and hardly a breeze blew. And not a single word was uttered by any of the more than thirty high school students walking those consecrated grounds.

I've walked the battlefield at Gettysburg and stood among the headstones of Arlington. I was once lucky enough to stand in the house on Mt. Koressos near Ephesus, Turkey, the house that many believe is the place where Mary, mother of Jesus, lived her final days. And I've stared down at the rusted gun turret of the USS *Arizona* from the memorial that floats above.

All of those places felt holy to me, like sacrosanct slices of human history that require humility and reverence when within their bounds. But walking through the gate at Dachau, there was nobility and dignity to the sense of sorrow that washes through you. It's as if the souls that reside there ask nothing more than to be remembered. And your mere presence within those walls fulfills that humble request.

It's impossible to be of human DNA and not recognize the beauty in a place like that. What evil that did lie in those barracks and bunkers and near those ovens those many decades ago is no longer present. But the strength and humanity of the victims who had their lives stolen at that place still remain. It's in the memorials, markers, and chapels that dot the landscape. And it's in the air you share with the others who are there to pay their respects.

Some people get through their hours of darkness by comparing their own struggles to those of people much worse off. I call this the "At least it's not . . ." defense. At least it's not a lay-off. At least it's not a sick child. At least it's not cancer.

I agree with the principal idea that there is always someone worse off than you are. It does allow for natural perspective, or at least it should. And perhaps there is some comfort in the acknowledgment of those worse off, although I never felt good about the merits of easing my pain by focusing on the even worse pain of others. It's the beauty and humanity that remains in those in pain that I find worth celebrating. It's the comfort in the knowledge that love still exists in the darkest corners of places, like Dachau, that gets me through my midnight hours.

The most beautiful moments in life are often found shrouded in packages of great ugliness. But if you can find the patience of mind and the clarity of heart to look past the cloak, you will see them.

With the iodine in place and the lead blocks back from the shop, my Monday-through-Friday radiation regimen was ready to begin. After school. As much as I would have liked to get that first treatment over and done with as quickly as possible and break the seal on the road to recovery, I had to wait until 3:45 PM. As soon as the bell rang to end the day, I was in my car, driving across town to the hospital, and then into the waiting room, patiently awaiting my first of many turns under the radiation beam.

I'd had a calculus quiz that morning. I'd been to choir practice, attended English and government classes, and met with my debate team as we prepared for that weekend's tournament. As was normal for me, I'd gone to lunch at Bionic Burger with a handful of friends—one of four primary lunch places that were in our noontime rotation.

From the outside, my day was no different from any other. I was no different from any of the other students in Mr. Riley's calculus class. I was just like everyone else eating Bionic Burger's double-cheeseburger special at lunch and then carrying its smell back to fifth period. And when I got in my car at five minutes after three, I looked just like everyone else who was trying to flee the parking lot for the freedom of the fall afternoon.

Internally, however, I couldn't have been more antithetical to the day's external facade. Every minute, every moment, took me closer to the unknown of radiation. Even the grease and fat high brought on by a basket of freshly cut French fries couldn't break the spell that the specter of my afternoon's activity had cast. Treatment day had arrived, and all of the mundaneness of high school couldn't change that.

Sitting in the standard doctor's office, clinic, or hospital waiting-room chair that is sold in every state in the country, I nervously bit my fingernails. What does a radiation beam feel like? What would I feel like, knowing that ions, protons, neutrons, oxymorons, and photons were all bouncing around inside my body, altering the DNA of my cells? How would I feel after five months of this?

Before I had time to ask too many of the burning questions that were consuming me—an eighteen-year-old with the kind of cancer you want—a mother and her five-year-old son, clearly being treated for a brain tumor, walked in and sat in the chairs directly across from me.

What does a radiation beam feel like? This young kid, who's hardly had time in his short life to learn anything, knows the answer to that question. And how would I feel after five months of this? Well, I'd probably at least feel something, because the odds were heavily in my favor that I'd be alive in five months.

By the looks of the five-year-old and by the body language of his mother, for him the odds were stacked the other way.

He sat there, like almost any other little boy, playing with a toy train. And she sat there, like almost any other mother, stealing glances at her son with a love that filled the room.

Where is God when a young child like that is stricken with terminal cancer? Where is the beauty in having a promising life snatched away before it begins?

It's in the humanity that that mother and son still maintained in spite of a lot in life that could have easily stripped them of it. It's in the love that they shared in that small room, on that particular afternoon, that I was privileged to witness. It's in the hundreds of thousands of people that deal with daily struggles so immense that surely their spirits should collapse— yet not only does that spirit endeavor to endure, it flourishes.

As I was called into the room for my first blast of radiation, I couldn't help but think of myself as lucky. Lucky to have just witnessed such staggering beauty, and of course lucky to have been handed a diagnosis that awarded the one thing every cancer patient longs for: a fighting chance.

I was ready to rumble.

THE VERY FIRST thing you notice about the room is the nuclear symbol on the side of the giant machine that dominates the space. It's hard to see that symbol and not have your breath catch. Or, in my case, picture a hybrid blend of Mad Max characters fighting it out with the Sand People of Tatooine in a postapocalyptic battle of sci-fi characters.

A couple of small chairs line one wall, but there are no plants, no windows, and no doors that lead to any other rooms or hallways. Of course the reasons for that are obvious. Radiation has to be completely contained, or we would in fact be forced to deal with the marauding gangs of a kinder, gentler Mel Gibson's Australian youth. But the obvious needs of the design don't make it any less disconcerting to see or walk into.

I had to lie down on the floor, because the transformer-looking machine literally leaves no room for a regular-sized table underneath it (which would be a design more reminiscent of an X-ray machine). The technician used a beam of light to line up the lead blocks with the painted lines on my chest.

A week earlier I had learned that when doctors tell you something usually doesn't hurt, be very, very suspicious. On this day I learned that doctors have a remarkably elastic definition of the word "precise."

The radiation beam, it was said, was very "precise." It would only affect and treat the very specific areas in which it was aimed. The lead blocks would do a more than adequate job of protecting the surrounding lung and thyroid tissue. As for the rest of the body that was well outside the machine's field of operation, no worries. Like I was already told, the beam was very "precise."

The doctor and technicians then left me in the room alone, closed the giant six-foot-thick steel door (which looked more like NORAD closing up the mountain as international tensions mounted and our rising DEFCON level indicated an imminent full-scale thermonuclear launch), and watched me with the comfort and convenience of closed-circuit television.

Not exactly how I define "precision."

The actual blast of radiation lasted no more than a handful of seconds. The directing beam of light clicked off, there was a slightly menacing low rumble, followed by a discernable whir, and then, as quickly as it began, it ended.

I felt nothing. There was no burning flesh and accompanying cries of agony. When I sat up on the makeshift floor mattress and looked back at the pillow I'd been using, I saw that there were no clumps of hair left behind. In fact, to see me was to be completely clueless as to what had just happened. There were absolutely no outward tells of the DNA-destroying process that had just taken place.

On the drive home, I couldn't help but notice the blue skies of the descending October evening. It had been a beautiful early-fall day, and it was clear that the weather and mild temperatures were going to hold throughout the night. *What a great day to be alive*, I thought to myself as I tapped on the gas and pushed my Mustang up the short entrance ramp and onto the interstate for the fifteen-minute drive back to the west side.

Day one of radiation was in the books, and it was a piece of cake. Other than what amounted to a little more than an hour of total travel and wait time, which only served to delay me from joining my friends at our requisite hang-out house—a rotating honor bestowed predominantly on one of three homes, mine included—my day's itinerary hadn't noticeably changed from the month before.

I'd had the honor and experience of seeing the boy and his mother—a glimpse inside the remarkable window of life that I wouldn't soon forget—and I'd begun the active participation in curing myself of cancer. I humbly labeled it a terrific start to what was shaping up to be an easy run through cancer.

Teenage cockiness, of course, was not a new phenomenon in 1989, nor have we seen its decline in the two-plus decades since. Fourteen-year-olds have always been convinced of the idiocy of their mother and father, regardless of who that mother and father are. I'm quite sure that at some point during their teenage years, each of Stephen Hawking's three children thought of him as a clueless moron with scarcely a functioning brain cell.

Van-roof surfing, roller tackle basketball, and blindfolded bottle-rocket chicken are also all prime examples of teenage cockiness. The brain synapses that lead to an understanding of physics and the processing of pyro-pain probabilities are the last to develop. As are the connections to the lobe that handles all interpersonal male-female equations, which of course leads to the all-too-familiar scene of pimply teenage boys sitting in front of the television and declaring "I'd do her" each time an attractive woman appears on the screen, even though the associative physical law of mathematics that governs such things is very clear: women who are nines and tens do not "hook up" with seventeen-year-olds who have to borrow mom's car to go to the movies.

As I looked ahead to what was going to be an easy win over cancer, I definitely felt a touch of the teenage cockiness. Doctors, with their fancy degrees and years of clinical experience—what imbeciles. As someone who'd just been on the table and under the beam, I had real-world experience.

So instead of going home and resting, as had been suggested by the staff at the doctor's office, I went to join my friends, who were sitting in front of a television and watching for attractive women.

But as I sat there, engaging in the banter and cracking the occasional comment, something began to change in me. Inside I could feel a growing sense of what I can best describe these many years later as a hollowing. It was kind of like hunger pangs, but higher up and in my chest. It could have been confused for what feels like heartburn, but it came without the acid.

A hollowing, almost like a pumpkin being turned into a jack-o'-lantern, is really the only way to describe it.

I wasn't truly afraid of the feeling. It was mild in intensity, and anything that might be considered actual pain was not enough to distract me from the important business at hand: confirming to my friends that after carefully considering the long list of pros and cons, I would in fact "do" Alyssa Milano and Nicole Eggert. (All I needed was a meeting.)

But the feeling was enough to end my afternoon early. Instead of calling home and suggesting that I stay over at my friend's house through dinner, I left.

Arriving home, uncomfortable but also unclear as to what might alleviate the discomfort—even in the very moment it wasn't any easier to describe the sensation or brainstorm a list of possible solutions—I laid down on the couch. And then I fell asleep.

I am not a napper. I never have been. In preschool, when the lights would dim and the class would spread out across the room and unroll our floor mats, I never slept. With low lighting and a scattered pattern of prone children who made supervision by the one overworked adult in the room difficult at best, there was simply too much mischief about. Sleep would only deprive me of opportunity to assist in said mischief or be entertained by the creativity of others.

And as an adult, I've never been a napper. I'll lie down in front of the television and turn on golf—ESPN's version of the soothing-sounds sleep machine—but my mind just won't allow sleep. What if something amazing happens? I'd never forgive myself if I slept through it.

But in that evening following my first radiation treatment, I slept the sleep of the exhausted. All I had done was lay under a beam for a couple of minutes. In terms of physical activity, it wasn't much more than tanning. Yet while the cast of *Jersey Shore* still has the energy for gym and laundry and entire nights' worth of drinking and fighting, my turn under the tanning lamp left me whipped.

Radiation would not be a walk in the park.

As the days and weeks passed and my five-day-a-week treatment schedule progressed (I was given Saturday and Sunday off to recover), I began to understand the impact of the cumulative effects of radiation.

Outwardly I still looked like me and could easily pass for a typical teenager. And with that visible normalcy still maintained, my fears of unintentional exclusion from my classmates slowly abated. In fact some of my friends, incredibly supportive in the beginning, didn't realize that treatments were still ongoing just a few weeks in. This was either a great compliment to my own efforts to maintain the stiff upper lip of regularity or a sign that I was becoming out of sight and out of mind. Perhaps it was a mix of both.

But while my outward appearances remained largely unchanged, inside there was a distinct feeling that I was becoming more shelled. The internal hollowing felt more pronounced. The exhaustion was becoming more chronic, no longer limiting itself to the immediate hours following treatment but extending into all hours and aspects of my life.

Underneath my shirts and sweaters, my chest, and later my abdomen, began to show the burns of radiation. At first glance it looked like little more than a summer sunburn. But a closer inspection revealed that the skin was bubbling in some spots and breaking down by color and texture in others.

And there was the emptying mental fatigue of grueling daily treatments spread out over many weeks and months. It's one thing to get yourself psyched up to take on an afternoon's battle with cancer while you're filled with the strength of the fight. But when it's January and the days are short and cold, and you're exhausted and ready to drop, and the normalcy of being a high school student checking the mailbox for college acceptance letters has been so easily replaced with the anxiousness of remission reports on your cancer, the fight becomes a slog.

Pep talks, rah-rah speeches, and strongly worded verbal declarations of "kicking cancer's ass"—all things that you regularly did back in the beginning days of your life as a cancer patient—start to take on the amateurish quality of the uninitiated. You almost laugh at the naïve you, the poor sod who thought that by nothing more than strength of mind he could will himself to be up for this daily assault. What a fool that guy was, the me of two months ago.

FRIDAY NIGHT WAS for football at my high school. It's not Texas, with its pro-style artificial turf fields, stadiums that rival small colleges, and manic townies that relive the glories of their teenage years through this year's batch of varsity football players. But it is big, as it is in most of small-town middle America. For out-of-town road trips, large busloads of fans would follow the team. Nearly everyone in the school would attend home games. And Friday afternoon was filled with pep rallies and excitement about that night's action under the lights.

My Friday afternoons, like my Mondays, Tuesdays, Wednesdays, and Thursdays, were spent under a radiation beam, then back at home recovering. I mustered the strength to make it to every single football game and even many of the parties that followed the games when my depleted energy levels would allow. And then that next Saturday morning I was always at the debate tournament that was on my team's schedule.

The topic that year was prison reform and what the federal government could do to ease overcrowded populations. Our plan was to tackle the issue by dealing with the illiteracy that plagues most prisons. Illiteracy leads to recidivism, which keeps the population's revolving door of overcrowding spinning but prevents the prison from ever emptying.

Borrowing from a plan that I'd concocted the year before to deal with the previous season's topic—the encroaching insolvency of Social Security (how prescient high school students were in debating that in 1988 and '89!)—I tasked our nation's elderly with teaching prisoners how to read. They get a little extra coin to supplement their shrinking retirement payments, and nonviolent criminals gain the skills to function in society within the bounds of the law. As Michael Scott of *The Office* would say, it was win-win.

It was normal, I was functioning, and my days and weeks away from the hospital continued forward in uniformity.

My second life, away from the fun of football games, double-cheese-burger lunches, and debating the viability of turning North Dakota into a giant prison colony, à la *Escape from New York*, was also filled with ordinariness. Each day there was the drive over the same streets and through the same intersections. I waited in the same waiting room, with many of the same patients. (I no longer saw the mother and the son with the brain tumor. I was afraid to ask where they'd gone.) And there was the same routine to get me ready for the same blast of radiation that I'd received the day before. And the day before that.

And then, as quickly as it began, it ended.

The world doesn't stop rotating on its axis when you are diagnosed with cancer. And it doesn't stop to celebrate your completion of treatment either.

Don't mistake the blasé nature of my sentences to suggest that it isn't a great day when you finish radiation therapy. It is indeed. But physically you don't feel any different than you did the day before. You are sick and tired and wrung clean of all energy the morning of your final day's treatment. And you feel that way the next morning. And the morning after that. And so on.

For me, the real marker of the end of my time as a cancer patient came a few weeks later.

In the final couple of weeks of my radiation, when the treatment had moved down to my abdomen and thus introduced into the mix an element of severe nausea that had previously been absent, I began rehearsals as one of the leads in the school musical, *Brigadoon*. It's the story of two American hunters who are traipsing the Scottish countryside when they stumble upon a village that only pops up one day every hundred years. One of the Americans falls madly in love with a Scottish villager, while the other Yankee drinks booze and cracks jokes.

Once again, when it was time to cast the romantic lead, I was not considered. I was instead cast as Jeff Douglas, the sarcastic alcoholic.

It had been tough to go from school to the doctor for treatments and then back to school for rehearsals, especially since I was on the severe back end of treatments and it was all I could do to stay awake in class (and I swear it had nothing to do with the content of the syllabus).

My body wanted, demanded, a break. But I needed to be with my peers more, doing normal things, even if I was just "playing" a normal teenager who was playing a role in the school musical. At that point I wasn't above posturing, even if the only person who was being fooled was me. I didn't care what members of the American Psychiatric Association might say about my self-delusion. For me, it felt good.

But on opening night of our modest one-week run, nothing was pretend. The only role I was playing that night was that of Jeff Douglas, as portrayed by the great Van Johnson. (As a big fan of *The Caine Mutiny*, I was tickled to be playing a part that Johnson had previously mastered.)

The "me" part of that night and the me that was reflected onstage were both very real. I was back to being my normal self, happy, healthy, and with a long life to look forward to.

And the best part of the entire evening was that sitting in the middle section of the fourth row, in seats that were set aside by our director, were my doctor and his staff of nurses, who had been caring for me the previous five months.

It was my night to celebrate, and with them.

During the closing ovations, it was hard to look at them and keep from crying.

4

COLLEGE

You can't live a complete life and stay clear of moments of embarrassment. The private humiliation can be bad enough between you and the person you know you are. But when that embarrassment leaks beyond the discrete and into the cooperative, the person who gets to control where the labels of "standard" and "anomaly" fall is usually not you—which is why we're all very desperate to cling to those secret failings and maintain control over that proverbial label maker.

One such moment for me came in fifth grade, which has been scientifically proven to be the age that such a moment leaves the deepest scar.

It was Halloween, and our class assignment was to write a scary, funny, or otherwise entertaining Halloween-themed story that we would then read aloud to the class. I loved creative-writing assignments, so naturally I was eager to sink my Halloween-style vampire teeth into this one.

But for some reason—I honestly don't remember why—I didn't.

The day came for us to read our stories, and I had nothing but a blank piece of paper on my desk.

Once by one my classmates were called up to read their stories, and one by one we got closer to the inevitable calling of my name. I had no plan for what I was going to do when that humiliating moment came. These were rising floodwaters, and there was no higher ground left for me to climb. My fate was unavoidable.

But then, a flicker of hope. As offered by my teacher, a wonderful woman named Barbara Firestone, many of the students were setting up mood lighting in the room—aka, turning off the lights—and reciting their written stories from memory. This presented me a fortuitous opening on two very important fronts: (1) Who's to say what was from memory and what was made up on the spot, seeing as it was my story? and (2) with the lights off, no one would see me sweating, searching for words, or panicking that my hatched plan was failing.

So when my name was called, under the cover of the darkened room I began to "write" my story—a five-minute version of the Transylvania news, complete with weather, traffic, and a sports report from Count Dracula. (Instead of final scores and game-day commentary, Dracula focused on the number of blood-inducing injuries while railing against the dreaded Chicago Cubs and their insistence on playing games in the "cursed light of day.")

It ended up being a huge hit. The class laughed at all of my punch lines, and I could hear the subtle but very positive affirmations coming from my left, where Ms. Firestone sat. Not only had I expertly covered my behind, my "story" was a runaway success. Only moments before I was slinking from my desk, terrified of the public humiliation that awaited me at the front of the class. Now I was pridefully striding back to my writing lectern, the author of comedy genius. Life could indeed turn on a dime.

And then turn again, as it did the very next school day.

Not all of the stories could be read on the same day as mine. Five or six stories were bumped back to the following Monday. And, as luck would have it, since only a few had to be bumped, that left plenty of time for the rereading of some of the class's favorites. Mine was on that illustrious list.

Once again I was slinking to the front of the class, a comedy genius stripped to the bone. I spent about half of a minute trying to fumble my way through the parts of the story that I could remember, but of course all of the timing and punch were gone. Finally, after my stammering and stuttering transformed the faces of my classmates into a pack of very confused eleven-year-olds, I threw in the towel. Turning to my teacher, I explained that I couldn't remember the rest, then quickly sat down.

Of course it didn't make any sense that after only three days I could no longer remember a story that I'd memorized just a few days earlier. My teacher knew it didn't make any sense, and I knew she knew. She probably even knew that I knew she knew. And that was the circle that completed my humiliation. There was the initial deception, then the closing lie. And all parties were aware of both.

On the scale of shame, however, my fifth-grade impromptu triumph turned tumble barely makes a dent on the mountain of dishonor. I climbed that summit during my first year as a cancer survivor.

I CLOSED OUT my senior year well enough. I finished my classes, even attending a few of the ones that I liked along the way. And I was acquitting myself as a new survivor fairly well. I'd entered writing contests with essays about my cancer experience in *Guideposts* magazine and *Reader's Digest*, winning savings bonds and an electronic typewriter in the process. (And boy, was it state of the art. You could see up to fifteen characters on the one-line display before it actually put the words on paper.)

Physically I was bouncing back as well. My energy was slowly returning. It did feel a little like watching the spring buds blossoming in March and April. From up close and day to day, you'd swear that no progress was being made. But when you stood back and observed it from week to week, you could see the changes in growth were much greater than mere perceptions. And I had finally showered, much to the relief of my classmates, who no doubt feared what would happen with the daily rise in temperatures that signaled the coming Kansas summer.

Then two things happened in early June that I did not handle well. First, we graduated. School was over, college was still an entire summer away, and I now had idle hands.

Second, my parents moved to Kansas City. My dad, now armed with his doctorate from Columbia University, was opening a Kansas City satellite of the degree completion program he'd been running at Friends University in Wichita. It was a move that had been in the making for some time, but it was delayed a year by my parents so I could finish high school with the friends I'd grown up with. I was class president and had established myself in my high school. Thankfully, I didn't have to give all of that up in my final year.

It was a good move for my parents. My mother had gone to high school in Chicago and had always felt more comfortable in bigger cities. Kansas City was by no means a return to the Second City, but much of the big-city flair that was absent in Wichita could be found in Kansas City, one hundred eighty miles to the north. She took a job with an educational book company in Topeka, setting up a seventy-mile commute each way.

My dad had grown up in Kansas City, Kansas, and it was an opportunity for him to return to the city of his youth. It was also a good step in his climbing career as he continued to take himself away from music and toward adult education. My parents would be leaving behind a core set of friends that had been made during their thirteen-year stint in Wichita. They didn't travel in a large social circle, and the times when they did entertain at our house were limited to small dinner parties with a few select invited guests. But the circle was tight, and they would be missed. The pros, however, heavily outweighed the cons, and for the fifth time in my short life, the moving vans came to pack up our house.

The house being left behind, though, did not sell quickly. Hurt by increasing mortgage rates and falling prices, the housing market in 1990 was for buyers, not sellers. So while our house was on the market that summer—empty of nearly everything except for a bed, a television, and my clothes—I was allowed to live there.

Our house on Maus Lane had been a social gathering spot for many of my friends over the years. There were essentially three houses in the main rotation—Pete's, Matt's, and mine—and then a few others that would pop up on the radar from time to time. So it was well known and already on the evening route long before it became empty of furniture and parents. If you were looking for "the gang" (no one was nerdy enough to ever actually call us that), you'd go by Burger King. If you struck out there, then you'd make the house drive-by circuit, more likely than not to find us at one of the three homes listed above.

With my parents now living nearly two hundred miles away and the number of breakables and valuables reduced to near zero, the summer drive-by circuit shrunk to one.

It was the right and kind decision of parents who knew that snatching me from the neighborhood where I'd lived since kindergarten and transporting me to a strange city where I knew no one would make for a lonely and miserable summer. I was already the only one of my friends heading off the University of Missouri. Most of them were bound for KU, K-State, or Wichita State, which would make me the "new kid" in search of friends soon enough. No reason to jumpstart that process twelve weeks early.

It was going to be my very own "Summer of George," à la George Costanza's summer following the discovery that he was getting a severance package from the Yankees that should last him about three months. I didn't have grandiose plans like "reading a book from beginning to end, and in that order" or taking up "frolf"—Frisbee golf—as George did. But the actual execution of my summer was quite similar to his.

George bought a new recliner with a refrigerator built into the side. My empty living room was filled with seats that looked an awful lot like the beverage crates sitting outside the QuikTrip four blocks away.

George put his summer plans on hold initially because he needed time to "decompress." My first job of the summer was third-shift cashier at the 7-Eleven three miles out into the country, allowing me to decompress while actually at work from the hours of 1 AM and 5 AM, when the only customers were Kansas Highway Patrol officers on the hunt for a cup of fresh coffee. (A Slurpee machine, a 7-Eleven cooler filled with sandwiches, and an entire aisle full of Doritos makes for quite a decompressing break room.)

And George's summer of discovery and rejuvenation ended largely unrealized after he slipped on some stairs while retrieving invitations for a party. My summer also ended with a party that turned the neighborhood around my house into a scene out of *Full Metal Jacket*, complete with hovering helicopters and scores of fleeing teenagers being caught in the beams of scattered spotlights.

If ever there was a summer devoid of all responsibility, this was it. And if ever there was a teenager who took full advantage of the washing of those responsible hands, it was I.

Sure, I didn't end up in front of any judges, and no one ended the month of August with their fall plans derailed. No one was wounded, at least not permanently, and property values on our block remained largely unchanged. But I had been class president, a member of the debate team, and one of the leads in the school musical. My mother was a well-known member of the television community. My father was our church's choir director and one of the most respected college band directors in the state. What was I becoming?

It's not that I didn't care about the answer to that question. As it was happening, and as I was living it, it really never occurred to me that there was a question being asked.

My complete lack of concern for responsibility, or maybe it was an intentional shirking of responsibility (even now I'm not certain), was carried with me from my "Summer of Kyle" to my fall across state lines in Columbia. Dorm life at Mizzou awaited me with open arms of freedom and untapped deposits of irresponsibility just waiting to be mined, and I was ready with pick and auger in hand.

A series of eye-opening and semester-shaping revelations set me upon the long and fun-filled year to come. My dorm, a coed building, plus two all-female dorms shared my dorm quad cafeteria. As a journalism major, I was taking a statistics class—one of my favorites—and I was able to figure out that for a nineteen-year-old college freshman, a cafeteria filled with five girls for every one guy was a very good thing.

I also discovered that a couple of the bars that lined the district on Broadway accepted an MU student ID as drinking age ID. I wasn't a law student, so I didn't allow myself to get too bogged down in the legalese of a state-issued driver's license versus flimsy laminated cardboard with a photo snapped at orientation or twenty-one versus a lot of years shy of twenty-one. I'm sure it was all on the up-and-up. This was college after all.

The all-you-can-drink draft specials for $1.99 lent them even more credibility.

College was off to a roaring start. There were parties in Greektown, parties in our dorm, and parties at bars, followed by late-night trips to Burger King. We sat around and played Tecmo Bowl, ordered pizza, and drank dorm fridges full of beer. Hours of ESPN were consumed by our superabsorbent polymer-like brains.

I was never alone in partaking of these activities. And when they stretched beyond orientation week and well into the semester or beyond the weekend and well into Tuesday, I had company. But depending on what was happening, where we were going, and when the night was expected to end, my company changed faces. But for them, the accompanying face was always mine.

I was becoming one of the most well-known and visible guys on the floor. When the football players wanted to play cards in the commons area, they knocked on my door. When our floor "bookie" needed some help in setting lines for that evening's slate of basketball games, I was on his short list of visits. And when our dorm needed a commissioner to help set up its Whip-It Olympics—a series of competitions held between athletes who have just inhaled a canister of nitrous oxide—I was the chosen guy.

I was having too much fun trying to be all things to all people while being absolutely nothing worthwhile to myself.

I did do normal college things, like intramural sports. And when it came to academics, in classes that truly interested me, I did go, study, and make sure that I had the grades to match. Unfortunately for my GPA and me, the moments when I was able to locate my motivation were too few and far between.

I consumed incredibly large amounts of alcohol, but I hadn't become an alcoholic. It wasn't the drinking that appealed to me as much as the companionship that came with it. Introduce a twelve-pack into a room with four guys, and you can guarantee that the laughter level will rise while the depth of the driving conversation will shallow out. I liked that. I craved that. I needed the mindless and mundane. The fact that it came with beer and Nintendo attached was just a bonus.

I was also chronically absent from class, opting instead to stay in my room and blow off the walk into campus anytime it was cold, raining, or snowing . . . or warm, sunny, and pleasant. I was like the antipostman, never delivering and definitely not the person you would call if you absolutely, positively had to have it overnight.

I obviously knew how little I was making it to class, yet I was still able to convince myself that in the end, I could pull something worthwhile out of the semester. I knew my grades were sinking and my college career was dangerously close to the edge, but denial is an easy river to navigate, especially when you're sporting a beer-induced buzz.

I had some great college-experience moments in that first year at Missouri. There was a communications professor who I developed a memorable collegial connection with. He liked a paper of mine, we bonded about being from Kansas, and I think he recognized my floundering as something much deeper than the typical student on the clichéd voyage of young-adulthood discovery. He never actually called me on it, although he was always probing for an opening. But my previous year remained hidden. I never allowed for that opening to materialize.

I also made some unyielding friendships during that first year. The two guys across the hall from me were two of the most standup men I've ever met. If I needed something, anything, Brian and Bill would say yes first, then ask about the details. They were also two of only three guys that I ever had any meaningful conversations with about cancer.

My trust in the two of them grew slowly at first and was built around our mutual love of sports. Bill was from Chicago and loved all things Bulls, Bears, Blackhawks, and Cubs. Minus the extra poundage of George Wendt and Chris Farley, the old *Saturday Night Live* skit featuring "Da Bears" superfans who worshipped at the feet of Mike Ditka and Michael Jordan could have been written about Bill. Although to my knowledge he never survived a heart attack through self-administered CPR while eating a Polish sausage.

Brian was from a county seat in southern Missouri of less than two thousand people and came with the small-town sensibilities that resembled an earlier generation. He always told it like it was, and he did so in the colorful language that straddled the line between his Ozark Highlands upbringing and his obvious intelligence and learnedness. He was a big guy with the heart to match. And because of that, his direct manner and style never cut or wounded.

I eventually trusted them enough to tell them about my cancer. One night the good times and laughs turned serious, and after they each shared some of their own griefs, I spilled the details of Hodgkin's disease and radiation. But my details stuck strictly to the facts of the nuts and bolts. I remember feeling almost as if I was talking about someone else as I detailed the diagnosis and following treatment. There were no feelings behind my words. They were clinical. It was a point-by-point account that connected to me like a third-person retelling of a tale with wrong pronouns. It wasn't my Hodgkin's or my radiation. It just existed apart from me.

From September through the following May, that part of my life was sinking ever deeper into my hardening core, getting tamped down by the meaningless superficiality I was piling onto it. Cancer, its meaning, and my emotional self were parts of my person that I was losing all connection to.

During that football season, Missouri lost a game to eventual NCAA national champion Colorado on one of the most controversial finishes in sports history. The Buffaloes, down 31 to 27 with the ball inside the MU five-yard line, scored the winning touchdown on the game's final play. The only problem—and it was a doozy—was that the winning touchdown was scored on fifth down. Five downs in football happen about as often as four outs in baseball, which is to say that they only happen when someone screws up royally.

That one football game stirred more passion in me than an entire year of thinking about my brush with mortality. As far as I was concerned, Colorado head coach Bill McCartney was the enemy of all that was good and holy. He knew that his Buffaloes didn't earn their win. If he'd been moved enough by the lessons of sportsmanship and integrity, which he could have passed on to the populations of two Big 8 campuses, he would have forfeited. Instead, he smugly held on to his win and watched his team win a national title it didn't deserve.

For CU and McCartney, as far as I was concerned, the ways to balance the universal scales of serendipity were obvious. But the required search to find *my* own inner plane of harmony was a journey into the depths of myself that I had no desire to take.

Let's talk more football. Or maybe open another beer. Where's tonight's party?

Eventually all chickens of disgrace do come home to roost. For months the vise that I was slowly tightening around my person was mine alone to bear. It was a weighty burden, but it still ran free of humiliation. The anger, disappointment, and shame were limited to growing self-flagellation. But that all changed when the spring semester ended, and my parents learned of my grades.

There were no explanations worth making, or that might be worth hearing. There were no words that could make it right. And I couldn't think of any deeds that might resurrect my reputation. I was a complete disappointment, and no one could argue otherwise.

For all that I had done right as a cancer patient—the genuine feelings of gratitude that my disease was treatable, my absolute refusal to ever say or think "poor me," and the very real connections that I made with my fellow radiation patients—I had done everything wrong as a cancer survivor. I had become an unexplainable embarrassment.

My parents, bless them, gave me the benefit of the doubt. "You had such a hard previous year," they said. "There were so many issues that you never really addressed," they excused.

Of course, their statements were true. I had unresolved issues sluggishly oozing out of every open pore. If ever there was a man in the middle of Missouri that needed a guest spot on Maury Povich's talk show, I was he. But "true" statements don't automatically equate to acceptable actions. Lots of people get terrible years thrown at them in far more direct and destructive ways. For millions, cancer is a way of life. For millions more, suffering is par for the course. But they don't drop into an emotional vacuum while rejecting society's conventional constraints.

I had lived almost an entire year not fulfilling one single responsibility. On the surface, that might sound great. But on the inside, where the human being is supposed to be cultivated, it kills. I'd survived cancer, but cancer was winning. And badly.

I STOOD IN the shower of our Kansas City home a couple of weeks removed from my year of misery. I hadn't flunked completely out of school. I was able to return for the fall semester with an opportunity to still set things right.

As the water poured off my head, pooling into the drain below, I imagined it as a cleansing. The elimination of the deeds that had consumed me, to be replaced by the rest of a life worth living. I was resolved to be a cancer survivor grateful for his second chance at life.

As I stood in the shower, my head swirling from the new direction that I swore that I'd be taking, my hands mindlessly touched my neck.

And there it was. Another lump.

5

MOPP-ABV

On a small patch of grass on the western edge of the Country Club Plaza—an upscale shopping and dining area in Kansas City established in 1923 that claims to be the first-ever shopping center designed to accommodate automobiles—lies Cancer Survivors Park. The generosity of the R. A. Bloch Cancer Foundation has led to more than twenty such parks being built around North America. But Kansas City's park, built in 1990 in the city where Richard Bloch (of H&R Block fame) was surviving his own cancer, was the first.

In 1978 Bloch was diagnosed with terminal lung cancer and given just ninety days to live. He ended up living another six thousand days, eventually passing away in 2004 of heart failure.

The first Sunday of every June is National Cancer Survivors Day, which began in 1991. And Cancer Survivors Park on the Plaza was the obvious and perfect location for all the festivities surrounding the celebration of lives saved from cancer.

There were bands playing and giant balloon arches against the backdrop of the beautiful summer sky. Laughter floated about the carnival-like atmosphere with the feel-good foods to match. And there was a survivors' registry, where everyone who was on the "alive" side of his or her cancer scare could etch his or her name into the permanent record of survivorship.

My parents encouraged me to go and add my John Hancock to the long and proud list of survivors who were publicly publishing news of their good health. So I did, only to be told that since I'd ended treatments for my Hodgkin's disease just sixteen months earlier, considerably less than the touted five years, I was not in fact officially a "survivor."

I left the table and then the park, making the ten-minute walk back to where we lived at Forty-Fifth and Walnut. It had been two days since I discovered the new lump on my neck, and I knew that the radiation I received in early 1990 was not what disqualified me from survivor status; it was the chemotherapy I was about to endure.

There had been no confirming diagnosis yet. In fact, no one other than me knew about the new lump. But I knew what it was. There was absolutely no mistaking it. Certain memories in life are tattooed into your consciousness. The voices of loved ones, certain smells, the bark of your childhood dog—all are moments in memory that don't get mistaken for others. The same holds true for the touch of cancer underneath your fingertips.

I just needed to gather myself for a couple of days before passing on the news to the powers that be. As soon as I did, I knew that everything in my life would change, and I wasn't quite braced for that. It was summer, and there were baseball games and long afternoons to enjoy. As soon as I mentioned cancer, it would all be ripped away.

A day or two later, I broke the news to my mom during lunch at Worlds of Fun, Kansas City's version of Six Flags. At the time I wasn't sure why I'd made that place the location of the big reveal, a disclosure that would not just change life for me but for my mother as well. Maybe it was because we'd been having such a fun morning. We'd gone on a number of thrill rides and eaten overpriced food that contained absolutely no nutritional value. It had been the perfect day. Perhaps perfect enough to mask the true severity of a recurring cancer. Or maybe so perfect that the news would seem less severe when seen in the light of a carefree and fun-filled June afternoon at a world-class amusement park.

Six-dollar sodas and stand-up roller coasters did not soften the blow. My mom had been with me during every step of the diagnostic process in 1989. She was there during staging, and she'd heard the doctors' explanations regarding the whens and whys behind a choice between radiation and chemotherapy. She briefly protested the inevitable by voicing the required, "It could be a dozen other things . . ." but without any belief or conviction behind her words. She knew, like I knew, what it was and what it meant. I wouldn't be going back to Missouri in the fall.

That evening we told my dad, and then we reluctantly let the medical people in on the secret the next day. As in 1989, a biopsy was performed. And just like in 1989, the malignancy was confirmed. Suddenly, my year of self-indulgence plummeted from our consciousness. Fear and worry consumed the embarrassment I felt and any lingering anger my parents still lived with. The "most curable cancer to have" had survived our first attempts to kill it. Could I survive our second attempt?

The radiation oncologist who was doing my follow-up at the University of Kansas Medical Center in Kansas City, Dr. Richard Evans, referred me to a nearby hematologist and medical oncologist, Dr. Richard Mundis. As I already knew but still hated to hear in concrete confirmation, the change in doctors meant that as a course of treatment, radiation was taken off the table. A medical oncologist meant that chemotherapy was on it.

But first things first—we needed to stage the disease once again.

Even though I was willing to assume the worst stage possible and be treated with everything including the kitchen sink, there was no getting around the required and dreaded bone marrow biopsy. My hips ached at the mere whiff of the suggestion, while my mind raced back and forth, wrestling with the notion that knowing what I was in for was much worse than the blissful ignorance of "It usually doesn't hurt."

Dr. Mundis, however, was a very wise man. He explained to me that doctors regularly use twilight medications like Valium and Demerol when they go into the holes that the human body already comes equipped with. Why would you not, then, use these same relaxing pain-killing agents when boring an entirely brand-new hole into flesh and bone? Why not indeed, I concurred.

So I had my bone marrow biopsy. It still hurt every bit as bad as it had on that cold exam-room table in Wichita. But this time, I didn't care. The pair of sedatives took me on a trip not unlike Ron Burgundy's journey through cartoon Pleasure Town, complete with rainbows, unicorns, and dancing pandas. Somewhere in the middle of that, there was a bone marrow biopsy.

At least I think so. The stick I felt in my backside could have come from a rogue unicorn tusk.

There was also another very long day spent with a fluoroscope and a lymphangiogram. But with the methods of my kindly old lymphangiogram specialist left behind in Wichita, the blue shots of dye between each toe had to be employed. To go hand in hand with the rainbows and unicorns of the bone marrow biopsy, I now had Smurf feet.

WITH CHEMOTHERAPY A sure thing and my being a nineteen-year-old with hopefully a long life to live and perhaps future children to sire, my doctor brought up something that had been the furthest thing from my mind: sperm collection.

When your typical soon-to-be college sophomore male (or third-semester freshman) thinks about children, it's usually in one of two ways: "Please shut that kid up. I'm hungover." Or, "Thank God I dodged that bullet. No kids for me."

On the list of written side effects that chemotherapy was sure to leave me with, the word "sterility" barely made a blip on my consciousness. The temporary hair loss, nausea, nerve damage, skin breakdown, and eye thickening all made far greater impressions on me than the inability to find myself starring in my very own real-life version of *Knocked Up*.

But I wouldn't be nineteen forever. At some point I would become an adult with the seriousness of life to match. And as I contemplated what that "me" might look like, it included kids. My dad had coached me in little league baseball and soccer, and I think it's only natural to picture ourselves as the type of husband or father we see in those we love and respect.

So it was on to the fertility clinic, where we had two weeks to collect what was necessary before the advancing cancer dictated that we move forward in trying to save the current generation as opposed to future ones yet to be conceived.

Since those days in the summer of 1991, my mom has gone on to earn her PhD and has had a hand in creating online teacher licensure and professional certification in nearly all fifty states. She is an author and a speaker and has had the privilege of teaching on five different continents. I say all this not because she asked me to get her résumé in print, but because I want this next story to be seen in the unbelievable context in which it played out.

No need to get into the details of how someone goes about collecting sperm for future frozen storage. If you have reached the age of thirteen, you can fill in any possible remaining blanks. Suffice it to say, it's a solitary activity that requires very little skill.

The night before I was to go into the clinic for my first collection, my mother knocked on my bedroom door. She had the look of a concerned mother, searching for a way to help her struggling child. "I picked up some things today that might help you out tomorrow."

She then left me with a brown paper bag as she quietly exited the room.

Unsure of exactly what to expect, I probed the top of the bag, trying to get a glimpse of what was covered inside. The bag slipped open enough for me to see the top of a magazine cover. A magazine covered in plastic. The plastic covering that only comes on one of type of magazine—adult.

There were three magazines in all, and they weren't your garden-variety mainstream classy porn. No *Playboy* or even *Penthouse*. We're talking off-off-brand, with the models to match. They were the kind of magazines that even I'd be too embarrassed to purchase for fear of being judged by the pimply-faced minimum-wage worker behind the counter of the 7-Eleven, which had been me just twelve months earlier.

So how did my well-respected, professional, college-professor mother pull it off?

There is no denying the powerful love of mothers. Orangutans build brand-new nests every day for their babies' afternoon naps and then do it again every single night before bed. With as many as two hundred thousand eggs to protect, clean, and oxygenate, octopus moms don't have any time to hunt for food during the month leading up to birth, so they'll often eat their own arms for sustenance. And elephant moms are pregnant for twenty-two months before giving birth to two-hundred-pound babies. I've not been pregnant, nor have I given birth, but I'm told this is a pretty extreme commitment from mama pachyderm.

Now add to that list human mothers and the positively tasteless and trashy porn they buy for their children. Love knows no bounds.

WITH THE PREGAME out of the way and future generations of Garletts safely ensconced in liquid nitrogen vapor at –196 degrees Fahrenheit, I was ready for the main event: the surgical implanting of a Port-A-Cath—the catheter under my skin that would allow easy access to my veins for chemotherapy administration—and my first dose of chemo.

The port consists of a small reservoir with a silicone rubber bubble on top, which is used for needle insertion, and a solid metal backing in the rear to ensure that the needle isn't able to puncture through the back of the reservoir into vital organs. The connecting plastic tube attaches the port to the vein. This occurs so that when chemotherapy is injected, there is no risk of its leaking out and damaging the surrounding tissue.

My course of therapy was going to be a seven-drug combination cocktail (called MOPP-ABV), including some of the old standbys of Hodgkin's and lymphoma fighters, as well as a couple of the newer kids on the block in 1991 hematology. It would be broken into twenty-eight-day cycles: day one was two injections and the beginning of fourteen days of two other oral medications, while day eight would be the injection of three more chemotherapies. After finishing the oral meds on day fourteen, I would then get another fourteen days off from everything before moving onto the next cycle. But in chemo, just as in war, no plan ever survives first contact with the enemy.

It was month one, day one, and my body was already rebelling. There were the obvious bouts with nausea that came on the heels of that first injection—which were admittedly made worse by own bullheaded decision to go have a cheeseburger for lunch, despite a doctor's admonition against all things dairy. (I thought, *Mind over matter*, and *Chemotherapy be damned—I'm going to eat cheese.* My bad.)

There were the sensations of chemotherapy coursing its way through my body, vein to vein, muscle to muscle, and in and around my brain. And when I say "sensation," I really mean "sense." I could smell it, I could taste it, and my inner self was able to perceive its presence. It was like a freshly poured soda over ice, but into a glass that had just contained vinegar. Volume wise, the vinegar is hardly perceptible. And when you taste the soda, its flavor is still dominant. But something isn't right, and the more you drink it the more you're sure of it, until eventually the drink makes you sick.

My volume of fluids was off kilter and only getting more so.

The real rebelling came in my body's physical reactions to the chemo-therapy. By that evening my scalp, still covered by hair, had broken into a raging rash. A fever spiked, making an already warm summer evening sticky and close to unbearable.

I was sore from the minor surgery to implant the port and getting more so as the chemo worked its way through my body, which interfered with the mild pain medications I was taking. And my head was becoming thick and heavy. It was the thickening that I most remember, as if heavy winter gloves had been put around my head, dulling its dexterity.

As I began my course of chemotherapy, I tried my hand at early visu-alization. The idea that I would do, at a minimum, six twenty-eight-day cycles with the possibility of as many as ten was exhausting in its reality. Instead of thinking about the possibility of twenty total injection days spread out over ten months, I had a scale on the mantle with twenty mar-bles. A marble is harmless and unobjectionable. It doesn't cause pain or affliction. All it does is slowly but surely tilt those scales toward comple-tion as one by one they're moved from one weighing pan to the other.

After moving marble number one from one side to the next, signaling the end of day one of chemotherapy, I climbed the stairs to my room and collapsed on the bed.

Six months.

I was in it barely six hours.

Things had been moving quickly since I first called my doctor to tell him that a swollen lymph node had returned to the side of my neck. I'd visited six doctors, counting surgeons, since placing that call. There were procedures to remove the node, to implant a catheter, to test my bone marrow, and to find lymph nodes for the lymphangiogram. But now that chemo was officially underway, the freneticism of diagnosis, staging, and daily trips to the fertility clinic had been replaced by the drudgery of daily treatments. I now had hours to think and reflect on where I was versus where I should be or wanted to be. The cancer that had been distant and held at a long arm's reach during my freshman year of college was now my entire life. And it was all mine. And it was all consuming.

I'd voiced relief in 1989 about avoiding chemotherapy. I wasn't sure that I could survive the months of torturous poison. And in the hours of nausea and misery that followed each injection in 1991, I would again question my ability to withstand the barrage and navigate chemo's dark path. Those hours were ones of loneliness, though I was surrounded by my family. Those afternoons and evenings were ones of isolated with-drawal, though I spent them in fellowship with friends.

The dark hours would eventually pass, and something good would come along. It could be small or insignificant. The taste of pepperoni. The smell of baking cookies during an hour when I had an appetite. And then the doubt would lift. My reserves of energy would recharge, and I'd be ready for the next battle, the next injection, the next step toward reclamation.

With one eye always searching for the good and beautiful and the other eye trained only on the here and now, I remained confident and determined to proceed. There would be an end . . . eventually.

LIKE RADIATION, CHEMOTHERAPY has cumulative effects, and the days off from treatments can best be compared to a slow-draining sink. Fourteen days away from chemotherapy is good, but the sink only drains about 10 percent of its water during that time. When the next treatment rolls around the sink is refilled at a much faster rate than its levels had been decreasing. Enough of these refills, and eventually the sink runs out of room for more water, causing an overflow. The same holds true for chemotherapy and the human body.

Medication levels were adjusted down to compensate for some of the more serious infections and side effects. The schedule was constantly being adjusted to allow more time for blood counts to rebound—not once in what turned out to be six cycles did I actually make it twenty-eight days with the previously prescribed dosages. And I was constantly being treated for other ailments caused directly by the chemotherapy.

Of course, I was also dealing with all of the many side effects that come along with being a chemotherapy patient. I lost all of the hair on my head, and over time my eyebrows came out too, dramatically altering my appearance. I was fighting nausea from day one. Some days were better than others, and eventually I figured out the rhythmic balances between what medications I was taking on any given day versus what I was eating for particular meals that day. But for the most part, nausea and vomiting became a way of life.

What affected me the most on a day-to-day basis was the extreme loss of strength. No one was going to mistake me for one of the noted German strongmen Hans and Franz. I wasn't in the gym "pumping myself up" before I got sick, and I wasn't there after I got sick. But as a regular nineteen- and later twenty-year-old guy, there was a certain amount of muscle strength and fitness that I had grown accustomed to.

Slowly, but steadily, that strength was taken. From the effort my legs had to put forth to climb the stairs to my bedroom, it was noticeable. My ability to lift simple things like suitcases or books became compromised. Doors became heavier and more unwieldy. A couple of times when I stepped off high curbs, my legs gave out, and I dropped to the ground. I was becoming the dreaded girlie man.

The most disquieting moment came when my parents had to stop buying gallons of milk for our refrigerator. I'm a cereal fan, always have been. I was a Honeycomb Kid before I was a Cub Scout. I had a plastic Booberry ghost as a kid, thanks to a half-dozen proofs of purchase and a set of parents who didn't force me off sugary cereal. And Mikey liked it, but I loved it.

It sounds silly to attach so much importance to a morning's single serving of breakfast cereal. But when we had to switch from gallons to half gallons because I no longer had the strength to manage a full-sized jug of milk while pouring it into a bowl, I felt a part of me had been stolen.

It was a loss of freedom and independence, because cereal is the ultimate symbol of normalcy. What says "everything's fine here" better than a bowl of Kellogg's finest? In truth, the apple pie's origins can be traced back to Europe—perhaps the phrase should read, "As American as Mom, baseball, and Cap'n Crunch?"

When it was an injection day, my routine began with a long, hot shower. They put a line into my port as soon as I got to the doctor's office, and there would be no more showers the rest of the day. Later, when I would feel sick, when I could smell the chemo seeping out of my pores, the shower would be off limits. The line would stay in until late into the night so that my antinausea medication could be hung and dripped over the course of nine hours. So I began the day with a good, hard clean as my means of preparation.

On days when there were no injections scheduled, I would slowly roll out of bed and make my way downstairs. If I was up to it, I'd make a light and easy breakfast. If I wasn't, I'd make my way over to the couch in front of the fireplace and stereo and tune in to the local sports talk radio station. It was an off year for the Royals—the beginning of about twenty such off years. But I still hoped, and prayed, and listened. It was my escape. That couch and that radio made up my little spot of normalcy.

My off days continued on like that. I'd listen to the radio, fall asleep, try and eat lunch (or if the prednisone was really working, I'd eat lunch for five with plenty of room for dessert), read in the afternoons, perhaps try and catch a movie if my energy and stomach would allow, and then watch a little television before bed. One day bled into the next, and then the next, and then the next. I had very few friends in Kansas City. All of my high school friends were back in Wichita for the summer, and then they would be back at their respective colleges in the fall. My Missouri college friends were all from St. Louis and Chicago, or they were completely out of the loop regarding my recurring cancer, because originally I'd been too afraid to let them in.

The days were long and often lonely, but they rolled on. They were a means to an end.

OVER THE COURSE of six months, there were several huge moments of great pain and fear. None was bigger than when I developed an allergic reaction to the chemotherapy drug Bleomycin in October. It's a known potential allergen, so the first time anyone is given Bleo, the dose is manageably small. That way, if the patient is allergic, the doctors and nurses are only dealing with a very small infusion amount. If there is no reaction, then the full dose is given.

I showed absolutely no signs of an allergy the first time I received Bleo in July. My August dose went without a hitch, as did September's. But in early October, something serious began to happen.

I'd driven the three hours down to Wichita for my high school's homecoming football game. Knowing almost no one in Kansas City, it was an opportunity for me to go to familiar grounds and feel like my regular self. There was no hiding what was happening with me. I was bald and severely bloated from chemo and high dosages of prednisone. My skin was flat and dull and lifeless. I looked every bit as sick as I felt. But around friendly faces free of judgment, none of that mattered.

Upon returning to Kansas City the following day, after another long drive, I realized that I couldn't get out of the car. I was too exhausted to swing open my door. I felt like a prisoner behind the shoulder harness of the seat belt. It might as well have been a straitjacket. Even the slightest of movements, like reaching across my body to unlatch the belt, drained my lungs of oxygen.

The following day I was back in the doctor's office and ready for my next infusion. I couldn't walk more than ten feet without trembling from shortness of breath. There was pressure all throughout my body, though it was concentrated in and around my chest. My head was swirling, fuzzy, and unfocused. Fevers were recurrent, nausea was intermittent, and energy was nonexistent.

If you were looking for the definition of a patient on the brink, I was your poster child.

Luckily I had a doctor who recognized that what was happening in me went well beyond the fatigue of chemotherapy. Not only did he suspend my scheduled infusion for that day, he sent me straight to the hospital. He didn't say anything specific at the time, but later he revealed that things with me were critical—another dose of chemotherapy, especially one that included a full helping of Bleomycin, could have killed me.

I LOVE BASEBALL and grew up dreaming about getting the big hit in Game 7 of the World Series to win it for the home team. But admittedly, as far as sports go, baseball has a bit of a cream-puff element. You can't play in the rain. When players tweak this joint or that, they miss fifteen games. And the entire point of the sport is to run home.

Football, on the other hand, is better in the rain. Or—even better—the snow. Guys play games on broken legs. Instead of missing the playoffs, 49ers safety Ronnie Lott chose to have part of his pinkie finger amputated. If baseball is the Woody Allen of sports, football is Chuck Norris. And football expects no less from its fans.

The final game of the Kansas City Chiefs' schedule in 1989 was played under the blanket of a Midwest snowstorm that hit the region on Saturday. But two friends and I made the one-hundred-eighty-mile drive up to Kansas City on snow-packed highways that Sunday morning to watch the Chiefs . . . well, come up just short of the playoffs.

A few years later, after moving out to California, I braved the prison riot known as the Los Angeles Coliseum to watch the Chiefs and Joe Montana beat the Raiders in the final week of the season to win the division and make the playoffs.

These are the extremes that football fans are expected to exemplify. When the heat index is north of a hundred and your seats are in the blazing sun, there is no crying. When it's forty-two degrees in November and a driving rainstorm has you floating down the stairs of the upper deck, there is no complaining. And when you have tickets to the first Monday Night Football game in Kansas City in almost two decades but you've just been hospitalized with severe lung damage from a Bleomycin allergy, don't despair. Improvise.

That summer, I learned a lot about becoming a proactive patient. Often you are limited in what you can do or what you should do. But if you are armed with the appropriate knowledge about your illness, your treatment, and your options as a patient, you have power. It may be contained power that only serves to sanction your own mental survivability, but it is power nonetheless. And it is immensely important.

I contacted the Leukemia & Lymphoma Society (at that time it was just called the Leukemia Society) to get information. On a day when I was especially full of the vigor to take on the fight of cancer, I went to their offices and devoured as much information as possible. I learned about my disease and chemotherapy, but also about what the Society could offer me.

One thing they did offer was a contact in the Kansas City sports world. The executive director of the Kansas City chapter of the Leukemia Society was the wife of a former Kansas City Royal. I called her, she called him, he contacted his friends at the Chiefs, and my outdoor tickets, which would have had me sitting in the cool October evening air, were instead switched to a luxury suite where I would be sitting with some of the all-time great Chiefs. I'd responded quickly to treatments, and pneumocystis pneumonia, something often seen in patients with immune-system issues, had been eliminated as a suspected cause. So following the appropriate begging and pleading and promises of absolute medical-advice compliance, I was released from the hospital and allowed to attend the game.

Football expects no less from its fans.

I SURVIVED MY brush with Bleo death and continued on with my chemotherapy, now minus one drug. My lungs were bruised and battered and to this day still retain the scars of the scare from 1991, but that was the price of admission. The fact is that Bleomycin is very good at battling Hodgkin's disease, and there are quite a few people walking around today because of its usefulness. Some, like me, may not be walking at one-hundred percent, but limping along is far better than being six feet under.

October passed, and I continued to deteriorate. More nausea, more vomiting, more weakness, and more infections. Doses were adjusted again, my body managed its way back to acceptable blood levels, and then the next hit came. There was always another hit.

November came and went, and cycle number five was now in the rearview mirror. I had massive pains in my joints from being on high doses of prednisone, then coming off the prednisone. Every cycle there was the same up and down high of the drug and subsequent crash from its removal.

I'd become unrecognizable in appearance. Bald, badly bloated, and colored a pasty bright white that even my Northern European–rooted brethren would be blinded by, I looked like a depressed and despondent Michelin Man. I was also moving around with all of the vim and vigor of an osteoporosis-afflicted octogenarian in desperate need of caffeine.

December came, and December went. As I sat across from my doctor preparing for my seventh cycle in early January, he broke the news. I was done.

My body had been beaten to hell and back, and he didn't want to keep pushing it. There was no doubt that I received strong doses of the prescribed chemotherapy drugs and that to keep piling on at this point would result in diminishing returns. Six cycles was the minimum, but he assured me that based on the amounts and the intensities of what I'd just experienced, we weren't cutting any margins close. I'd received more than enough chemo.

Then, motioning to me in a very matter-of-fact and genuinely direct way, Dr. Mundis said, "This is the face of courage."

It's the face he sees in all of his patients. People like me, just normal Joes and Janes, dealing with the upheaval of normalcy in the most sobering of ways. None of us signed on to be cancer fighters, clawing tooth and nail and digging down into our souls to call on the final fibers of our natural survival instincts for no other reason than we'd like to see another sunrise.

I saw that same face of courage in the patients who shared that office with me during my six months of chemotherapy. I saw it in the nurses charged with treating us on good days, on bad days, and on some of the worst days imaginable—days when some patients lost their fight.

And that face is ever present on the families who support those patients. As the chemotherapy receivers, our job was fairly simple—sit still while the doctors and nurses did their thing. But our families' roles were largely undefined. They were left bumping into corners in a dark and unfamiliar room, trying desperately to find their fit but having no roadmap to guide them.

Trust is one of the most precious gifts, both given and received. It's the handing over of control with the acceptance of another as the keeper of all things favored and treasured. It's the glue that binds all relationships—the relationships between loved ones, the relationship between patient and doctor, and the honest relationship you have with yourself.

Trust is also the fuel that burns to power the tasks of inordinate importance. Trusting in the course that has been plotted. Trusting your instincts, your abilities, and your courage. And trusting that the effort that you put forth will not be in vain.

Human beings are equipped with a number of tools that enable us to survive a thing like chemotherapy. Or worse. The ability to give trust, and keep trust, are among the most important.

The night that chemotherapy was officially completed, my family and I went out to dinner at one of our favorite Mexican restaurants in Kansas City for a celebration. The laborious drudge was over, and no one could deny that physically I was much worse for the wear—I bore all the badges of combat with cancer. But mentally I had survived the daily assault on my sanity, for the most part. I'd kept it together long enough to slip back into remission and into a life free of cancer, and now I just wanted my life back.

We went to dinner that night to celebrate, but I sat silently throughout the meal. I was happy, of course, but not celebratory. For me, there were no champagne bottles to pop or loud laughter to engage in. Instead, I sat there picking at my burrito, desperate for an appetite and suddenly acutely aware of my absolute exhaustion. My head was heavy, my eyelids drooped, my mind fell from focus to focus, and my legs were like trunks sunk into the ground. I was a drained pond, emptied of vitality.

Every day for six months I had been steeling myself for the fight of my life. The physical, the emotional, and all points in between had been braced for the battle. Now I could finally drop that fortress and allow myself to relax. I was that fourth-quarter team in the playoffs, giving it my all because there was no tomorrow. But now, with chemotherapy behind me, tomorrow existed, and I could finally rest.

Half because they thought I wanted it and half because they did, my parents went to the restaurant that night ready for a celebration. They too could finally exhale, but the lack of the same physical toll that I endured left them with the energy for revelry. But they took my lead in the early stages of the evening. The table volume dipped to subdued, and we all just sat silently in front of our plates, thankful for the finish.

I went home that night, shared a quiet cry with the family dog, and then slept for the next three days.

6

THE ROAD BACK

Each year the arctic tern, a sub-Arctic seabird found in Asia, Europe, and North America, completes a yearly migratory round trip along the oceans and across Antarctica that covers more than forty-four thousand miles. With an average life span of twenty years, the Arctic Tern will log more than 1.5 million miles in its lifetime, all because of its instinctual draw toward home.

The call of home is a strong one in animals, human beings included. You can see "home" invading almost all aspects of our lives because of the comfort the place, the idea, and even just the word provides. In school we have homeroom, except of course for the kids who are homeschooled. We have home pages for our home computers, and many of us are homebodies working on our home brews with help from our homies. In sports, it's all about home runs for the home team and its home-field advantage. With some help from Home Depot, you can set up a home office, home gym, or home theater. And lots of people swear by homegrown homeopathic remedies harvested from the homestead.

Maybe our DNA lays down a homing pheromone that draws our attention anytime we stray too far from home, either actually or inherently. Maybe it's metaphysical and involved with animalistic needs that are far more profound than the comfort found within four walls. Or maybe it's the memories that spring forth from those walls, like warmth, security, and the smell of baking chocolate chip cookies.

Whatever the source of the allurement, the pull is undeniable, even when memories of home aren't filled with Christmas carols, birthday cakes, and a fridge full of orange soda.

But you can't go home again, as writer Thomas Wolfe tells us through his creation George Webber. You can try, as I did following my year of chemotherapy. But the "you" of your youth is nowhere to be found. I'd had a year of radiation, a year of self-destruction, and a frightening and formidable year of chemotherapy. The "me" in the mirror didn't look much different. The "me" inside would never be the same.

By March of 1992, I had recovered enough physically from chemotherapy to take my first tentative steps back toward life. With full-time school not an option until the fall semester, I took a job working midnight security for a high-rise office building in downtown Kansas City. From March till August, I walked the forty-two stories of One Kansas City Place, the tallest building in Missouri, for eight hours a night, five nights a week.

The irony that I—a guy who just recently switched back to curling full gallons of milk—was the security guard for millions of dollars in property was not lost. But it was also the perfect job. The pay was good, I got to carry a really heavy flashlight and big jangly key chain, and I had the time to exercise in solitude.

For my social outlet, I began working with a start-up improvisational troupe, performing in a variety of local theaters and coffee shops. That was how I was reintegrating myself into the world of healthy young people. But the security guard job, which featured coworkers who were ex-cops, ex-military, or ex–you don't want to know, was my private rehabilitation.

I walked all forty-two floors, including two parking garages, twice a night. By the end of the five months, there was a total physical transformation. I was slim, fit, and full of energy. Other than the very thick, dark, wavy mane of new hair that had grown to cover my previously bald head—the color and waves looked strikingly different from the hair I'd sported in my pre-chemotherapy life—there was no physical evidence of the previous year's poisoning.

I also spent each night wandering through law firms, accounting firms, and a variety of very successful businesses that boasted vibrant workforces. Other than seeing a few of them in the morning when they came by to pick up their copies of the *Wall Street Journal*, my glimpses of the tenants I shared space with were limited to desk photographs. But in those keepsakes I saw the success of hard work in their faces, their vacations, and their families. (If you worked at One Kansas City Place in the summer of 1992, please accept my apologies for snooping. I didn't open closed doors or drawers, but if it was out on a desk or secured to a wall, I saw it.) They gave me hope that there was still a life out there for me beyond the pain I'd just endured. I didn't just feel connected to the people, the desks, and the jobs that I was walking among at midnight—I dreamed of those things for myself.

So I worked and I walked each and every night. And when it was time for me to head back to college, I made the only decision that felt comfortable: I went home to Wichita.

I enrolled in Wichita State University, found an affordable apartment on the east side of town, and reconnected with several old friends, even my old high school on-again, off-again girlfriend, Angie. These things comforted me. They were familiar, safe, and guaranteed, I thought, to provide me with the one thing I craved most: certainty. I hung out at the same places and went on the same dates that I had before cancer, back when I was innocent to the reality that my life's path was not set at the age of seventeen. Back when I thought that wanting something and expecting something were enough to best the indiscriminate deviations of life.

But as George Webber discovered, you can't go home again. "You can't go back home to your family, back home to your childhood, back home to a young man's dreams," or "back home to the escapes of Time and Memory."

My journey home didn't come with expectations of escaping time. But I was hoping for a return to the simple life I used to know, to a life that was dominated by backyard football and lunch at Pizza Hut. It was easy, light, manageable, trouble free, and light years removed from cancer follow-ups and the risks of future malignancies.

But you can't go home again. Attempts to return to your previous way of life and relive youthful memories, regardless of what new directions you've taken since, will always fail. And for me, they failed miserably.

I was going one way, and life in Wichita was going another. One wasn't better than the other, just different. It was the ride of my youth that always struck me as exciting, scary, and unpredictable. But since I'd become an adult, that same ride had become anticipated, even hollow, and discomforting in its constants.

You can't go home again, and as Thomas Wolfe himself explained, it may be a uniquely American paradox "that we are fixed and certain only when we are in movement. At any rate, that is how it seemed to young George Webber, who was never so assured of his purpose as when he was going somewhere on a train. And he never had the sense of home so much as when he felt that he was going there. It was only when he got there that his homelessness began."

Back in Wichita, the place I knew the best, I felt the most lost. Whatever life I thought I was going to reclaim had long since disappeared. Whether it was gone to other means or from cancer's hands, it didn't matter. It no longer existed; of that much I was sure.

You can't go home again. But you can go west.

When I moved down to Wichita, my parents moved out to California. They both took faculty positions with Azusa Pacific University (APU) in the foothills of the San Gabriel Mountains just east of Los Angeles. It was another positive move for both of them. Richard Felix, the patriarch of the family that had been our oldest and closest friends, had become the president at APU a couple years earlier. He had been looking for a way to bring my dad to the university to create programs for continuing education and degree completion. My dad would get to build the program from the bottom up, and he would get to do it for a man he loved and greatly admired.

With a résumé that had been further enhanced by stops in public education and corporate education, my mom returned to teaching college by accepting the position of director of elementary education at APU. On a personal level she was also thrilled to be reconnecting geographically with Richard's wife, Vivian, one of her dearest friends.

The move to Kansas City, while good for my dad's career advancement and full of possibilities, had been weighted with the baggage of cancer. Their first year in Kansas City was all adjustment. The second year was all chemotherapy. There was no need to see what a third year would bring, especially with my being back down in Wichita. The sunshine of California is inviting enough under the best of circumstances. But when you're escaping the kind of clouds my parents had been living under, it's irresistible.

The pressures of the previous year and the obvious difficulties of watching me go through something so painful and traumatic—all under the very real uncertainty of success—united my parents. They'd always been close. Always the couple that would spontaneously hold hands while walking in a mall. Always quick to say "I love you." But as the battle-tested and weary parents of a cancer-stricken son, they'd grown even closer. The relationship pitfalls that far too often accompany life-changing struggles had spared them as a couple. But just as I had done by returning to Wichita, they went to California in need of a reset.

During my year in Wichita I'd gone out to visit them over Thanksgiving and Christmas   both featured dinners outside. I went snow skiing one day and to the beach the next, and I became painfully aware that I couldn't do either activity in the state where I was currently residing.

I was twenty-one and searching, not for who I was but for who I wanted to become. Wichita was the old me, the me of my youth. But it was gone. Southern California allowed me to start fresh. Not in reinventing myself; I had no interest in doing that. But I could reinvent the expectation of others. My slate—in terms of cancer, college, and how I handled survivorship—would be clean, and I'd be the only one adding to the ledger.

So after two semesters in Wichita and a summer of relaxing with my KU friends in Lawrence, I packed up my car and made for California. I would attend class at Azusa Pacific University, work in the school's athletic department, and live in winter temperatures that constantly hovered around seventy-two degrees. I'd also be living less than ten miles from the City of Hope, one of the nation's most advanced cancer-research centers. It's where I'd do my follow-ups.

ONE OF MY life's crosses to bear has been my August 19 birthday. With parents in education, our family's moves revolved around the coming school year, which always began in late August. That occasionally left me to spend my birthday in a moving van, where I would fight for attention among the boxes and stacked furniture.

The week I was turning four we moved from Hillsboro, Kansas, to Nashville, Tennessee. I was sick the entire time.

My sixth birthday was spent in a U-Haul truck on I-70 as we moved from Nashville to Wichita. My grandparents were helping us drive the vans to Kansas, and we all spent the night together in the Motel 6 in Columbia, Missouri. It wasn't exactly the cake and ice cream and obnoxiously loud friends that most six-year-olds dream of, but it did qualify as an adventure. (It should be noted that the next day when we arrived in Wichita, I did get my vanilla ice cream.)

I'd moved to college just a few days shy of my nineteenth birthday. I turned twenty-one back in Wichita, surrounded by packing peanuts and half-empty boxes. And I made the move to Southern California just a week before I turned twenty-two. My first birthday in the Golden State was spent getting a new driver's license and bank account.

My history of birthday relocating did come with its advantages. I was an experienced assimilator, used to marking yearly milestones with unfamiliar faces. I'd started fresh a couple of times in my life, and with a new year beginning under the sunny, warm skies of Southern California, the transition to a new me was easy and comfortable.

It's a Los Angeles story as old as moving pictures themselves—a Midwesterner moves to the Pacific coast, sometimes running, sometimes chasing, but always looking for a transformation, be it in the spotlight of fame or the contentment of convention.

As I embarked on the new chapter in my life, I wasn't driven by a desire to rewrite my past. I didn't want to escape from what had happened or pretend I wasn't the guy who'd just come through the harrowing fires of cancer and chemo. And I'd decided to stop running from the person who had so poorly handled his first year of being a cancer survivor. It wasn't a proud year for me, but it was part of my history. It was one of the parts that made up my total sum.

As the school year developed and I got further integrated into campus life, I began to speak about my experiences with cancer. I was a member of APU's concert choir and orchestra, and through that large and very visible university group I was able to reach out to others with my perspectives. At first I spoke to the choir, a group of about one hundred or so college students. I went hiking and camping in Yosemite with a different set of students, and I shared my story with them over chili around the campfire. Then I spoke in classrooms and to the young-adult groups at a few area churches. Where there was an opportunity, I spoke. The stage-taking, student-government-running, commercial-appearing me of high school was reemerging, but now with a message. It was wonderful to be able to extend my own experiences and affect the lives of others. But more important for me, the talking that I did opened the doors to my own inner processing.

I don't pretend to know what it's like to be a soldier in battle and to know the hell that comes from dealing with constant death and destruction. But I have little doubt that cancer patients deal with the same problems brought on by post-traumatic stress disorder. The same fears exist, as does the same threat to life. And like soldiers sharing a foxhole, cancer patients are consistently making bonds through their shared struggle—only to have those bonds broken when a life is lost.

My speaking wasn't therapy. I don't know if you could place any kind of clinically defined importance on what was happening to me through natural self-reflection. Psychology 101 was one of the classes during my freshman year that didn't hold my interest and therefore didn't warrant my attendance. But the more I spoke, the better I felt. The moments, the memories, and the reality of what I'd been through were becoming more matter-of-fact.

I was also finding a very happy stride in the athletic department at school. Working in the sports information office gave me weekly writing responsibilities. I was covering all of our major sports and getting the increased access to our coaches, our teams, and the media that covered them. For a sports fan who still held ambitions of future broadcasting, it was shaping up to be a dream year.

When basketball season started, that dream clicked into overdrive. APU's nationally ranked men's team was far too popular for the small confines of its old gymnasium. A closed circuit broadcast throughout campus was the logical remedy, and since the cameras would already be in place, what harm was there in adding a play-by-play guy?

So that's how the rest of the year went. I was broadcasting basketball games throughout the remainder of the season, and I even traveled with the team to Oklahoma to send the national championship tournament games back to campus via satellite. I truly was living the dream.

As a part of the choir and orchestra, I was performing each weekend in different places around Southern California. At the end of the year we went on a three-week tour through Northern California, Oregon, Washington, and British Columbia. I'd established good friends, many that would be lifelong, but I had no notable girlfriends to speak of. I'd had a number of first dates, a handful of seconds, and a couple of thirds, but nothing that ever took.

In truth, I wasn't looking for any intensity in that part of my life. I was enjoying my integration into becoming a Southern Californian. The days were warm, the beaches were breezy, and the Dodger Dogs were legendary. I experienced a few of the Hollywood clubs, but they weren't really my scene. Most of my evenings were spent at the various sports venues on campus, working games, and then attending low-key student parties afterward.

As I advanced in the communications department at school, I got more involved with my fellow students. Gone were the large classrooms filled with three hundred faceless students; in were small-group projects and study sessions. I made connections with students, shared what I'd learned about life—and myself—during my year of chemotherapy, and I became comfortable with who I was again. I lived at home with my parents, and I'd occasionally bump into them on campus. But these were only minor intrusions into my being shaped into an independent young adult.

I was happy, I was healthy and strong (my follow-ups with my new doctor at City of Hope had all gone off without a hitch), and I was enjoying myself academically. I felt upbeat about my future, and the requisite motivations in the classroom came hand in hand with that.

That summer, I took further steps toward a long-term career in broadcasting when I landed an internship in the sports department of

Los Angeles's local CBS affiliate. Most of those hours were spent monotonously logging game highlights and sitting in a stuffy and windowless edit bay. It wasn't exactly the glitz and glamour you associate with working in a television studio on Sunset Boulevard in Hollywood, but it did have its charms. It also had its moments of excitement, when on occasion I was allowed to go with the crew to Dodger Stadium and collect postgame sound bites. Or when a news story broke, even though we were just sports and largely left on the sidelines of the frenzy, there was still an intoxicating energy to the newsroom that everyone enjoyed—including when a really slow-moving white Ford Bronco led police on a tour of the Southern California freeway system, ending in Brentwood.

Yes, it was that summer, the summer of 1994, when I worked for KCBS. Perhaps you remember the headlines. The New York Rangers won their first Stanley Cup in fifty years. The FIFA World Cup had come to the United States for the first time ever. Without a labor agreement in place, baseball was careening toward what many thought would be a sport-killing cancellation of the World Series. And O. J. Simpson killed a couple of people—allegedly.

It was quite a summer to cover sports . . . or to cover a freak show. The word "surreal" barely begins to scratch the surface.

I didn't have anything to do with our station's specific coverage of the Simpson murders. The news division commandeered it as soon as A. C. Cowlings told the LAPD, "You know who I am, God dammit!"

But a couple of weeks after O.J. had been arrested/surrendered to police in his front yard, a sports talk radio station out of New Orleans called the KCBS sports desk, and I answered. They needed someone to go on air and do a quick interview about what was happening with O.J. and how the city of Los Angeles was reacting. I explained that none of our reporters were in the office right then, but the voices from New Orleans didn't care. They just wanted someone, and I would do just fine.

For one afternoon in early July 1994, as far as listeners of sports talk radio in New Orleans were concerned, I was a big-city reporter from Los Angeles and an expert on all things O. J. Simpson, legal and otherwise. Thankfully I had a background in improvisation and real-world experience in the art of BS. I pulled it off. I was informative, concise, illuminating, newsy, and completely full of crap. For the first time, I felt like I really did belong in Hollywood.

It was a tremendous summer of education for me at KCBS. I learned the business from some of the best producers I've ever worked with. I was enlightened to the realities of how much actual work the on-air talent at that level of affiliate actually do, or how little, as the case may be. And my eyes were further focused on the future that I saw for myself in this world of sports broadcasting. It was where I belonged.

The following fall semester, I left the APU choir so I could continue to work down in Los Angeles at KCBS on the weekends. One was a lot of fun and had me rubbing shoulders with an awful lot of pretty girls, but the other was my future. I needed to keep those "ins" in the television world. Each semester there would be a new intern with new skills and experiences to draw from. I needed to stay in the fold. The reality was that jobs like these were rare. Guys like me, desperate for those jobs, were not. Choir was the necessary casualty.

School started, and my responsibilities with the athletic department continued to increase. I spent Saturdays working in the press box at our football games, and Sundays at CBS doing the drudgery that is unique to the intern experience. If ever there is glory in grunt work, it's when you know it's all a means to a very desirable end.

I was busy, but I was thriving. Slowly but surely, my work in the classroom was burying my aborted freshman year under an avalanche of purpose. I wasn't a 4.0 student, and I'm sure I could have, and should have, cracked the books harder. But I was becoming a whole person with an entire life outside of school—I was forging a place for myself among cancer survivors. I continued to speak about my past disease and even got involved with a few area support groups.

If you've never been to Southern California during the holidays, it really is an incredible time of year to be there, assuming you can get past the oddity of seeing Christmas decorations against the backdrop of palm trees and beach scenes. The skies are clear and blue, the mountaintops are covered in snow, and the daytime highs remain comfortably warm.

It fills you with confidence and optimism and serves as a daily reminder that despite all the problems that come with life in Southern California—smog, traffic, and eight-hundred-square-foot homes priced north of 1.5 million dollars—you're happy to be there.

That's how I was feeling in November of 1994. Cancer and its lingering effects had lost its grip on my future. The clear blue sky was my limit, and each day offered twenty-four new hours of further discovery.

Then, one morning, I found another lump.

7

STEM CELL TRANSPLANT

I wouldn't call myself a religious person. I do believe in God, and when it comes to the teachings of Jesus Christ, I'd consider myself a fan. Loving people and treating them as you would like to be treated seems like a pretty fault-free philosophy. But inside the world of organized religion, the core of those teachings gets layered in human failings, then loses much of its purity and most of its efficacy. The judgments of human beings will never be on par with that of the deity.

For lack of a better term, I am a Christian and have been since I was a child. In its strictest definition, I do fit the bill. But in terms of what it means in twenty-first-century America, in pop culture, and in the derision that so many Christians create, I hate the label. However, I really don't like the sometimes gleeful demonization that springs forth against Christianity either.

There's no denying that there are quite a few putzes who cloak themselves in Christianity. It had been suggested to me in late 1994 that I was continually being diagnosed with cancer because of something I'd done. God was punishing me for something; if only I had enough faith, I could figure out where I'd gone off the path, then correct the course. Never mind the asininity of following and worshipping a god that would be so petty and vengeful. A god like that would definitely not be worth my second thought.

But that wasn't the God I knew or know today. I don't believe he gives you a disease any more than I believe that he cures you of one. To believe that God chose to make me sick is also to believe he's actively taking a role in keeping the likes of Charles Manson disease free. To believe that he will cure me of cancer, if I pray hard enough, is also to believe that he consciously made the decision not to cure the six-year-old leukemia patient, even though her family prayed every bit as hard.

I don't believe God exists like this. I can't. For me to believe in a god like that is to believe that he is as random, cruel, and imperfect as human beings. The bar for my God is a lot higher.

The relationship itself, however, was severely strained when my Hodgkin's lymphoma came back for a third battle. I cursed at God, calling him quite a few names not fit to print. Fortunately he has a pretty thick skin and was aware of the context behind my anger. I don't imagine I hurt any feelings or made him particularly angry. I needed to vent, and I suspect he understood.

It felt good to be angry. I'd experienced sadness, fear, confusion, and uncertainty, but never before had I been angry at my cancer, the diagnosis, or the all-knowing and all-loving supreme being that allowed it to happen. It wasn't a consuming anger, or the kind of anger that fuels the settling of a score or the righting of a wrong. It was a cleansing anger that served to keep my emotions awake during my grappling with the confounding nature of God.

Where is God when things like this happen? Where is he when an airplane goes down? Does God not care when children are diagnosed with cancer? If you believe in a loving God who is all-powerful in all things, how does one reconcile the painful realities that highlight a life's timeline?

My questions about God's allowance of evil and his will were certainly nothing unique to me, to the time, or to cancer. Nor did it speak to a lack of faith, thought, or knowledge. Abraham Lincoln, a far deeper thinker than I am—and almost anyone else—had these very same ruminations during the Civil War about the shortcomings of human wisdom in relation to understanding God. He put them to paper in what is now known as "Meditation on the Divine Will":

The will of God prevails. In great contests each party claims to act in accordance with the will of God. Both may be, and one must be wrong. God cannot be for and against the same thing at the same time. In the present civil war it is quite possible that God's purpose is something different from the purpose of either party—and yet the human instrumentalities, working just as they do, are of the best adaptation to effect His purpose. I am almost ready to say that this is probably true—that God wills this contest, and wills that it shall not end yet. By his mere great power, on the minds of the now contestants, He could have either saved or destroyed the Union without a human contest. Yet the contest began. And having begun He could give the final victory to either side any day. Yet the contest proceeds.

God loves us, yet we suffer. God is with us, yet we often feel alone. So how do we know that he does in fact love us? How do we know that he is with us? Go and spend a day on a cancer ward at any hospital in the world, and you will see him. He's always present in the people.

I was devastated by the new diagnosis. Life had become great—then it was snatched away. It left me adrift, searching for the meaning in life that I'd thought I'd found but that suddenly looked like nothing more than a very cruel and tantalizing mirage. It had been almost three years since I'd finished chemotherapy—three years of building a foundation of health and happiness that was washed away instantly by the returning cancer tsunami.

But there were the people. Friends that I'd made at APU became unexpected rocks of support. Ted Tyman, baseball fan and brilliant tenor, became an anchor to that life I had built. My doctors at City of Hope did not despair, even though all conventional means of treating and destroying Hodgkin's had since been exhausted. Constantly searching for new avenues to the cure, these brilliant people had a plan to retain my life—they would give me chemotherapy so intense that it would wipe out my bone marrow, then a stem cell transplant to rescue me from those depths.

It sounded experimental, and, in truth, the stem cell transplant procedure I began in January 1995 was. It was a course of therapy being used to treat certain stages of breast cancer, and it had been yielding promising results. Doctors were also seeing very interesting effects to cancerous lymph nodes in those breast-cancer patients, so they felt that there was very good crossover potential.

When the doctors came to me with the plan, they were still adjusting the course of action. Which drugs, how much, and for how many cycles were all questions still being answered. But to know these minds and to speak with them about the realities surrounding your own chances at survival was to be reassured. I knew that torture was in my immediate future. But I also knew that despite the failures of radiation and conventional chemotherapy, I still had a chance.

The process began with the two-week daily collection of my own stem cells. After the staging, and yes, another bone marrow biopsy (they don't get any easier), my marrow was deemed to be cancer free. So I could be my own donor, which made the procedure viable. With two weeks of marrow collection, there would be enough stored stem cells to allow for four cycles of the chemotherapy and transplant.

Each cycle began as an inpatient with seventy-two hours of nothing but hydration. The constant IV drips would ensure that my system was filled to overflowing with fluid so that none of the chemotherapy drugs would sit too long in any one organ. They were all highly toxic, and while they were needed inside my body, too much exposure could be fatal. The extra fluids would help push them out.

Then it was time for a straight seventy-two hours of IV-delivered chemotherapy. That was three full days of chemo without so much as an hour to take a break. In comparison, the longest infusion that I'd received in 1991 lasted no more than four minutes.

After that, we waited. I sat in isolation in the bone marrow transplant (BMT) unit at City of Hope, waiting for the dying to happen. I was waiting for the chemo to work its way out of the body and for it to wash out my destroyed marrow and blood counts with it. And then, when those blood counts bottomed out—leaving me with no immune system, no red blood cells to carry oxygen, and no way to form the most simple of blood clots—I received a bag of stem cells.

A few more days would pass, and eventually those stem cells would start to work their life-saving magic. Slowly, and almost imperceptibly, my counts would begin to rebound. Once the counts had risen enough—to the point where I could safely leave the hospital without a serious risk of dropping dead—they'd let me go home for two weeks.

After two weeks and what was presumably more blood-count recovery, we'd do the whole cycle again. I was slated to have four total cycles of this chemo, then isolation followed by transplant misery. And misery may very well have been putting it mildly.

The reality of my third diagnosis was taking its toll. I had good days where I felt upbeat about the ability of the people at the City of Hope to find my way back to good health. But I had horrible days where I was convinced of the coming doom of my death. Some of that was mental, but much of it was physical.

The nights in isolation in the hospital aren't just lonely. They were often spent vomiting uncontrollably, which did more to baffle me than anything else because I knew just how little I was eating. At some point the numbers of "volume in" and "volume out" have to mesh on the same ledger. And if there is cheating to be done in one direction, it only makes sense that it would be in the area of less volume out. The body absorbs some food and fluid and discards the rest, and that should account for a deficit.

But who can explain a judicious discrepancy in the other direction? I wasn't eating. At all. In fact, there was one stretch when I remember I went without solid food for six full days. They supplied me with nutrients through IVs and other means, but my stomach was completely empty. Yet there would be hours at a time where that same empty stomach was filling up vomit pans.

There was a film of filth that also came as a bonus with each chemotherapy course. It was like a layer of invisible radioactive sweat. It had a very specific scent, and you felt dirty under its blanket. It was part chemical in nature, part self-produced enzyme that was secreted through fear glands, and part exhaustion materialized in liquid form. I felt its sickly weight constantly.

When it was shower day on the BMT unit, it was like Christmas. There was a chair in the shower, and even if it took all of my energy to walk the ten feet to the door of my room, I could always find enough reserve strength to get down the hallway forty feet to the shower. Once there, I would just sit in the chair and feel the warmth of the water run down my face and head.

A lot of senses take their leave when you're being treated with the harshest chemotherapies known to medical science while also being isolated for days on end. You can't taste anything. You shut off your hearing as a defense mechanism against the cacophony created by the many machines that fill your room. The only things you feel are the excruciating muscle cramps that wreak havoc in your body each and every night.

Except on shower day. The water was warm and cleansing. It's a simple pleasure, but a pleasure nonetheless. I would just sit there, partially exhausted from the walk to the shower room. But mostly I just sat and soaked in the twenty minutes of feeling normal. When every other aspect of life is running away from your control, the small victory of sitting under a hot shower can mean so much. It was my safe place.

But its safety—and the sanity that it restored—was only temporary. There was always another treatment. Always another beating to take. And always another lonely night in the hospital for you to stare at the ceiling and contemplate life's end.

At night, I would often dream about my funeral. It seemed an inevitability, considering just how weak I felt. I just couldn't imagine my body mustering up the strength in the morning to wake up. I just knew that each system was so close to total shutdown. By allowing myself to sleep, I would essentially be allowing myself to die.

The funeral was ever present in my mind. There would be lots of tears for the life that I wouldn't be around to live—and of course a long line of women mourning the eligible young man that had been taken from their midst. (Who says you can't have a fun fantasy stuck in the middle of a dream about death? It's your dream.)

There were even several nights when I felt compelled to sit down and write out good-bye notes to my family, thanking them for the years of support. But each night, when the fear of expiration moved me to the point where I thought about the letters, I would be too worn down to act on the impulse. I barely had the energy to manage my nurse's call button. Letters to my family felt like a climb up Mount Everest.

I'd initially been skeptical about my doctor's insistence that what I'd be going through in 1995 was "intense" chemotherapy. I was pretty sure that 1991 met the definition of "intense." I'd also mistakenly thought that the side effects I'd experienced three and a half years ago would be a good measure of what to expect now. That was a terrible miscalculation.

Most visibly was the difference in hair loss from one treatment to another. In 1991, except for a small layer of sickly little fuzz, I'd lost all the hair on my head. But that was where the hair loss ended. I still had to shave every day. To have some fun, I didn't. I had a bald head, but I also had a full-bodied goatee for a stretch. I could have passed for mob muscle that'd just been released from prison, as long as no one gave me the gallon-of-milk test.

But in 1995, I lost it all. The head was a smooth cue ball, and all of my body hair and whiskers fell out and stopped growing. I even lost my nose hairs. You might scoff at the loss of nose hairs. During this very moment, you might be deriding the nose hair as tiny and pointless and more nuisance than necessity. I forgive your ignorance. I have had to endure a runny nose minus that first line of defense, the tiny nose hair. And I say with no equivocation, the nose hair is and will always be a valuable member of my team.

There were differences in how my body could tolerate the nausea created in 1991 versus 1995. There were new anti-nausea medications on the market in 1991 that proved quite effective. The post-treatment nausea wasn't eliminated, but it was largely controlled. But in 1995, I felt like Mr. Creosote of Monty Python fame. When I was asked how I was feeling, the most accurate answer I could give was "Better get a bucket."

The effect on my family was starting to take its cumulative toll. My parents had been with me for each of my chemotherapy infusions in 1991. They'd watched my physical transformation as the chemo did its business, and it was obvious how hard that was to see. My mother is a wear-your-emotions-on-your-sleeve type of person, and her sleeves were quite full in 1991.

By 1995, her sleeves were permanently covered. There wasn't just noticeable emotional baggage that comes along with watching your child fight for his life a third time—there was emotional wreckage. Her relationship with God was equally strained, and I'm sure the answers she demanded were harder than my own.

The fact is, when families deal with consuming issues like multiple cancer diagnoses, those relationships get sick as well.

My mother struggled mightily during the months of my bone marrow transplant. She was in constant fear of my death and was terrified that when I was home from the hospital between cycles, I wasn't being adequately cared for, mostly because she was the one doing the caring. She feared her ability. Blood-count-wise, I was much better when I was home. But from an energy standpoint and every other layman's yardstick with which you'd measure someone's health, outside of the hospital I wasn't much different than I was when I was in it. I ate a little more and threw up considerably less. I slept in my own bed, so I was better rested. But my waning energy—and my own occasional slips into the defeatist sensation of just living to run out the clock—followed me home from the hospital.

Out of the hospital, I still saw my doctor regularly, and my mother came with me. When he'd asked for a report on how things were going at home, my answer and my mother's would be very different. I wasn't downplaying anything. I understood the importance of being honest. With what was a fairly experimental therapy, he needed to know exactly what was happening inside my body. But I didn't overemphasize the negative either, for the very same reasons.

My mom, however, only saw what was wrong with me physically, and she laid out all the gory details. Perhaps that's just being a mother, something I know nothing about. Perhaps it comes with being a mother who was now on her third go-around as the mother of a cancer patient. Whatever the case, my doctor was ready to rehospitalize me right then and there.

For me, being an inpatient was a little like being admitted to a death camp. All around me I could hear the moans of other sick people. I never slept more than two hours straight, because there was this machine going off, or that IV that needed changing, or it was time to be weighed, give blood, or check vital signs. In the hospital I was alone, with the only companionship coming from my all-too-active imagination. The hospital was my hell.

But my mother confessed to me that she felt more comfortable about things when I was in the hospital. She felt sure that the nursing staff in the BMT unit were meeting my needs better than she could do at home. And if something tragic were to go wrong, I'd be right there, just down the hall from experts.

These two competing visions for where I was better served continued to butt heads beyond that doctor's visit. There were harsh words and feelings to match, fights over rearranging the items on my bedside table (she needed to fidget while I wanted control over the one thing I could control), and finally a patient-imposed ban on who could and could not come with me on visits to the doctor. I was twenty-three. I was an adult patient going through cancer, and that chronological fact was very important for me. So ultimately I made the decision to see the doctor on my own. For the health of our relationship, which was becoming quite strained, it was a decision that had to be made.

It was self-interest that led me to impose the ban. And it was my mother's acting in her own self-interest that I objected to. In the end, it was my self-interest that won. If there was a time when meeting my needs was paramount to meeting those of the people around me, it was then.

The relationship between my mother and I hadn't experienced anything like this during my first two rounds of cancer treatments. As I reflect on our relationship today, I realize we haven't experienced anything like it since. But in the spring of 1995, the weight of being a chronic cancer patient with ever-decreasing odds of survival and the opposing emotional weight of being the mother of said cancer patient nearly fragmented our bond.

I tell this story because the stark realities of cancer are the casualties it takes. You can see the casualties in the actual numbers of people who lose their lives to the disease, but that's really just half the story. Families and relationships are quite often destroyed in the process. Life still advances normally. Jobs continue. Bills continue to pop up in the mail. Responsibilities remain. But like a fault line in the ground that hasn't seen an earthquake in several generations, the strain becomes too great, and something eventually has to give. Too often that something is a close relationship.

There are no good road maps to help you navigate through the vulnerabilities caused by cancer. We all do the best that we can, and hopefully we retain our dignity and compassion in the process. There is no such thing as the perfect cancer patient. I certainly wasn't. There were times when my temper was short. There were moments when my acting in my self-interest crossed beyond self-preservation and into the realm of selfishness. And there were certainly moments when I deviated far from being the perfect cancer survivor.

There is also no such thing as the perfect cancer supporter. We are all human beings thrown into the lion's den with only instinctual survival skills. It's a tough hill to climb once—climb it three times, and you start to feel the frustrations of Sisyphus. The strains of work didn't stop for my mother or father just because I was sick. Other family and personal issues, like the aging of their own parents, didn't slow because they were focused on my disease and treatment.

We were all human beings doing the best we could.

THE SECOND CYCLE through the stem cell transplant proved to be more difficult than the first. Getting my blood counts back up to acceptable levels so the doctors could then crash them again required blood and platelet transfusions. I developed infections that had to be treated before a start date could be set. And a battery of tests had to be completed to make sure that nothing too damaging was happening in places that couldn't be fixed.

One of the chemotherapy drugs I received was Adriamycin, which I'd also taken in 1991. Sometimes called "the red devil" by patients because it turns urine a very distinctive red tint, Adriamycin carries with it one very serious potential side effect—it can be heart toxic. Doctors of course know this and do their best to mitigate its possibilities. But that potential

side effect is rare, and if you don't attack the cancer with the best chemotherapy agents possible, future heart damage becomes a moot point.

After each cycle is completed, the strength and health of the heart
are confirmed before moving on to the next round. An echocardiogram,
which is essentially a sonogram of the heart muscle, is the chief source of
this info.

Following cycle number one, everything checked out. No damage, no
worries. And the swollen lymph nodes along the sides of my neck that
had been visible signs of the disease had retreated out of sight. Not only
had I survived round one of treatment, but I was responding to it. It made
the drive of the damned (the one back to the hospital for another stretch
as an inpatient) marginally tolerable.

Cycle two followed the same script as the first—days of hydration,
days of chemotherapy, and days of waiting for the physical crash, which
was then finished off with the transplant and days in total isolation. The
big difference, however, was that my body started cycle one fresh, rested,
and strong. I began my second round beaten, weakened, and wasted.

I developed mouth sores, a common side effect of chemotherapy, so
intense that they ran all the way down my throat, which caused a nearly
constant gag reflex. Even on the rare occasion when I did have an appetite, eating became next to impossible. I was given an antibiotic to gargle
with and swallow. It was supposed to shrink the sores to a manageable
level, but even swallowing a drink of water still felt to me like swallowing
large-grit sandpaper mixed with fiberglass.

It became an hour-by-hour exercise to make it through cycle two.
What little strength I did have was squeezed out, as if I'd been put through
an orange-juice press. The mere mention of food made me sick to my
stomach. The walk down the hall to the shower felt three times as far.

The hourly grind eventually turned into passing days, which added
up to weeks, and then, finally, to sweet release. When I returned home,
nothing felt better than the clean sheets of my own bed and walking
through rooms with carpet. It is the lack of the small, simple things that
most remind you that life hangs in the balance. The fear, the pain, and the
fatigue are always there. But being able to walk down the hall to the refrig-

erator or go to the bathroom without having to drag along an IV pole laden with full bags of medicine made a light-year of mental difference.

Inside or out of the hospital, I didn't have much in my daily routine. Even when I was deemed recovered enough to go home, I was still incredibly sick. I couldn't go anywhere; there was always the danger of infection because of my compromised immune system. With nausea ever present and a trip to the bathroom possible around every corner, I didn't want to go anywhere. My bedroom was on the second floor of our house, and it was a trip up the stairs that I didn't want to make more than once a day. When I came down in the morning, I was down for the day. At home there was the couch, the recliner, and the television. That was my day.

There were frequent trips to the hospital to check blood counts, and sometimes they resulted in the infusion of blood or platelets. I'd have friends come by to visit when they could, but classes sometimes kept them away, as did basketball games, choir trips, or social lives. I knew they cared, but they also had lives. It feels unfair, but in truth it isn't. It just is what it is.

You just keep working each day as the means to the end. You get up each morning and eat when you can. You do what you can to stay positive, and you accept the moments when you can't as OK and not to be feared. And then you go to bed at night.

The next series of midcycle tests were completed and passed. My blood counts rebounded, and my body recovered enough by early April for me to begin cycle number three. And I once again made the ten-minute drive to perdition.

Human beings at their capacity are capable creatures. I was entering the third month of intense treatment for what was then my third bout with cancer. Existing in a vacuum with nothing but the starkness of that reality, I'm not sure I could have managed to begin that third cycle. Where does that commitment of purpose come from when the trail feels destined to end in certain failure?

For me, and I think for most people, it comes in the ability to still find joy and beauty in the other surrounding areas of life. Even when you're immersed in pain, there is always a place for laughter. My good friend

Ted would come often to the hospital to visit, and almost never did we talk about cancer. He never asked how I was doing or how I was feeling. It wasn't because he didn't care—he cared immensely. And on many occasions those types of questions were pointless in their making. If you spent five minutes with me, it was pretty obvious how I was feeling.

The main reason that cancer never dominated our conversations was that, as far as he was concerned, there were a number of topics far more pressing. Baseball season had just started, and we both had favorite teams and fairly strong opinions. Why waste time talking about my plight when there were pitching rotations to discuss? Or, in his case, the pitching rotation of my favorite team that was primed to be mocked and ridiculed.

For Ted, I was still just Kyle. Though bald, weak, and barely recognizable, I was still the same guy who just six months earlier commiserated with him over the canceled World Series. I was still the same guy who'd introduced him to CheddarWurst, the best cheese-infused smoked sausage available on the open market today. I was still someone he could laugh with.

Where is God when suffering threatens to crowd out life? He's still there and very present in the people.

VISITING HOURS DON'T really mean much on the BMT unit. Each room is private, so guests are flexible. And because of the nature of the unit and the types of hospitalizations they deal with—touch-and-go battles for life—the nursing staff is highly sensitive to the patients' need for as much human interaction as they can get, when they're allowed to get it.

Jessica was a friend who I'd made through the athletic department at APU. My boss in the sports information office, Gary, had been kind enough to schedule her to work stats at the same time that I was doing them. She was a cute and athletic first-generation Mexican American with a huge smile and a sense of humor that closely mirrored mine. Gary knew I was interested, and I greatly appreciated his efforts to work wingman magic. And it was working, at least as far as my very limited powers of perception in regards to women could discern.

But then I got sick again, and everything that a normal twenty-three-year-old planned for his life had to be put on hold.

Jessica and I hadn't had time to forge much of a relationship beyond the ancillary connections through the athletic department and a few mutual friends. And there were of course my rather weak perceptions that admittedly could have been nothing more than wishful thinking. But when I began my series of lengthy hospitalizations, she began making regular trips to see me. She'd come, often later in the night after my parents or others visitors had gone home, and just sit on the end of my bed and talk.

The physical connection of her sitting on my bed meant everything. Here was someone who had very little personally invested in me. Our friendship was quite casual and could have very easily been pushed aside. She was busy with school and the social life of a college student, and at my best I made for an uncomfortable presence. The easy road was one that ignored me.

But she came anyway, always sitting on the end of my bed. We could have been lounging on a couch in someone's living room. We could have been sharing a booth at a local coffee shop. We could have been anywhere, having regular conversations with the body language to match. The fact that we were inside a hospital room was inconsequential.

As the only child of parents who divorced when she was young, Jessica had seen many of her own difficult days. For a long stretch when she was younger, her mother worked multiple jobs to make sure that food stayed on the table and that a private-school education away from the troubled classrooms of East Los Angeles could be hers. She'd known friends who weren't as lucky, friends who'd fallen victim to the dangers that infect many of those in urban neighborhoods. Like me, she had become a survivor.

Months later, Jessica would tell me that she kept coming to see me in the hospital not because I needed her, but because she needed me. She found normalcy and solace in her BMT-unit visits and our conversations that defined them. They were her sessions of therapy. She has claimed that I did more good for her than she did for me during those weeks in the spring of 1995. I respectfully disagree.

Despite my circumstances and the personal suffering that dogged all of my moments that spring, there was still beauty to be found. I had friends who loved and cared for me, but, more important, I had friends who saw past the cancer patient sitting in my bed and into the heart of the person still living underneath.

BEING A NURSE on any cancer ward is tough enough. But to be the main caretaker of people in the midst of a bone marrow transplant takes a special kind of saint. Without complaint and with absolute serenity and total patience, I was cared for as a person, not a patient. They didn't treat my disease—they treated me.

On April 25, 1995, I was released from the hospital following the completion of my third stem cell–transplant cycle. Just days earlier I was stuck in isolation, lying in bed and watching early-morning television, when programming was interrupted for a special report from Oklahoma City. A bomb had exploded in front of the Alfred P. Murrah Federal Building, killing 168 people.

Where is God when sanity is replaced by evil? He was in the rescuers and first responders who pulled out more than fifty injured victims within the first hour. All told, more than twelve thousand people participated in the rescue and relief effort. Nine thousand units of blood were donated, as were more than two hundred thousand meals to feed the people involved in the rescue and recovery.

In great moments of tragedy, the beauty of the human spirit will always shine through. As I rode home with my father six days after the horror of Oklahoma City and on the heels of the completion of my third cycle of torturous chemotherapy, I knew this to be true. Watered by the people around me, my spirit was still alive.

8

BLISS AND IGNORANCE

American philosopher, genius, and world-class dissenter George Carlin famously complained that life has its order all wrong. "Life is tough. It takes up a lot of your time. And what do you get at the end of it? A death."

Carlin suggested that death come first to get it out of the way. Then you work your way through an old-age home, get a gold watch, work forty years, spend time partying, move onto high school, then finish it up with a responsibility-free childhood before spending the final nine months of life floating in peaceful bliss.

The ends of all things can be a jolt to the system. Anything to make the transition a more gentle going into the night is welcome. Life; any long-term, worked-toward goal; relationships, both good and bad—all leave an emptiness when they abruptly come to a close. The same holds true when a long and protracted battle comes to a sudden and unexpected end. In its place is left a hole.

After my blood counts had rebounded from the third cycle of my stem cell transplant, I was once again put through the battery of tests to make sure that I had come through the torture relatively unscathed. To me, it had a ring of logic about as sound as when a prisoner on death row has his execution stayed because he's running a fever. Death can only be inflicted institutionally on the totally healthy, and I could only get more poisonous medication after being given a clean bill of health. You try and do that math.

I was all geared up for cycle number four and one more trip into the fire. But the echocardiogram came back with some very troubling results. After cycles one and two, my heart had been unaffected by the Adriamycin. But when cycle three was completed, the strength of my heart had been severely compromised. My ejection fraction—which is an essential measurement of the strength of your beating heart at rest—had gone from the normal range of 55 to 60 percent down to a very scary 22 percent.

I wasn't exactly sure what that meant for me long-term. The cardiologist who I was referred to wasn't big on sharing information. But in the short-term, it had one very sudden consequence: my bone marrow transplant was over. A fourth cycle would be too dangerous.

My hematologist reassured me that there was no evidence that four cycles was any better than three. That had just been the medical best guess when the team of hematologists was creating my protocol. But what they could be sure of was that a fourth cycle would very likely be fatal for me. We had to stop, and stop immediately.

After getting over the initial shock of the sudden cessation of transplant activities, I decided that I didn't care. The whys and hows didn't mean anything when compared to the whats and whens. Being done with the treatments—and, as far as anyone could tell, also being free of Hodgkin's disease—overshadowed any possible heart condition. A bum ticker I could live with; I wasn't sure that I could live with more chemo.

Part of the plan had always been to top off the bone marrow transplant with a few more weeks of radiation. My disease kept returning on my neck near the top of the radiation field from 1989, and since I hadn't quite reached the limit on total allowable lifetime radiation, they wanted to raise that field on my neck and fill me up with all of the remaining rads.

Six weeks after the chemotherapy and the stem cell transplant were stopped, I began three weeks of radiation. There was another giant six-foot-thick steel door strong enough to house a terminator, but no purple lines this time. Instead I wore a mask specifically fitted to my head that was outfitted with radiation-beam directional maps. There was a Hannibal Lecter–esque feel to wearing the mask and having it locked tightly in place on the table. I couldn't move my head, neck, or shoulders—or eat any fava beans—during the fifteen minutes of radiation each day. But I was able to retain the last citadel of that year's indulgence, the shower.

As BEFORE, I began to rebuild my life. I now had a cardiologist and a heart medication that I took each day, but as life passed my twenty-fourth birthday and I went back to school in the fall for what would be my senior year, things began to take on the feel of normal. I had a class schedule again. I was back and working in the athletic department, looking ahead to more broadcasting. And I began to date Jessica.

Her visits to me continued after I left the hospital. It was obvious to both of us that a special relationship had formed and was still forming, unlike any that either of us had experienced before. The connection was initially feelings of need born inside the intensity of the bone marrow transplant unit. Outside of the unit, we had feelings of want and desire that added to the need. On the Fourth of July, under a popping sky filled with fireworks, we shared our first kiss. For me, it meant everything.

My hair was still growing back in early July. To look at me was to see the days and nights of the nightmare I'd just endured. The radiation along my neck had further damaged my salivary glands, making eating, talking, and kissing dry and difficult. It had been almost ten weeks since I'd finished the transplant, but I was still losing weight. It would take me six glasses of water and more than thirty minutes to get through a simple sandwich. And I carried with me the unknown future of a damaged heart and the very real possibility that my third battle with Hodgkin's would not be my last.

Yet here was this beautiful and intelligent and exciting woman wanting to date me. The circumstances surrounding our bonds built inside the BMT unit led to long and intense discussions. By the time we shared that first kiss, I knew just how deep Jessica went. I was moved by her as a person and affected a great deal by the trust that she was putting into having a relationship with me.

But there was always the threat. It never went away.

I was living life again, but very little of it felt real. It was if I was no longer in the picture but watching it from the stands. I had normal days and weeks and moments when I was able to move past the fear of cancer and build life toward graduation. But there were the terrors of an unknown future that was ever present. There were days and weeks and moments when I felt like there was no future other than more illness and greater struggles that were destined to end in my death.

My plan had been to be working as a major-league play-by-play voice or the sports anchor in a major television market by the time I was thirty. But that future goal now looked like the haziest of pipe dreams. Forget the fact that I'd had to sit out three semesters to battle cancer, knocking my self-imposed schedule off its track. There was no way I would still be living by the age of thirty.

I didn't know when, or exactly how, or what it would eventually look like. But I knew that cancer was going to claim my life. In just over five years, I'd faced it three times. And while I ultimately won each battle in the end, I was losing the protracted war. My body was paying a price that it would eventually be unable to pay. So what was the point? What was I working toward? What were my ends?

I sleepwalked through that final year of school. It had its moments, and there were certainly times when I was able to psyche myself into believing that life could be healthy, normal, and long. I continued to work as a sports intern in L.A. television. I was able to continue with the play-by-play gig for APU basketball, and I even added the job of doing the broadcasts for Long Beach City College football. In May 1996, I graduated from college.

At times, it all felt like a facade.

Even when I was offered a full-time job with the new cable start-up Fox Sports Net that following fall and then moved into my own apartment in the Los Feliz area of Los Angeles, I knew it was all temporary. These things I was adding to my life—the job, the apartment, the illusion of a future—were all just momentary placeholders, filling space in my life until the next cancer shoe dropped.

I continued to grow in my relationship with Jessica, who'd also graduated that May and earned employment as a social worker in Los Angeles. She was the main thing that kept me grounded and focused on a possible future. Days with her were always good, so I tried to have as many of those as possible. My family rebounded from the fear and pain of 1995 and moved on with life, continuing to be as supportive in the process. New friends entered my life, old ones solidified, and I lived normally.

Søren Kierkegaard said, "Repetition is the reality and the seriousness of life." I spent day after day repeating my reality. I went to work at Fox and laughed with my friends at the good fortune we had of working in sports, living in Hollywood, and being in our midtwenties. Then I went home.

Day after day, that repetition began to crack my self-predicted reality of impending doom. I actually allowed myself to believe in that good fortune of job, friends, girlfriend, and future expectations. Time passed, life continued to remain good, and the external of my reality began to seep into the internal. I didn't just have the x's and o's of a good life forming. I began to feel it.

In October 1996, a comedy about coming-of-age in Los Angeles, *Swingers*, was released. A little-known cast appeared in the movie, which was made for an estimated two hundred thousand dollars—a sum so low that even the tightest of K-Mart wads would call it cheap. (That little-known cast now prints Hollywood money in the persons of Jon Favreau, Heather Graham, Ron Livingston, and Vince Vaughn.)

It was ninety-six minutes of new-to-L.A. friends going to bars, parties, and late-night pancake houses in Hollywood and Los Feliz. It was my neighborhood, and while it was not exactly my life—I wasn't trying to break into show business, and I never went swing dancing with Heather Graham at the Derby—I could relate to Mike's (Favreau's) plight. He was trying to get beyond his ex-girlfriend of the past several years and move forward with the new life he was making for himself in L.A., which included PlayStation hockey, burritos, and pizza.

My proverbial "ex" was my ex-life of compulsively walking the plank toward condemnation. I also had PlayStation as an integral part of my social life and the high-fat, high-carb, late-night barhopping lifestyle that came along with working a job that didn't end each day until midnight. And like Mike, I had a good core group of friends who did everything they could to open my eyes to the light forward.

I found it in the people, in the places and opportunities, and at work with Fox. If you ever want to feel alive, be in charge of full-screen graphics during a live sports broadcast that coincides with the NCAA revealing its matchups for March Madness. There is a special energy inside a control room during live television. But when that live TV takes place at the same time that the sports world focuses all of its intensities on basketball brackets, it's explosive.

I was working long hours, weekends, and holidays. It was exciting to be working with a start-up sports cable network that was attempting to be the guerilla army in the war on ESPN. We did as many as five hours of live television each night, bringing targeted sports news to each time zone and region across the country, often not ending until almost 1 AM, which was after the next day's morning show had been taped and put to bed.

Those late nights meant even later nights out with my coworkers, a group of people like me—young, energetic, in love with sports, and with what felt like bright futures in television. When Barney's Beanery, Cat 'N Fiddle, the Troubadour, or whatever the Hollywood bar of the night was would close (the Fox Sports studios were on Sunset Boulevard back then), I'd get home at 3 AM or later, depending on if we hit a twenty-four-hour pancake house before calling it a night—or morning.

On my days and nights off, usually a Tuesday and Wednesday, I made sure to see Jessica. The weekends, however, were always wall-to-wall sports television. It was the nature of the business, and most of us loved it.

I was getting to do more play-by-play on the side of my main gig at Fox. When I had nights off or when I could work it into my Saturday afternoons before needing to be at Fox that evening, I was in Long Beach calling football and basketball games. I got a special charge out of doing play-by-play, and I saw it as my ticket to the big time, so I did it as often as possible. And of course as someone who fancied himself a writer and had a Los Angeles mailing address, I engaged in the inevitable writing of my first screenplay. (Living in Los Angeles and having a couple of screenplays under my belt makes me about as unique as an Angeleno with a headshot—which I also happen to have.)

Two years earlier I'd discovered the lump in my neck, which led to the bone marrow transplant. But in November and December of 1996, that moment and those memories felt like a lifetime ago. Just one year earlier I had been on autopilot, waiting for the next and final shoe to drop. I didn't even know that guy anymore. The great thing about being down in a deep and dark valley is that there's always another mountain peak just on the other side. Start with steps, which turn to strides, and eventually you'll be at a jog. Before you know it, you're climbing up the other side, the valley below long forgotten.

The calendar ticked over to 1997, and that spring I marked the two-year anniversary of the end of my bone marrow transplant by heading out to City of Hope for its annual BMT reunion picnic and celebration. I was most looking forward to sitting down over a hot dog with a fellow stem cell survivor named Tom. We began our treatments at City of Hope on the exact same day, and our diagnosis history had been nearly identical. We'd stayed in touch the first few months after treatment, and I'd visited him at his home in Santa Monica. He was a commercial director who'd just landed his first feature before getting sick, and we'd bonded in the hospital over our shared misery. But truth be told, the interruption to my life was nothing when compared to his. The father of two was about to achieve his ultimate dream, only to have it abruptly crushed. I was impressed by the way Tom handled the disappointment of his misfortunes, and I was drawn to him because of it.

I checked in for the picnic and picked up my two-year survivor's button—an oversized adornment that proudly announced to everyone the number of years since my transplant. I then made my way over to the nursing coordinator, Karen, who'd been in charge of scheduling my treatments and hospitalizations. She was the taskmaster general who made sure that the nuts and bolts behind the medicine stayed lubed and operational. She also knew Tom and would know where I could find him. We'd lost touch for most of the last year, but I knew he wouldn't miss the reunion.

I found Karen greeting other patients over by the rose garden. She was kind, soft-spoken, and always carried with her the nurturing air of a lifetime caregiver. She greeted me with a smile and a hug, as always, and I asked if she'd seen Tom.

With a slight change in expression, she moved me over to the side of the garden and away from other patients. "Tom died a few weeks ago. I'm sorry."

My head started swirling. My breath caught. Tom was dead. Tom was me, and I was him. Our diseases and treatments were nearly identical. Yet he was dead.

Karen may have told me in greater detail what specifically caused his death. I honestly don't remember how the rest of the conversation went, or most of the day that followed. It might have been a return of the disease or that it was never successfully fought back during the transplant. He had none of the side effects that I did. When I was struggling to get my body back into shape for the next round of treatments, suffering might-ily from its poisons, Tom breezed through to the next round. His counts never crashed like mine. His schedule was never delayed. I was always envious.

Were those eases a sign that the treatment had been less effective inside his body? It certainly had done more damage inside mine and to my healthy tissue. It only stood to reason that it did more damage to my cancerous tissue. Or were those thoughts the rationalizations of just hav-ing had the rug ripped out from under me, mixed with the silver-lining desires of wishful thinking?

I walked over to the far side of campus to be alone, away from my parents and Jessica, who all had made the trip to Duarte to "celebrate life." I sat down under a tree and stared blankly at the ground. I didn't cry for Tom or for the reminder that death still lurked nearby. I just sat quietly, alone with my thoughts, replaying my own standing in life.

I was happy to be alive. I was glad it wasn't me; yet those very real and honest thoughts left me feeling empty, as if a part of my humanity had been leeched out through chemotherapy. Where were my emotions? How deep had they been buried?

When you are used to thinking of things in terms of life and death, those become your bookend benchmarks. When mere survival is the foremost driver in your life, the scales of perspective get calibrated quite coldly.

I was of course sad to lose Tom. My heart was breaking for his kids, who would over time eventually lose the vivid memories of their father. What a tragedy, that our minds can't retain those most important of reflections.

I was sad for the loss of Tom's future and the gifts that he had to offer the world. He was a brilliant and kind man who befriended me, a fledgling college student seventeen years his junior. He was a film director, now granted with an incredible perspective, who no doubt had important works still to do. Now he was gone.

But I wasn't. Same diagnosis, same treatment, but with starkly different results. I felt selfish, and a big part of me still feels that way as I write this. But as I sat there alone, mourning his passing, I couldn't push away the sensation of relief that it wasn't me. Do instincts of survival become so strong at a certain point that we become willing to accept anything that isn't our own death? I hoped not then, and I hope not now. But I was disturbed by how unsure I was of the answer.

At the news of Tom's death, I was shocked instead of saddened. I was numb instead of grief stricken. I found myself detached and not distraught. And all of that disturbed me.

After about twenty minutes of reflection, I gathered myself and rejoined the celebration. I saw my doctors, and we exchanged smiles and greetings. I swapped life updates with a few other patients I knew from my time in the hospital, and it was pleasant and nice to see them. But I left City of Hope that day feeling noticeably somber. A life ended—a good life at that—and we should all be more heartbroken. Including me.

My emotions of relief and consolation were all wrong. I was afraid that it signaled within me a dying of certain human emotions. Is this what happens to people terrified by thoughts of their own demise?

I began the summer of 1997 learning how to compartmentalize the fun me—the Kyle who had hopes, dreams, and expectations for the future—with the survivor me, the Kyle who was singularly focused on staying alive. The compartments were fairly easy to separate and remained safely locked away from each other. And the survivor me wasn't called upon much, if at all.

I still spoke about my experiences with small groups and newly diagnosed patients needing to see someone, anyone, who was still alive after getting that news. But the further along I went into my current life and the more distance that gathered between where I was going and where I had been, the less important those speeches became for my growth. Before, it had been the necessary cultivation of who I wanted to become. Now it took on an air of nuisance.

The fun me ended up so separate and disconnected from the survivor me, the guy who was still a heart patient, that I stopped taking my daily medications. Being a patient was becoming exhausting. It wasn't normal to be twenty-five and be on the same heart medications as your grandparents. It wasn't normal to have a hematologist on speed dial and have the names of chemotherapy drugs roll off the tongue as easily as the selected starting infields for the two Major League Baseball All-Star teams.

As much as I lived like a normal person, or attempted to, there was no denying my differences. Normal was not in the cards, yet it was the only thing I truly craved.

So I stopped taking my medication. It was a nonsensical and futile effort to try and be a nonpatient, but I didn't care. I just wanted to be without that tether, even if it was momentary.

I'd not heard much from my cardiologist about the specifics of my condition anyway. How much I really needed the medication had never been fully explained, so I considered it up for debate. I rationalized its exclusion from my daily regimen as a minor health blip that came with huge emotional payoffs. Physically I didn't feel any different not taking it in that first week. But mentally I felt lifted from its burden. I found it ironic that the removal of something measured in milligrams could make me so perceptibly lighter.

That's how life went through the month of June and the first week of July. I was medicine free and generally guilt free. There was still a rational person living inside of me who knew that my break from the medication could only last so long. My senses had taken a brief leave, but my medical IQ had not. I knew, eventually.

But the break that I was getting from patienthood, albeit small and indiscernible to those on the outside of the observation glass, was sedative to me inside. It made me feel ordinary.

Until that second week of July, when I had my first nosebleed.

9

JULY 23, 1997

When you have a workday that begins at 3 PM on most days and ends at or beyond midnight, solitude becomes your friend. Before you head into work, your days are spent largely alone. After work, most of the world is already asleep. And when the daily grind includes full workdays on Saturday and Sunday, midweek days off leave you with the lifestyle of the unemployed and friendless.

Living that lifestyle, you can't be too proud to go to the movies alone. Meals are either takeout or tables for one. And if you want a vacation that extends beyond a twenty-four-hour road trip to Vegas or that contains some actual relaxation not found during overnight drives to and from Tijuana, you'd better be open to traveling alone.

That first week of August, I had such a vacation planned for myself. I was going to take a week to drive and tour the California coast, ending with a few days of solitude spent exploring the city of San Francisco. My mom had recently taken a job in the Bay Area and was renting a small apartment just a few blocks up from Fisherman's Wharf in the North Beach area. She had also been hit with the same "God must have a plan; that's why Kyle keeps getting cancer" bromide that I'd experienced from a few of the more cut-and-dry die-hards at Azusa Pacific, which soured her on some members of the faculty. She took a job back in corporate education, away from Christian higher education, and my parents became a bi-city couple. Half their weekends were spent in San Francisco, the other half in L.A., and most weekdays they were apart.

It wasn't an ideal setup in the least. My mom needed my dad, and I don't think either of them quite knew just how much he needed her. I was now gone, living about forty-five minutes away in the heart of the city. After making a move to Kansas City for his job and then a move to California, also largely for his job, she was entitled to do a little career chasing of her own. She'd recently completed her PhD work at the Claremont Colleges and was ready for a new professional challenge.

Beyond the professional, there was also a personal experience that she was chasing. Married to my dad at nineteen and a mother just a handful of days before her twenty-second birthday, she'd never been on her own. My mom had never experienced adult life as an individual. She was always a part of a family. The move to San Francisco wasn't an effort to get away from my dad or the family that she'd always had, but it was an opportunity for self-discovery. I also think a part of it was to recharge herself after the exhaustion of our multiple cancer battles.

For the weekend that my planned vacation had me in San Francisco, my parents would be together in L.A. I'd have a free and private place to crash in a great location. Missing out on a good portion of my early twenties because of cancer, I was also in search of a little adventure. I was hopeful that my week along the Pacific would provide a small taste of it.

But there was one major problem looming. My mind was ready and willing to have its batteries recharged along the cliffs of the Central Coast, but my body was not. For more than a week, I'd been dealing with nosebleeds and body bruises. They weren't the small bruises that everyone gets from time to time when running inside a television studio filled with moving chairs and desk corners—these were big bruises that made me look like I'd been beaten by a baseball-bat-wielding gang of Little League toughs.

My breath would leave me after just the slightest physical exertion. I first noticed it walking into the studio from my car. Next, stairs and hills became unmanageable. After traversing even the tamest of inclines, I would find myself bent over double, gasping for air. It even got to the point where I would delay going to the bathroom as long as possible when

I was sitting at home watching television, because the short fifteen-foot walk to the toilet was taking all the air in my lungs.

I broke down and called my cardiologist. From experiences with chemotherapy and the stem cell transplant, I'd learned enough about how my body reacted to differing blood counts to figure out where the source of the problem could be found. After nearly five weeks off, I'd recently restarted taking my cardiac medications. One of the potential side effects of those drugs was shortness of breath. I couldn't imagine that it would have manifested itself in such a severe manner, but obviously it had. Or the sudden reintroduction of the medication into my system had done something sinister to crash my blood counts.

Whatever the source of my collapsing counts, I needed to have the ship righted as quickly as possible. If I didn't have the strength or energy to make regular trips to the restroom, how could I pull off a solo coastal vacation?

I called my cardiologist and explained to him my symptoms, my thoughts on a blood-count diagnosis, and my belief that the heart meds were the most likely suspect. He listened but took almost no time in offering his counterargument to my medication theory. "You need to call your hematologist, not me."

The specific hematologist who had treated me through the duration of my stem cell transplant had since left the City of Hope. But one of the strengths of their treatment philosophy is their team concept. Each patient has one primary doctor, but an entire group of a dozen or more MDs know your case, your history, and the chosen course of therapy. They present the details of each case to the group at a weekly staff meeting, giving you, the patient, the benefit of their collective brilliance.

I had a new hematologist, Dr. Anthony Stein, whom I'd only seen a couple of times in follow-up to my stem cell transplant. But I knew the stock that the stable of City of Hope hematologists came from quite well, and I was comfortable with him as my doctor. He's a quiet but confident man. And that fills you, the patient, with confidence.

I called him and explained my symptoms, and Dr. Stein decided that he wanted to see me the very next day.

On July 23, I made the now twenty-five-mile drive out to Duarte and managed to muster enough oxygen to shuffle my way into the outpatient clinic. I gave a quick vial of blood to the lab, then found a seat in the small waiting room attached to the hematology clinic. (The City of Hope has since expanded into a beautiful outpatient facility with large open-floor waiting rooms. In 1997 it was all still contained in its much smaller and older original hospital building.)

Waiting, I couldn't help but engage in clock watching. I was still planning to go to work that afternoon. The other guys in my department were already going to have to cover my duties when I went on vacation. That wasn't a huge deal; it was simply the system we worked in. But I didn't want to force them to cover sick days around my trip on top of it. It was also a really beautiful summer afternoon, and there would be suspicions that I was taking a bonus beach day before heading out on vacation.

Finally an exam room was available—it was very much like that original exam room all those years ago when I was first introduced to life as a cancer patient. It was ten foot by ten foot, with a small expandable table to one side and a pair of chairs and a sink on the other to provide balance. As I sat and waited for the doctor, my mind raced through the probability that I might not get out of there as quickly as I'd hoped. Receiving a unit of blood, or even a bag of platelets, was a distinct possibility. I only hoped that one or the other—or both—would be enough to stabilize my blood and get me back to normal.

The door opened with a quick clatter, breaking me free of the waiting-room trance that so often absorbs those who are used to hours of waiting in hospitals or government agencies. It's like a computer's sleep setting, but for people. You're on low power and mostly shut down, but you can quickly snap out of it and back to full alertness without having to wait for a full system reboot.

Back on full, I greeted Dr. Stein, and he did the same in return. He then asked me a couple of quick questions about how I was doing. Although since he had my blood results in his right hand, I suspected he already knew.

Getting to the point and not mincing any words, Dr. Stein revealed the results. "You have an acute leukemia."

The little breath that resided in my lungs was suddenly gone. I couldn't think. Then I couldn't stop thinking, my mind awash with a thousand thoughts but none of them in one place long enough for me to focus. Then the room started to close in.

I knew instantly what it meant for me to have leukemia. I was just finishing my eighth year as a cancer patient. I'd read every pamphlet and handout written about Hodgkin's disease, lymphoma, chemotherapy, and the side effects that can sometimes show up years after treatment. I knew about chemotherapy-induced leukemia. On the scale of desirable diagnoses, it would be better to hear that my Hodgkin's had returned than to find out that I was now facing leukemia.

I finally found my voice. "But it all came on so quickly. Just two weeks ago I was fine."

Even as I said these words, I recognized the unmistakable sound of useless protests. It's an acute leukemia. Of course it came on quickly.

Dr. Stein asked me if there was anyone he could call. My dad was just down the road in Azusa, no more than fifteen minutes away. I gave Dr. Stein the number. After dialing, he handed me the phone.

My very first memory of ever feeling or being sick dates back to when we were living in Nashville in the mid-1970s. I stayed home from kindergarten with the flu one day and was allowed to lie on the couch, watch television, and drink soda through a silly straw. It was awesome. It's also one of the earliest memories I have of getting a gift from my dad. On his way home from work that day, he stopped at a store and bought me a Dopey figurine, my favorite of the Seven Dwarfs. It was plastic and blue and probably quite inexpensive. But in the long list of presents that I received as a child, it's one of the only gifts I remember.

It was fitting, then, that when I was driven home after my final hospitalization for the bone marrow transplant, it was my dad doing the driving. We didn't say much on that short drive. We never said a lot to each other in serious moments like that. He's not an open gusher in regard to his feelings, and neither am I. There is no doubt that we love each other very much, and we seem to both be from the school that believes if it's obvious, where's the need to voice it? In this respect, we are perhaps too much alike.

"Hey, Dad."

"How did it go at the doctor?" I'd seen my parents for lunch the weekend before, and my exhaustion was hard to hide. They'd asked and I'd evaded, but I did update them a couple nights later when the appointment was scheduled. The overall severity of my symptoms, however, had been a tightly kept secret.

"It's not good. I'm still here, and I'm going to be here awhile." And then I paused a second, my throat constricting with dryness, before I verbally admitted the defeat of reality. "I have leukemia."

With no pause on his end, my dad replied, "I'll be there as soon as I can."

Dr. Stein took the phone and finished up with a few more answers for my dad, but I heard none of it. My head was swirling and the entire room was spinning, as if I was being flushed from the face of the Earth and into the obscurity of the damned.

"Can I call anyone else?"

Dr. Stein had finished with my dad and was now looking at me with the heavy eyes of someone acting as a reluctant executioner. There was one other person I needed to call, but someone who I also felt compelled to protect from what would surely turn into an out-of-control freight train destroying everything in its path.

I gave him Jessica's number.

She'd given of herself so freely and with so much devotion during my bone marrow transplant two years earlier. And with so little obligation. Now she had everything to lose, and I had every responsibility to try and protect her. I loved her, and because of that I wanted to keep her life as free from pain as possible. Yet here I was, about to invite her to another nightmare, one I knew she couldn't—and wouldn't—say no to. How could I tell her? How could I not?

"Hey, Jess."

"Are you at work yet?"

"No. I'm still at the hospital." Breaking, but summoning the strength, I released the trapdoor on the gallows: "They say I have leukemia."

"What?!"

It was part question, part protest, and part curse. Within those four letters, there was shock, disbelief, and panic. For a split second, the clocks of the world stopped ticking, and we both sat on the phone, numb and incredulous. It was horrendous on my end of the phone, where I sat surrounded by context. I can only imagine what it was like going from the banality of a workday, sitting in your office engaged in the mundane, to the sudden axial shift of hearing a leukemia diagnosis.

"Just please come after work. I'll explain it to you then."

But what was there to explain? I'd been handed a death sentence. I knew what it meant to have leukemia. I knew what it meant to have leukemia caused by chemotherapy. And I knew that based on how suddenly we had to stop treatment in 1995 because of my heart damage, the options this time around would be even more limited. It was a death sentence as sure as if they'd handed me a hood and a noose.

There would be no life to look forward to. There would be no future for me, or with Jessica. She'd seen me through some of the most difficult moments of my life. Now she was going to be there for my final moments. It was cruel, but it was life. It happens every day. Now it was happening to me.

I'd felt for some time that I was going to die before celebrating my thirtieth birthday. Now I knew that my twenty-sixth birthday, just four weeks away, would probably be my last.

DURING MY STEM cell transplant of 1995, I had been privy to the most amazing and beautiful display of human grace and dignity. One afternoon I was receiving a pair of platelet bags to replenish my own depleted reserves. I sat in a chair in the infusion room next to a bed behind a curtain. A young woman occupied the bed, and the muffled voices of her and her family revealed that she was a cancer patient who had been fighting for some time. She sat with her parents, who, it was clear, had been exhausted by the struggle as much as she.

Her doctor entered the room, then ducked behind the curtain to have the very talk that every physician dreads. Her disease wasn't responding to treatments as they'd hoped. Other than more chemotherapy, her options were few. They'd been running on a treadmill for months, and there was nothing to do but either keep running or stop.

With her parents by her side, this young woman summoned the courage that can only be found in the most human of our species. She told them and her doctor that she was ready to go home and enjoy her final days the best she could. There would be no more chemotherapy treatments and no more nights of nausea and vomiting. But there would also be no more hopes of a cure. She would die, but it was going to be on her terms.

Her voice never cracked, not once. For their part, her parents seemed to stay strong and supportive. They had been through so much as a family, so much pain and anguish, but now they were unified in their readiness to be done.

I felt like the ultimate intruder, being in the room that day. This was the most private of human moments taking place between people who knew the tightest bonds of love. I was an outsider, trespassing on their privacy. But I couldn't stop listening either. The strength and courage in her voice was mesmerizing. I was in awe of this woman who seemed to feel such peace at the very moment that she made the choice to die.

Could I ever carry such a burden with that kind of dignity? Could I ever make that same decision to stop treatment and die in the place and time of my choosing? Could I ask the same of my family, to have them be there when I told my doctor that enough was enough?

For millions, hope is the last thread of human dignity they hold. Without hope, they are helpless. The continuing of life feels pointless. But what would it take for me to get to that place? When does the pain of struggle tip the scales of life beyond its moments of beauty? As bad as things were during my bone marrow transplant, I never reached that place. There was always a chance at a cure, so that drove me. And there was always another coming moment, no matter its length or significance, that would make me glad to be alive.

If that time of futility ever came, I hoped to be as dignified. I hoped to be as strong and as at peace. But most of all, I hoped.

I WAS USHERED out of the exam room with Dr. Stein and put into the very same bed that had been the sight of such humanity more than two years earlier. How many other great people had passed through its sheets, filled with the grace that you can only find in humans in the final stages of life?

Physically I was at the bottom of the blood-count barrel when I drove out to City of Hope that afternoon. The normal hemoglobin count in the red blood cells of a healthy individual is in the 14.0 to 16.0 range. My count was 4.5.

A platelet count in someone with healthy blood can range from 160,000 to more than 400,000. On the afternoon of July 23, my platelet count was 12,000.

I was put into bed and immediately hooked up to an IV. The order was for three units of red blood and two bags of platelets. Before anything else could be discussed in terms of a long-term therapy or prognosis, we had to deal with the critical problem of my failing systems. Within fifteen minutes of first hearing the word "leukemia," my IV was in and operational.

When I learned about Tom's death a few months earlier, my body didn't respond with many tears. I had red eyes and maybe one or two tears actually fell, but the emotions of the moment were simply too deep to drain out in any meaningful way. Something in my physiological response system had deadened, keeping me too composed for the meaning of the moment.

Once I'd made my phone calls and moved to the bed and into the relative privacy of the sliding curtain, I emotionally fell to pieces. I was dying, and it was as if the life in me was pouring out in liquid form. I wasn't just crying—I was sobbing the guttural sobs of the damned. I was in mourning for the life that I had allowed myself to picture but that was now fading from the light.

I had a career, a family, and a list of adventures that I'd started to imagine. But in an inverse of having your life flash before your eyes, the life that

I would never get to live was fast-forwarding through my consciousness. I wasn't picturing the places that I'd been or the memorable moments that I'd had. The images of the "never would be" were crashing my cognizance.

As I lay there suffering with my not-so-silent sobs, the nurse who'd hung my first bag of blood sat down beside me. She verbally acknowledged that I'd gotten "some really tough news," then didn't say another word. She didn't need to. She sat and stroked my hand, and it was everything.

Looking back, I don't remember the details of what she looked like. I don't know her name or if she was a nurse who I'd seen previously at City of Hope. I was seeing through tear-soaked eyes and looking at life through the refracted light of heartbreak. Nothing was clear, especially the images in front of me.

But I do remember the specifics of her touch. It was the simplest of acts, stroking my hand. There was less dread in my heart because of its reminder that people, including total strangers, still cared. I'd been condemned to die, but at least I wouldn't have to make that walk to the end alone. The world still had beauty in the touch of those who cared.

My father arrived a few minutes later, still wearing the coat and tie from work. The Azusa Pacific University community is fairly small. With my parents in the faculty and me a visible member of the student body during my stem cell transplant in 1995, most people on campus knew what was happening with our family. So when the leukemia call came from Dr. Stein and me in 1997, the scab was easy to pick. His office was hyperaware of what it meant for him to have to rush off to City of Hope unexpectedly.

I explained to him the best that I could about what was happening with me physically. The emotional state of things didn't need to be discussed. It was written all over my face with a thick-point black permanent Sharpie. Everything I was feeling on the inside was readily visible on the surface. He just sat, listened, and supported silently. What could he say? It was a shot to the gut for all of us. He was as stunned into silence as I was into tears. Reassurances of "It's going to be all right" would have been hollow and disingenuous. Rah-rah speeches about taking the fight to cancer would have been too soon. I was told that whatever I needed, he would provide, and then we sat. (At some point later, he called my mother in San Francisco.)

Following the dropping of that hammer of a diagnosis, the words and emotions of the moment behind the privacy curtain were implicit. There was no lack of emotion from either of us. But the words were unnecessary, almost to the level that they were unwanted. The silence passed, and it was preferred.

Next in was Jessica. I'd settled down into the normal rhythms of a postdiagnosis existence with my dad, even allowing for a stilted joke or two. But when Jessica walked through the door, I was hit with another wave of the life that was slipping away. She had been such an important rock for me in 1995 as a friend. Now she was much more than a friend, and I couldn't help but once again go in spirit to my inevitable demise.

We shared a cry together as I filled her in on the details as I knew them. Much of what I knew, or thought I knew, was conjecture from the layman's knowledge I had about leukemia. No one had any details about my particular case because there were so many disease-specific unknowns. The exact type of leukemia that I had was still to be determined.

Jessica was with me no matter what it took. No matter how long it took. No matter the price. It had been her instinctual reaction the moment she heard me utter the word "leukemia." Now, following what had to be one of the longest drives in from downtown Los Angeles, both literally and figuratively, that conviction remained and had become more resolved. I don't know if my father or Jessica had the same feelings of doom that I did. I don't know if they truly realized at that moment just how precarious my life and future were. I couldn't stop thinking about it, but I wouldn't put a voice to it. And neither did they.

As the platelets and blood units did their duty and rescued me from the brink, it became time to do further testing and find out exactly what kind of leukemia we were dealing with. Of course, the favored test to help solve that mystery was a bone marrow biopsy.

There was a certain amount of poetic irony to the entire scene. I'd survived the initial blow of diagnosis and managed to turn what was slipping into a day of despair into one with limited laughter and smiles. Then up popped the dreaded bone marrow biopsy.

I couldn't help but think of *The Simpsons* episode when Krusty the Klown's half-brother, Luke Perry, gets shot out of a cannon during Krusty's big comeback special. Perry goes flying out of the studio, through the museum of sandpaper, through a display of acid at the Kwik-E-Mart, and lands safely on pillows at a pillow factory. Seconds later, the pillow factory is demolished.

I was Luke Perry in this scenario, minus the quiet scowling breathiness.

Punched in my own pillow factory but eventually done with the procedure, I was finally removed from the infusion room and given a regular hospital bed in the inevitable private room. The blood and platelets still came in bunches throughout the evening, but even that ended before the calendar clicked. I was back from the brink, alive but with a very cloudy future.

I WAS INTRODUCED to the cycle of life when I was a young kid spending summers at my grandparents' home on Lake Barkley in Kentucky. It was a beautiful rural property covered in trees on top of a short hill that led down to a dock on the lake. Our summers there were long, slow, and as predictable as the coming of the mayflies, which would show up suddenly by the millions in early June, then leave just as quickly.

Hatched from eggs laid along the bottom of the lake, adult mayflies live for no more than a day. They have no mouths, and their digestive systems are filled with air. They exist for no other reason than to reproduce and advance the species. It's the ultimate in organic phenomena.

But the life cycle on the lake didn't end with the mayfly's procreation and passing over. We discovered that a writhing mayfly on the end of a fishing hook helped pass on life to the fish in the lake. Or perhaps it's more accurate to say that the mayfly helped bring the fish into the human life chain and onto our dinner plates.

When humans get involved, however, the biology of the life cycle starts to encounter resistance. After I hauled in my first-ever fish, a whopper of a bluegill every bit as big as a fully grown hamster, my grandfather taught me how to clean it. Since I was an inquisitive six-year-old with natural curiosity, that led to the next progression in the life cycle: questions about why it's called "cleaning" a fish, since there didn't seem to be one clean element to the process.

Sitting on the dinner table that night were several beautiful catfish filets that my grandfather brought in on his trotline earlier in the afternoon. They'd been cleaned, breaded, fried to a perfect golden brown, and served with all of the fixin's of the quintessential Southern fish fry. Sitting on the plate next to the perfectly shaped catfish filets was a lone little bluegill filet, now reduced to the size of a breaded silver dollar.

I was proud of my bluegill. My grandfather was bigger than me and had many more years of lake experience under his belt. If we broke it down by a ratio of body weight to hours fishing to actual ounces of fish caught, I stacked up pretty strong. But when it came to the next test of the evening—the eating of our prized catches—I forfeited any of the fisherman cred I'd collected on the boat that day. I couldn't bring myself to eat my sad little bluegill. On that plate that night, the cycle of life that began with the hatching of a single mayfly—which lived for the one day I used it as bait at the end of my fishing pole—came to its hopeless and unsuccessful conclusion.

Life is more than just biology. The death of one in the sea of millions is still the death of one. And for someone, that one is the entire world. The cycle of life does not just roll along in a protected vacuum of inevitability. When human emotions and connections are involved, the cycle gets corrupted.

IN MY HOSPITAL room, with my world turned upside and with nothing beyond the next two hours of my future assured, I saw the cycle of life rolling by outside my window. Cars filled the 210 Freeway as thousands of drivers headed home after another boringly normal day of work. In homes across the country families were sitting around the dinner table, and kids were giving one-word answers to questions about their day.

The next morning would begin with alarm clocks, coffeemakers, and monotonous commutes to offices filled with cubicles. People would be involved in inane conversations about what clothes are hot and what dates were not. Lawns would be mowed, groceries would be purchased, and the days and nights of life would seamlessly blend together into endless uniformity.

The cycle of human life in America continued unchecked on July 23, 1997. It looked exactly like it had the day before, and it was exactly like it would be on the next. But for me, nothing remained the same. It was the cruelest of realities. My life ended that day. Everyone else's rolled on as is. It was cold and unjust, but a stark reminder of the authenticity of life's randomness.

10

ACUTE LYMPHOCYTIC LEUKEMIA

The port that was implanted in my chest for chemotherapy infusions in 1991 was the perfect solution for that particular course of therapy. It only had to be accessed twice a month, so keeping it tucked below the skin and away from the hassles of daily cleaning was ideal. Other than when I had to remove the access line at the end of each long day of in-office chemotherapy and at-home anti-nausea IVs, it was virtually maintenance free. I could get it wet, go swimming, and not have to worry about infections.

During my chemotherapy and stem cell transplant in 1995, it was a different story. There were daily chemotherapy treatments and blood draws as well as frequent infusions of blood and platelets. The added step of having to access the port with a large-gauge hooked needle made the port highly impractical for regular use. (The large-gauge hooked needle did not just go into the port. It had to go through the skin of my chest first. So it was both unworkable and unwanted, at least as far as the patient was concerned.)

In 1995 a Hickman catheter was implanted to solve this problem. It's an external line that essentially serves the same purpose as the port, allowing access to veins without the worry of needle sticks or leaking IV lines. It comes with two contact points, making it the perfect tool for long-term chemotherapy treatments—like the seventy-two-hour chemo drips of the stem cell transplant—while still allowing for blood draws. The only downside is that since it is external, the connection site (where the catheter enters the chest wall) has to be cleaned daily. It's essentially an open wound the entire time the line is in place.

The day after I was diagnosed with leukemia, I was back in surgery and getting another Hickman catheter. The jury was still out on the exact course of therapy I'd be undertaking in the coming weeks and months, but there was no question that it would involve more chemo. I hadn't had the line during my day of mass blood infusions on the twenty-third, and my veins had paid the price in bruises. It's hard not to feel like a cancer patient when you have a chemotherapy line swinging freely from your chest, but it's far better than presenting yourself as an all-access pincushion for trainee phlebotomists.

With the Hickman in place and my blood counts stable, the doctors made the compassionate decision to let me leave the hospital and go home. It was now Friday, two days since I had been diagnosed, and the doctors wanted to give me a weekend at home and away from the hospital before what we all assumed would be a lengthy stay as an inpatient. I couldn't help but think of the weekend at home as an unspoken opportunity to say my good-byes. I was convinced that when I returned to the hospital that next Monday, it would be for good.

AT MY PARENTS' house that night—I wasn't allowed to go to my apartment in Los Angeles, as it was too far away—my mom (now home from San Francisco), my dad, Jessica, and I pretended that it was just another night around the dinner table. We are not good actors.

Jessica had been a major part of my life for more than two years at this point, and she was accepted and embraced by my parents as a part of the family. All parents, especially mothers, are protective of their sons when it comes to the women they choose to love. Because of what I'd been through, it was safe to say that my mother's antennae were especially sensitive in this area. But the progressive tightening of the bonds that had been created at the beginning of my relationship with Jessica were more

From the time I could walk and talk, I could swim. Although like me, kids' goggles circa 1975 weren't made to be very "aquadynamic."

One of the things I loved most growing up was sports—in this case the St. Louis Cardinals football uniform I was given for Christmas in 1978 (quarterback Jim Hart wore number 17). Another was our beloved family dog, Cricket.

Nothing gave me more pride as a kid than pulling on the stirrup socks of my baseball uniform. Sadly, it was obvious by the fourth grade that my baseball abilities weren't keeping pace with my love of the game.

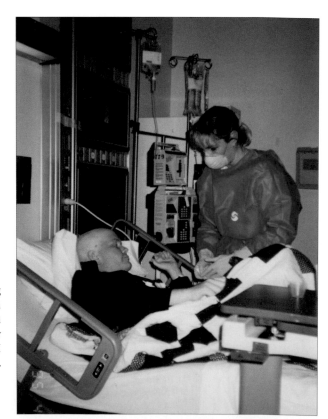

Receiving chemotherapy during my bone marrow transplant in 1995. The nurse is protected from the poisons of the chemotherapy with a gown, a mask, and gloves. I have pajamas.

One of the many times during our concurrent bone marrow transplants that my friend Tom Coyne beat me to the hospital release. Less than two years later, the father of two lost his battle with recurrent Hodgkin's disease.

A year after my bone marrow transplant and my third battle with Hodgkin's disease, with hair back on my head, I graduated from college flanked by my parents. It was a day that seemed an impossibility just twelve months earlier.

In 2005 Carrie and I were married on ABC's *Extreme Makeover: Wedding Edition*, which featured a bachelor party with Chiefs tight end Tony Gonzalez, a dance lesson from choreographer Cris Judd, and a reception performance by the one and only Liza Minnelli.

PHOTOGRAPH BY VIVIAN ZINK

Surrounded by a motorcade of police and personal bodyguards, I carried the Salt Lake City Winter Olympic Torch when it came through Los Angeles in January 2002. My weak and damaged heart never felt stronger.

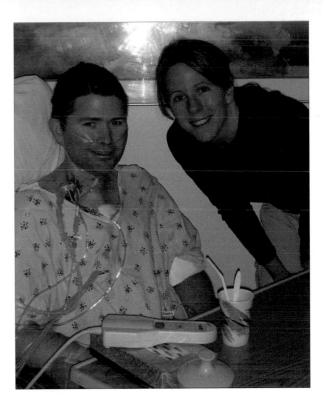

On October 12, 2006, just thirty-six hours after heart transplant, I was sitting up, feeling strong, and making plans with Carrie on how we were going to fill our now limitless future.

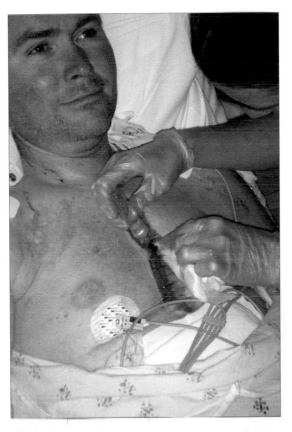

Of the many scars that populate my body, I wear none with more pride than my heart transplant scar. It is a daily reminder of the life that I was given by the man who beats below.

Just eleven months after my heart transplant, Carrie and I took to the beaches of Malibu for our first official triathlon. September 16, 2007, was a life-defining day.

My first Team In Training triathlon coaches, Tim Petlin (left) and Todd Weinstein (right) were instrumental in getting me to that initial finish line and instilling in me a love of the sport. They continue to be trusted and supportive friends.

Moments after my seven-second miss at the Ironman swim in 2009, I was mercifully removed from the crush of the television cameras and given some alone time with Carrie and my mom.

You won't find a more impressive group of athletes than those who gather every two years for the U.S. Transplant Games. I was honored with a request to address the hundreds of kidneys, livers, hearts, and lungs that convened for the 2010 U.S. Transplant Games in Madison, Wisconsin.

Minutes before the start of the swim at the 2010 Ironman World Championship in Kona, Hawaii, and ready to settle a twelve-month score. I am the one with his goggles already strapped in place.

Just across the bike-mount line at the 2010 Ironman World Championship, I was happily out of the water and ready to brave the Queen K Highway.

than enough to win over my mother and father. They loved her for her commitment and devotion and for the stabilizing force that she'd become in my life. She also happened to be a hard person not to like.

We sat there as one unit, engaged in as much mindless chitchat as we could safely get away with without it devolving to the point of intentional insipidness. We ignored the leukemia elephant in the room and talked about sports, work, and the headlines of *People* magazine. This was still a few years before the reality television wave swamped network schedules, but if somehow a camera crew had been in our living room that evening taping a pilot for the genre, it would have been rejected as cheap and empty entertainment for the dull and feebleminded. (Good thing the world dodged that misdiagnosed bullet.)

Dinner and the evening eventually came to a close, and I said good night to my parents. Each time I said good night, it mattered. It was one less night that I would be home, and maybe one less night that I would be alive. This didn't feel like the defeatist me dominating my assumptions. It felt like the pragmatist me grappling with reality. I'd had my legs knocked out from under me with the stunning diagnosis on Wednesday. I wasn't about to be staggered by more of the unexpected.

Jessica stayed the night, and we fell asleep at about 9:30 PM. I was fitful as sleep descended, unable to shake the closing suffocation of dread. Nightmares are a common side effect of certain chemotherapy drugs. Considering the state of your mind in the midst of chemotherapy, you can imagine just how vivid and upsetting those nightmares can be.

That night, I wasn't on chemotherapy yet, just a mild painkiller to ease the discomfort from the procedure to implant the Hickman. But the nightmares returned.

A few hours later, I was awake. It was dark, and I was sticky and wet. I reached up to feel the shirt that I was wearing, and it was soaked through. Jessica stirred awake, then fumbled for the lamp to turn it on. We were both shocked into complete consciousness by what we saw. My shirt looked as if I'd been bathing in blood. The expanding stain had soaked its way through the sheet and onto the mattress below. If I had been shot in the chest by a high-powered rifle, there couldn't have been any more blood.

The sight of the blood, its quantity, and its source added a huge new wrinkle to an already anxious situation. It was obviously leaking from the hole where the Hickman had just been implanted. I'd never before bled from a catheter, and I'd never faced such an immediate emergency during the many years as a cancer patient. The acute stress of the moment released the requisite adrenaline in the both of us, resulting in immediate action.

Like a battle-tested field nurse from the U.S. Army, Jessica didn't hesitate. With wits fully about her, she sprang from the bed, found a closet with a towel that was deemed blood-stain appropriate, then helped me out of bed, down the stairs, and out to the car. I thought to myself right then and there, *If I ever do get shot in the chest by a high-powered rifle, I hope Jessica is beside me.*

Not quite sure what to do or where to go, we headed to City of Hope. The hospital did have doctors on call at night, but it wasn't set up as a traditional emergency room. It certainly wasn't the place to go with a broken bone following a car accident—or after getting shot in the chest. But since it was clear that the blood was coming from the incision site for my Hickman and I didn't want to get a first-year resident at some lesser ER who'd never seen one before, City of Hope seemed our best bet.

Pulling around to the west side of the main hospital building near the entrance to the urgent care but far away from where we'd always parked before, Jessica slammed my Jeep into park and ran inside to get help. By the time I'd removed myself from the passenger seat and exited the vehicle, one of the nurses on late-night duty had responded to Jessica's presence and came out to retrieve me. A bed was quickly found, and the on-call doctor was alerted to my arrival.

In medical science, not all is obvious. First, I was given a bag of platelets, which was to be expected. The blood trickling out of the open hole in my chest was showing no signs of clotting, so low platelets—considering my diagnosis—was a good candidate. But what came next, which I did not expect, was a twenty-pound sandbag for me to hold over the hole.

And hold.

And hold some more.

From the time we arrived at the hospital around 2 AM until about 10 AM, I held this sandbag against my chest as if we could create a tiny sand Hoover Dam to hold the flowing blood at bay. I understood the physics behind the idea. I'd done enough Cub Scouts and Webelos work as a kid to know about compressing an open wound. But by hour two, when not much had been accomplished besides getting the bag nice and bloody, I was hoping for new ideas. This was not a regular ER, though, and it was now Saturday. I'd stack the City of Hope's weekend team up against almost anyone. However, triaging a gusher was not their specialty. Since the bag of platelets had not started a clot to stop the flow, our medical options were limited.

Finally on Sunday, after I went home Saturday night only to turn around and return to the hospital a few hours later with more bleeding and another ruined T-shirt, a weekend surgical resident discovered the problem. The Hickman is held in place by a cuff of sutures attached to the chest wall. One of those sutures had come loose. Five minutes and one short stitch later, the bleeding had stopped.

Just in time for my relaxing and reflecting weekend of good-byes at home to be over.

ELEANOR ROOSEVELT SAID, "You gain strength, courage, and confidence by every experience in which you really stop to look fear in the face. You are able to say to yourself, 'I have lived through this horror. I can take the next thing that comes along.' You must do the thing you think you cannot do."

When I finished chemotherapy in 1991, I remember thinking to myself that there was no way I could endure something so difficult again. I simply wouldn't be able to muster the courage for the fight if I was faced with that challenge a second time. Luckily I was wrong.

In 1995 I encountered far greater hardships. The treatment was more debilitating. I was forced to walk closer to the edge of life, occasionally teetering at the precipice. And my body had clearly paid a greater price. Yet I got through it with the majority of my good humor and spirit intact. It turned out that I could endure something so difficult a second time.

And now, with yet another long fight laid out before me, I knew I could do it again.

Don't mistake my feelings of fear and the perceived inevitability that I would die as a sign of my capitulation. I did believe that eventually my fight would end in defeat. The house was against me; the deck was stacked. If you play the game long enough, eventually the odds work themselves out, and you end up a loser. Now here I was, being forced to play through a fourth cancer diagnosis. That was the very real truth that I couldn't escape.

But I'd also already endured so much. I'd muscled that stone up the hill multiple times, pushing me back into the safety of remission on each occasion. I'd lost years and opportunities that only youth presents, and I'd done it with the promise that my days were still to come. What would it all be for if this time through I didn't also come out swinging?

I almost felt trapped by the fight. It was the bar that I'd set for myself, and that led to certain expectations. My standard, my norm, was to try with all my might, regardless of the ultimate outcome. I had to do things that I thought I could not do.

Our survival instincts are strong. I think much of the desire to fight that I felt then is innate to all of us. But I'm also an incredibly competitive person. I hate to lose at anything. I've been known to yell at my PlayStation. I once got into a fight during a church-league basketball game (he had it coming). I loved test time, be it the Iowa Test of Basic Skills that we took every year in elementary school or the SAT and ACT, because for me the tests were a competition, even if it was only a competition with myself.

I couldn't stand the thought of giving into cancer. Losing might have been the probable and eventual outcome, but it would not come because I didn't give myself every chance to win. I would not give up. I would not quit. For the thousands of diagnosed patients with no chance at survival, for the families of those patients who were all facing the inevitable, I would fight. I owed it to them. I owed it to myself. I owed it to the people around me who were ready and willing to fight alongside me. I would fight for the rest of my life.

ON MONDAY I was back in the doctor's office to get test results and hear my therapy sentence. Unexpectedly and to my great benefit, I was declared to have acute lymphocytic leukemia. It remained a serious diagnosis, but it left Dr. Stein with options. He could conceivably treat me without the chemotherapy drug that had caused the leukemia. He could also create a viable course of therapy that had the possibility of success without Adriamycin, the drug that damaged my heart, or the immediate need of an allogeneic bone marrow transplant, a transplant involving someone else's marrow cells. (My stem cell transplant in 1995 was autologous, meaning that I was my own donor.)

I had a chance, and that was enough.

When I asked him to quantify that chance at surviving the leukemia into hard statistics that I, as a sports guy, could wrap my head around, he placed my odds at 40 percent. To me, that was about the best news I could hear. A 40 percent chance meant a .400 batting average. That was Ted Williams. I had one shot, one at-bat to get the win of my life, and I was going to have the greatest hitter of all time taking the swings on my behalf. I honestly don't think I would have felt any better if he'd placed my odds at 80 percent. I just wanted to know that the fight wouldn't be in vain. I just needed to have a chance.

But it wasn't going to come easy.

That week I began a three-year course of chemotherapy to battle my leukemia. It would start with what was called induction chemotherapy— an intense daily regimen designed to bring about remission in a month's time. Following induction, we moved on to consolidation chemotherapy. It's also intense, and it was expected to last for eight to nine months. The idea behind consolidation chemotherapy is to keep the intensity going so that if remission was achieved during the induction phase, it could be maintained.

The final stage of treatment would be maintenance chemotherapy. Assuming that I was still holding a remission after both the induction and consolidation phases, I would begin maintenance chemotherapy and remain on it for as long as two years. It was less intense and limited to oral chemotherapy agents, but it was lengthy. I knew that if all went well and according to plan, I would be on chemotherapy well into the year 2000.

But at least I had a chance.

"CHEMOTHERAPY" IS AN all-inclusive word that means "treatment by chemicals." It was first coined by a German scientist in the early 1900s. The actual number of drugs that fall under the broad chemotherapy umbrella is well into the hundreds. They all work essentially the same way, killing cells that rapidly divide. But some are more commonly prescribed, others seem to work better on specific types of cancers, and almost all have differing side effects.

Hair follicles rapidly divide, making hair loss one of the most common and recognizable side effects of chemotherapy. But hair loss is not automatic. In 1991 and 1995, I experienced different levels of hair loss, from just the hair on my head to every possible hair follicle (including those nose hairs). But in 1997, as I began induction chemotherapy for my leukemia—the most intense of my scheduled phases of treatment—not a single hair fell out. I'd expected to lose my hair, as had my doctor. But for whatever reason, this time around, my hair held firm.

It was not, however, a sign that the treatments were easy on my body. I was fighting nausea, immune suppression, fatigue, sleeplessness, and a host of other issues as soon as treatments began. The injections were daily and for hours at a time. They were outpatient, allowing me to sleep in a regular bed and have some semblance of normalcy, at least for a few hours each day. But the assault on my body and the cancerous leukemia cells was incessant—and, on occasion, quite invasive.

Leukemia cells can be found everywhere. There are no tumors to surgically remove or areas of the body to target. The treatment plan is completely comprehensive, because that's how the disease invades. No stone can be left unturned if remission is to be achieved. That means that not only did injections have to be intravenous, there needed to be spinal injections as well. The membrane that protects the spinal column and contains the spinal fluid cannot be penetrated by in-vein chemotherapy treatments. The only way to break that seal is with a needle.

As discovered during my first bone marrow biopsy in 1989—and confirmed again in 1991, 1994, and 1997 (my hip bones must look like Swiss cheese at this point)—I have thick bones. But not just thick hips or ribs or bones in my arms and legs—I also have very thick vertebrae. Typically, the spinal tap required to test spinal fluid and inject chemotherapy can be taken care of on a standard exam table, with nothing more than the knowledgeable touch of a doctor to guide the needle home. We tried that initially with me as well, but we met with very painful and unsuccessful results.

A special room in radiology equipped with a fluoroscope was option number two, and an especially skilled doctor was given the needle to work his magic. In theory, he could look at the picture and see where my bones were in relation to the needle. A quick poke to puncture the membrane should be an easy finish to the process.

What happened, however, was something more akin to the techniques of bamboo torture. Each time he thought that the needle was lined up with an opening between vertebrae, he would push. And each time he did, he pushed his needle directly into bone—or worse, right into a cluster of nerves coming from the spine. It felt like a shot of lightning going from my spine down my left leg and into the floor below the table.

He'd pull back between attempts, reassess, then strike again.

I could see that it was becoming frustrating for the doctor. He was the best, and I was proving to be an unsolvable puzzle. He tried to keep the moment light, telling me that if I was ever in a car wreck I had a spinal column that would be well protected. But with each attempt and each flash of intense pain, I grew more defeated. There were going to be at least five such spinal tap treatments as part of my chemotherapy regiment. The thought of that left me decimated.

Finally, after more than thirty minutes of torture, I heard the pop of the spinal membrane. He was in, and so was the chemotherapy. It was finally finished—for today.

THE DAYS AND weeks passed, and by the end of August I was nearing the end of induction therapy. I'd been forced to move out of my Los Feliz apartment and into my parents' home. My apartment was too far away from the City of Hope, and since I'd been forced to go on disability, it was no longer affordable.

At her own insistence, Jessica sacrificed her job in downtown L.A. so that she could be my chauffer, daily caretaker, custodian, Sherpa, or whatever other role might be most needed on any given day. It was a huge gesture—she was giving up her financial freedom, her professional stimulation, and a large portion of her personal privacy by moving back in with her mother in Highland Park, about twenty-five minutes away from me. It was hard to predict how I would feel or what I would require from one treatment to the next. But her presence and flexibility eased those daily transitions and allowed me to remain an outpatient. It also underscored her level of commitment to me and our mutual fight. I hated what she had to give up, but I couldn't imagine doing it without her. It wasn't what I wanted for her, but it was what I needed.

We spent most evenings together at my parents' house, recovering physically and emotionally from that day's time in the infusion room. There were always other patients in there with me and other stories being written. I became friends with some and was affected by them all. The patients who were outwardly ill were the most sympathetic. It was hard not to bond with them, even if those bonds remained unspoken.

August 30 was one such night of chemotherapy decompressing and attempted reenergizing for the next day. As usual during that first month of induction therapy, I was exhausted but unable to sleep. I was hungry but equally incapable of finding a food that sounded good and would agree with my stomach. No matter which piece of furniture I was in, sitting or lying down, I couldn't get comfortable.

Then across the television came the bulletin that Princess Diana had just been involved in a serious car accident in Paris. The randomness of life once again.

We sat there in front of the television that night as the story unfolded. Details of the wreck, the paparazzi's involvement, the death of Dodi

Fayed, and then the passing of Diana in the hospital were all slowly revealed as if it was a Hollywood miniseries meant to hold an audience for several nights of programming. None of what came out of the television that night felt real. It smacked of the worst kind of gratuitously mass-marketed pulp fiction.

But it was all too real. Lives were shattering before our very eyes and before the eyes of millions of others around the globe. The cycle of life rolled on, unflinching in its indiscriminate tally of casualties and without regard for the fame of its victims or the unjust nature of their demise. Not that we needed a lesson in life's preciousness or the value that every moment holds. I was in my own battle against the encroachment of mortality. It was just that the accident that claimed Diana that night was so capricious and arbitrary, yet also methodical and systematic in its capture of the human condition that it glared at me in its instruction.

Human beings and their spirits are strong and resilient, yet life itself is frail and easily extinguished. Those coexisting contradictions make life all the more beautiful to behold.

BY LABOR DAY weekend, we'd achieved remission and were able to move on to the consolidation stage of chemotherapy. The days of treatment remained long and punishing; the nights were spent recovering and reloading for the next morning's fight. I reloaded through as much normalcy as my physical being would allow. We'd go to movies when possible, or we'd just drive through some of the foothills of the mountains to explore neighborhoods and enjoy the California sunshine.

I could never escape from the cancer; wherever I went, it came with me. But on good days when my energy was up and the nausea was held in check, I could picture myself, years in the future, healthy and strong and cancer free. I wouldn't try to masquerade as something that I wasn't. But I would visualize the man that I expected to be again.

The further into the fight I went, the more assured I became of an eventual cure. Medically speaking, the cancer was responding in every way we'd hoped. September and October remained leukemia free, and every piece of literature about blood cancer agreed on one central point: for each day that I could hold the remission, the realization of success inched closer. My own realizations that this was not a fruitless fight further crystallized.

But there were still challenges, treatments, and the side effects that came with them to manage my way through.

Nausea, vomiting, and fatigue get most of the press when it comes to the side effects of chemotherapy. But the truth is that chemo rolls through your body like a bull in Pamplona during the festival of San Fermín. No space is safe, and at any given moment one of your body's systems could be gored.

Digestively speaking, anything and everything was fair game. Foods would be fine one day but the death of dignity the next. You could go from dehydrated and chronically constipated to the complete and total opposite in a matter of hours.

Infections are common, from skin lesions to scalp rashes to upper respiratory contagions that hang around for weeks. Skin begins to break down, resulting in stretch mark scars that betray the fact that you are actually losing weight. The nerves in your extremities begin to deaden and die. It's not uncommon for fingertips to lose feeling, making the simplest things, like tying shoes or writing a note, irritating and onerous. Feet go numb, and walking becomes a chore. Forget about tasting food—mouths take on a chalky, metallic feel with even the strongest spicy flavors.

It's a grind getting through the daily difficulties presented by chemotherapy. But you laugh at *Seinfeld* and focus on your friends and family, and before you know it, it's Thanksgiving. It sounds counterintuitive for those who've never been there, but you only really understand the meaning of Thanksgiving when you're on the verge of losing all of life's blessings. The people who know suffering make all of the best toasts.

When I was in the hospital on July 23 wrestling with the new reality of my fourth cancer diagnosis, I thought ahead to Christmas. My illness had come on in less than two weeks, which was so quick, and I started to do the march-to-death math in my head. Treatment would probably slow the leukemia's progress. But the treatments themselves couldn't be too aggressive because of my heart condition, so the slowdown would hit its ceiling in no more than a month or two. In my mind, that meant a likely October or November death.

So I began to make a bargain with God about getting me through the holidays. I just didn't want to die in November and screw up Thanksgiving and Christmas for everyone (it's hard to explain the thoughts of someone who thinks he is dying). As I was being pumped full of blood in the bed, I asked God for just one more Christmas with the family; then I could accept whatever fate he had in store. (Days later, I realized that I didn't offer up anything in return. I hoped that wouldn't nullify my request.) As it turned out, I did make it all the way to and through that Christmas.

It's always been a special holiday for my family, from the extended gatherings at my grandparents' home in Kentucky when I was little to smaller adventures with my immediate family, which included a snow closure along Interstate 70 and a night huddled on the floor of a Holiday Inn in Dillon, Colorado. We'd also celebrated Christmas in 1991 just a few days after I finished chemotherapy, and Christmas of '94 was spent counting down the days through the holidays before I'd begin marrow collection for my stem cell transplant.

Christmas was special, but never more so than in 1997. I was alive and daring to be so bold as to set my sights on Christmas of 1998.

THE STRESS AND strain of being a cancer patient is ever present. It permeates every part of your being, including your relationships. The stress, strain, and heavy burdens that come along with being a patient's primary caregiver can be even more demanding. You are the physical and emotional support for the person dealing with the disease, but all too often there is no one else in line there to support you.

Throughout the spring and throughout my consolidation chemotherapy, Jessica shouldered a world's load of issues. She had virtually no life that was separate from my leukemia or me. It had become her full-time job, but there were no weekends, no vacation, and you never clocked out.

It was her twenty-four-hour-a-day life. For even the strongest of people, at some point it becomes too much.

In the summer of 1998, I finished consolidation chemotherapy and was still holding strong to my remission. That meant that I would move on to the milder maintenance chemotherapy in July, and I could even begin to look ahead to returning to work at Fox by early fall. With injections ceasing and all chemo switching from IV to oral medications, my body would begin its recovery. The maintenance chemotherapies would keep me in a low-grade state of illness for the next two years, but I could play through low-grade. More important, I wanted to.

Jessica, on the other hand, had already returned to work a few months earlier and was making noise about the possibilities of taking a job in Philadelphia. She'd been born in Los Angeles and had never lived anywhere else, so initially I didn't place much stock in it. But the noise continued to get louder, and the opportunity in Philadelphia continued to look sweeter. Before long, she took it and was packing up her car.

Throughout the first two years of our relationship, everything was moving forward. From the recovery from the bone marrow transplant to graduation from college to entering the workforce to thinking about a long-term future together, we were constantly advancing and growing. But for the year that began on July 23, 1997, we were running in place. I'd gone from being on the verge of promotion at work to being on disability. Jessica was back in the workforce but also back to the bottom of the totem pole. Any permanent plans we had been making as a couple had long been shelved. It didn't seem prudent to get too caught up in thinking about the future when it was muddied and uncertain.

So to Philadelphia she went. I made the drive across the country with her that August, and it was a special time for the two of us. We stopped at the Grand Canyon—her first-ever visit—and we worked the trip's itinerary so that we'd be in the bleachers at Wrigley Field to watch the Cardinals and Cubs on my August 19 birthday. Baseball fans will remember the summer of 1998 as one of the most amazing seasons in modern history. For me, that afternoon at Wrigley made the previous year a distant memory. Mark McGwire of the Cardinals hit two home runs that day, taking his season total to forty-nine, and the Cubs' Sammy Sosa hit one, his forty-eighth. (They of course would both go on to shatter the single-season mark of sixty-one, which Roger Maris held.)

Jessica and I never talked about it in specific terms. During our cross-country journey, we still said all the things a couple planning to give a long-distance relationship a serious try would say. But neither one of us was so obtuse as to not really see what was happening. She needed a fresh start in all possible ways—job, city, and cancer-free existence. Maybe in some ways I needed a fresh start too. The year of leukemia had stolen so much of our excitement and passion and love of life. We had been doing nothing but existing and surviving. People cannot grow and thrive under those conditions, and relationships will inevitably suffer. We hadn't grown apart. She was still my best friend, and I was hers. We still loved each other. But the hangover of cancer and chemotherapy fatigue infected everything, including us.

I was heading back to work at Fox as soon as I returned to California, and normal life was just days away from rebooting. I needed the complete system restart just as much as she did. We weren't actively seeking new starts from each other. That was never the driving force behind her move. But the fact that she was willing to go—in spite of what we knew would inevitably happen—and that I never asked her to stay spoke volumes. Our relationship had changed; we just weren't ready to admit it. That finality wouldn't come until the middle of 1999.

BACK AT WORK but still living with my parents, I was only limping back towards normal. I was enjoying my days and nights at Fox in our new building on the main 20th Century Fox studio lot in Century City (although it did make for quite the commute to and from Azusa). But much of my life was stuck in pause. Where was I going? Where did I want to go? I couldn't answer either question.

I realized in early 1999 that much of what I was dealing with was depression. It was a mild case; I was still a highly functioning depressed person. But there was no denying that the years of cancer and the loss of so much of my twenties were taking its toll. I considered myself a strong person who could withstand the worst that life could dish out. I was proud of my survivorship and four battles with cancer. But I figured out that recognizing depression and admitting to needing the help of others do not make someone weak.

I asked a trusted friend for the number of a therapist who specialized in treating cancer patients and survivors. I had been a disbeliever in the effectiveness of therapy my entire adult life, which caused a delay by a couple of long months in my asking for the number after first acknowledging the need. Then I sat on the number for another six weeks before summoning the courage to dial the phone and make an appointment. No one was dragging me into therapy, but I definitely wasn't running into it with open and welcoming arms.

That first meeting between my new therapist and me was just a casual conversation that I used to feel her out. Her husband was currently battling cancer, so there was no denying her cancer credibility card. But I was still a cautious skeptic. This was not an inexpensive undertaking, so I needed to be doubly sure that she was right and I was reachable. If either side was less than authentic, then it would be a colossal waste of time for both of us. Well, maybe not hers; she was getting paid.

After one week, it felt to me like it had the makings of something suitable, so I promised to give her another three weeks. I ended up going weekly for the next four months.

It was an empowering time for me and without a doubt some of the best money and time I've ever spent. I began my time with her scared, confused, and struggling to see beyond my tomorrow. I enjoyed my job at Fox, but producing graphics was not what I wanted to do. It was not why I went into broadcast journalism, and it was never going to fulfill me on a deep level. But since I'd returned to work from my disability absence, I'd become content to safely tread water. I'd moved up to the lead in the department but was making no moves or plans to go elsewhere.

I'd heard through the grapevine that a writing job would be open in the coming weeks. With my therapist's encouragement and reinforcement, I went for it. Through my time in therapy, I progressed from scared to assured, from confused to confident, and from ignorant of the future to positive about its possibilities. I began my sessions with her as a twenty-seven-year-old who was passively waiting for cancer to strike its final and fatal blow; I ended my time with her as a twenty-seven-year-old who viewed his life as an open and empty book, waiting to be filled with whatever I myself deemed worthy.

There were of course no guarantees when I left her office for the final time that cancer wouldn't return. The possibility that my life was ticking down toward yet another diagnosis was still very real. But that I couldn't control. There was, however, still so much of my life that I could.

One of my all-time favorite films is *The Shawshank Redemption*. I am drawn to it as a story of atonement and salvation that treats two men, one innocent and one guilty, as equally deserving of redemption. And I relate to Andy Dufresne, an imperfect man but one who assuredly suffered far greater punishments than any of his transgressions should have allowed. At the pivotal point in the film, when Andy realizes that deliverance from the unjust hell in which he's trapped will only come from his own actions, he says to his friend Red, "Get busy living, or get busy dying."

Like Andy, I chose living.

A week after finishing my therapy sessions I accepted a staff writing position at Fox Sports. Armed with new confidence and a clear outlook, I had gone to my bosses and asked to have my hat thrown into the writers' ring. There was a future for me as a writer, whereas just a few months earlier I was too consumed by foreboding and doubt to see it. Now I had the job, the future it promised, and less than a year left of maintenance chemotherapy before I could finally put that behind me as well.

The fall of 1999 passed, and the world united behind its series of millennium celebrations. The first half of 2000, filled with positivities and possibilities, flowed by without interruption. Life was good.

My final bottle of maintenance chemotherapy was set to run out on July 20. I am, however, a sucker for an anniversary. To this day, I celebrate the passing of each July 23, which marks the milestone of one more year since the day I knew I was dead. So I rationed out my final few pills of chemotherapy, skipping a couple of days, then taking the last one on July 23, 2000, three years to the day after diagnosis.

My lifetime total tally in treatment—with radiation, chemotherapy, or a bone marrow transplant—now stood at fifty-four months.

11

HUMPTY DUMPTY

Like the average guy—one who enjoys the occasional cold beer and the decidedly male ritual of ripping his friends to their faces—I like golfing. I enjoy the actual game, although you can count my career birdies on one hand. But really it's the camaraderie of playing a full eighteen holes with a colorful cast of fellow hackers who aren't too thin-skinned for a little salty language and in-group putdowns, the type I find most appealing. You'll never get more laughs than when having your manhood consistently questioned by a group of guys who also can't hit the green in regulation.

The beautiful thing about golf in the age of technology is that the hacking and bashing don't always have to cost an arm-and-a-leg green fee. Video-game consoles come with golf incarnations that are packed with courses from around the world, and there isn't a sports bar worth its beer nuts that doesn't have the game Golden Tee. There also isn't a sports-bar patron worth his rising cholesterol who doesn't fancy himself a Golden Tee master.

I am one such guardian of Golden Tee and devotee of the deep-fried who is happy to take on all comers.

In May 2000, just a few weeks before I said good-bye permanently to the chemotherapy and leukemia, I was playing a round of golf with my friend Ted. I'd since moved myself and my cat, Mordecai (he'd been with me since I picked him up as a rescue kitten just a few weeks after my bone marrow transplant in 1995), to a little one-bedroom apartment out in

West Los Angeles to be nearer to the Fox studios. Mordecai made for a great roommate—I worked odd hours and wedged a social life into even odder ones, but he never complained. He was also self-cleaning.

Ted still lived out east in the San Gabriel Valley, and that's where we were hitting the links on this particular afternoon. I had a decent day on the course—by "decent" I mean that I was playing close to bogey golf—and I seem to remember beating him rather handily. He might remember it differently, but who's to really say which memory is more accurate all these years later.

After golf, we went to a local sports bar to watch a little baseball, eat a couple of cheesesteaks, and naturally play a couple of rounds of Golden Tee. Eighteen holes of the real thing in the heat of East Los Angeles County hadn't satiated our jones.

I had just played a full round from the back tees, which means I recorded about ninety-five swings over the course of four hours, not including practice swings. By round two of Golden Tee, which involves a trackball and a male urge to hit it as hard as humanly possible, I'd added another one hundred twenty swings of stress to my shoulder. That shoulder, my left, began to throb with each use.

My biggest mistake that night was to tell Ted about my shoulder pains. I believe I heard the phrase "Does your husband play?" There was a following serious discussion about whether or not I'd just recorded the first ever Golden Tee injury and if that meant that I would forever have to order light beer and substitute a side salad for French fries.

I laughed about the injury initially, but as the next few days passed, my shoulder got worse. When reaching for glasses or cans in my kitchen cabinets, my shoulder would catch, as if the smoothness of the joint had been replaced by a toothed set of gears that didn't quite fit. As my left arm became further immobilized, washing my hair became a one-handed job. Reaching across my body to fasten and unfasten the seat belt in my Jeep hurt every bit as much as going sans seat belt and getting thrown through the windshield.

After a week of dealing with shoulder shutdown—fortunately when seated and typing I was generally pain free—my right hip got in on the act. With my heart condition still an issue, I did what I could to avoid serious stair climbing. I was a confirmed elevator and escalator man whenever possible. But on the occasional step up into a building or out of a car, I was starting to have the same joint catch in my hip.

An MRI revealed that I had developed avascular necrosis in both joints (my right shoulder and left hip remained healthy), a disease that involves bone death due to the interruption of blood flow. Like other tissues, bones need blood and the oxygen it carries to remain alive. Obstruct that flow, and the part of the bone that is cut off from the needed sustenance slowly begins to die. It's common in long bones, like the femur or humerus, and it's often a side effect of prolonged steroid use, like the prednisone that I'd taken as part of my chemotherapy regimen.

There was no way to reverse the damage; when a bone is dead, it's dead. There was also no way to stop the continued deterioration. When the ends of the bones are dead, the round end of the ball joint loses bits and pieces of bone tips, flattening out those areas and causing the once easily operating joint to catch painfully. It was degenerative and guaranteed to get worse.

The only way to treat the condition, in my case, was with total joint replacement surgeries. I'd been on the same cardiac medicines that my grandparents took each day, and now I was going to have the fake joints to match.

In June 2000, a month before my battle with cancer ended, I began the long and slow process of rebuilding my body from the years of punishment that it endured. Because I could mitigate my shoulder joint more easily than the hip, my hip surgery came first. As surgeries go, it's fairly routine. Total hip replacements are done every day in almost every corner of the country. They aren't, however, usually done on guys in their twenties who are also dealing with weak hearts. That made my surgeon's job a little beyond the routine.

After surgery, I was in the ICU so that my heart could be monitored for the first forty-eight hours. Once I got past that hurdle, I was moved into a regular room for a day, then out of the hospital the next. The joint was set and the cement had dried, so as long as I stayed off snow skis and avoided any serious yoga for the first six weeks, I was good to go and ready for rehab.

Within two weeks I was off crutches, and by the time I had taken my final dose of maintenance chemotherapy on July 23, my hips were back to normal and pain free.

The shoulder joint is a much trickier animal to tame. The hip joint is just your average ball in a socket. Cut off the ball, replace it with titanium, cement a sturdy cup in the socket for the new titanium tip to rotate around in, and you're set for several years. But the shoulder has a clavicle, scapula, and humerus all working in concert with a series of muscles that allow lateral and medial rotations as well as extensions and flexes. The shoulder is the most mobile joint in the human body, which makes it also the most difficult to replace.

The surgery went well, and once again my heart came through with flying colors. But in place of the easy, almost nonrehab that accompanied the hip replacement, rehabilitation for my shoulder joint was long and intense.

For weeks I worked on basic flexibility each morning in the shower. With the steam helping to loosen up the traumatized muscles, I would slowly make my left hand climb the shower wall like a spider. Every few days I would notice that I was getting a tile higher with less pain and resistance.

Once I'd reestablished my basic flexibility, I began to work with a physical therapist at UCLA, the nearest hospital to me. I did hours on the hand-crank stationary bike and set after set of lateral pulls and seated rows. I even worked out with an as-seen-on-TV sensation, the Bodyblade. (This provided me with an extra bit of comedy, since one of the anchors who I worked with, Steve Lyons, was then starring in the Bodyblade infomercial. I made sure to mock him, even as I was using the product with trained professionals to strengthen my repaired shoulder.)

Unlike my titanium hip, my replaced shoulder joint has never regained its full range of motion. It operates anywhere between 90 and 95 percent, depending on how well it's been stretched or how ambitious I am in making a motion. But I've been told that the range of motion I experience is at the top of the expected range. Once again, I was the beneficiary of a really great doctor.

The gradual refurbishing of my damaged body was taking place piece by piece, and my net worth on the commodities market was steadily going up. With one eye on the price of titanium (you never know when you might need to visit a pawn shop), in 2001 I focused my other eye on the heart condition that I'd been diagnosed with six years earlier. At the time, it was just there, not really affecting my day-to-day life. I was weakened because of the heart; there was no question about that. But after three years of wearing the ankle weights of chemotherapy, which had come on the heels of my stem cell transplant, it was hard to distinguish how I actually felt from how I could feel with a strong and functioning heart.

One time when I was seeing the cardiologist who had been assigned to me across the previous six years, I finally pushed him for an answer to the million-dollar question. "Long-term, what are my options? What is the prognosis beyond continuing to take medication?"

He'd always been chintzy with the information and not one to voluntarily pass on the latest news. He continued to keep his cards close to the vest. "Are you sure you want to know?"

I'm the guy who wants to know everything. If you tell me not to watch a particular video on the Internet because it will gross me out, you can be sure that YouTube will be my first visit the next time I log on. I confess to having watched incarnations of *Jersey Shore* and *The Real Housewives* because my curious nature and rubbernecking tendencies are simply too strong to resist. Televise a train wreck like either of those shows, and I'm like Odysseus trying to resist the Sirens.

I'm also the guy who just came through cancer four times and discovered that the things you don't know are far scarier than the things you do, even when those known knowns come packed with serious substance. And we're talking about my heart here, one of my top three favorite muscles.

"Yes. I'd like to know."

"I'm going to have to refer you to UCLA, where they will discuss your surgical options."

At UCLA the next week, there weren't many options to discuss. I had chemotherapy-induced cardiomyopathy; this I already knew. I knew that it was an enlarging and hardening of the heart muscle that made it far less efficient as a pumper. It still worked, just not as well. I'd actually adapted my life around the limitations just fine. I wasn't going to be a rugby player or scuba diver, or anything else that required above average exertion, and I had come to terms with that reality. What other choice was there?

My new cardiologist at UCLA explained that it wasn't as simple as staying on the medications and maintaining whatever status quo I'd become accustomed to. The muscle had already deteriorated further since I was diagnosed with the condition in 1995, and it was only going to continue to slide downhill.

So for the second time in a week I asked a second cardiologist, "What is the long-term plan?"

Dr. Jaime Moriguchi, one of the most confident and capable physicians I've ever met, said without missing a beat, "We want to list you for heart transplant."

After four bouts with two separate kinds of cancer and following a year in which I had both my right hip and left shoulder joints totally replaced, it only stands to reason that the next step would be a heart transplant.

I almost laughed at the absurdity of the thought. That's exactly how it felt to me at that very moment—absurd.

You sure you want to stop with a heart transplant? Surely there is a brain surgery that you could also perform while I'm under.

It didn't knock the wind out of me like each of the previous cancer diagnoses. I didn't feel any impending doom or the march of the Grim Reaper. And I wouldn't say that my level of fear spiked unexpectedly at the thought of the unknown processes and procedures that surround a heart transplant. It just left me numb. For six years I'd been living with this heart condition. Surely in those six years the reality of an eventual transplant had occurred to my cardiologist.

This is not the kind of information you keep to yourself. Maybe knowledge of the serious freaks out some patients. I'm sure there are those out there who prefer the dark of ignorance to the light of information. (Although in my experience the bogeyman isn't nearly as scary once he's been dragged from the closet and into the middle of a well-lit room. He's far more terrifying when he's being defined by the figments of your imagination.) But after six years of my being his patient, shouldn't my first cardiologist have known that I was not one of those people?

The past didn't really matter now, and his reasons, good or bad, weren't going to change my future. That was now in the hands of my new team at UCLA, who were going about the business of evaluating me for transplant-listing eligibility. This is not automatic, especially with my history of cancer. Post–heart transplant patients go on medications that make secondary malignancies a very real risk. Add my history of radiation and chemotherapy to that risk, and there were real questions about my viability as a transplant candidate.

As we progressed with the physical workup, there were things functioning in my favor. It had been six years since the Hodgkin's disease, six years since I last received radiation, and almost four years since the leukemia reared its ugly head. I'd held my remission since it was first achieved in September of 1997. (When leukemia recurs, it typically happens within the first two years. Medically speaking I was still a risk, but it had been softened to an acceptable level.)

The last stage of evaluation is psychological. There is a lot of care required for patients post-transplant, which is administered by others as well as by the patient. Do you have a network of support? Do you have the means necessary to get to the hospital, stay current with your medications, and take care of yourself physically? Are you mentally ready for the realities of heart transplantation? The biggest of those realities is that it will take someone else's death to give you life.

I passed my tests in June 2001, and the team at UCLA officially listed me for heart transplantation. I was average body size in both height and weight, and my blood type was O-positive.

My doctor's best guess had me waiting five and a half long years before transplant.

12

FIVE AND A HALF YEARS

In 1991, when I was first cutting my chemotherapy teeth in Kansas City, I read the book *Comeback* by San Francisco Giants pitcher Dave Dravecky. A cancerous tumor was discovered in the left-handed starter's pitching arm in 1988. Half of his deltoid muscle was removed, and the humerus bone was frozen as part of the treatment to get rid of his cancer. Doctors told him that he'd have limited use of his arm, and there was virtually no way that he'd ever pitch again. Less than a year later, he returned to the Major Leagues and threw eight strong innings in a win over Cincinnati.

By the time I was reading Dravecky's book, I knew where the rest of the story took him. Dravecky's cancer had returned, and he'd lost his entire arm and shoulder to amputation. That led to his second book, which I've also read, *When You Can't Come Back*.

For me, the story didn't lose any of its inspiration because of the ultimate outcome. He'd shown the resiliency of the human spirit and how the drive of athleticism can lead people to accomplish amazing things. Some years later, I met Dravecky when he was at Azusa Pacific, and we swapped cancer stories. I figured we could also trade baseball anecdotes—his from when he was selected to pitch in the 1983 All-Star game and mine from when I got a gold star on my hat as a nine-year-old for making the defensive play of the game (I caught a fly ball). Unfortunately we ran out of time.

By 2000 I was passing my hospital downtime with the inspirational book *It's Not About the Bike: My Journey Back to Life* by Lance Armstrong. Armstrong and I are only a month apart in age. As his book's subtitle states, we'd both been engaged in journeys back to life after frightening battles with cancer. The only difference between Armstrong's story and mine was that he won the Tour de France and I didn't. But if you ask me, that's really just a minor detail.

At the time that I was reading Armstrong's book in 2000, he was beating Jan Ullrich for his second of a record seven consecutive Tour de France wins. The Lance Armstrong Foundation has raised hundreds of millions of dollars for the cause of fighting cancer since it was first founded in 1997, and he's provided an unquantifiable amount of inspiration for cancer patients around the world, me included.

Without a doubt, these two men and their stories influenced my life, both in how they handled their cancer and how they've lived as survivors. The inspiration they provided not only helped propel me through my illness, it made me want to get involved in the cause on a more permanent and intimate level. I'd had an ancillary connection to the Leukemia & Lymphoma Society (LLS) since my days of chemotherapy in Kansas City. I did a little speaking for them then and was a cohost for the local portion of their nationwide fundraising telethon.

In 2001 I was ready for a more active role with the Society. I volunteered for almost every program that they had available—School & Youth, Light the Night, Team In Training, and others. I spoke to donors, to athletes raising money for LLS, and to high schools, middle schools, and elementary schools. I loved it, and I felt like I was getting quite good at it. With my connections to both Hodgkin's and leukemia—two of the four major types of blood cancers that LLS specifically fights—I had a platform from which to speak.

In early 2002 I was asked by LLS to speak to the US men's soccer team as they prepared for that year's FIFA World Cup in Japan and South Korea. LLS had become their charity of choice for that calendar year, and I was tasked with the job of putting a face on blood cancers for the players. It was a wonderful opportunity, and the team couldn't have been more gracious in how they hosted me. (It should be noted that in 2002 the US men's soccer team advanced to the quarterfinals of the World Cup, their best-ever showing. I'm not saying that my speaking to them and their performance in Asia were related, but I can't be sure they weren't.)

Also in early in 2002, I had the great honor of carrying the Salt Lake City Winter Olympic Torch as it made its way across the country and through Los Angeles. I'd been nominated by a friend of mine the previous fall because of my cancer history and new status as a future heart transplant recipient, and fortunately the committee that made such decisions was moved enough by her submission to grant me a spot in the relay.

I only carried the torch for a quarter mile, but with every step along my allotted stretch on Burton Way in Beverly Hills, I felt strong and healthy and whole. (And when I was in the middle of the caravan that included police, firefighters, media, medical personnel, VIPs, and personal bodyguards to protect against anyone who thought about trying to extinguish the flame, I felt like the most secure person on the planet.)

Motivational speaking was also beginning to stretch beyond my volunteer work with the Leukemia & Lymphoma Society and cross over into the professional. I developed a core set of keynote themes as a foundation from which I could then tailor speeches for a variety of companies and medical conferences. Those themes all spoke to my own experiences and learned lessons: "Obstacles don't stop us; they challenge us"; "How to tap your inner fire"; "Treating failure as a means of finding success"; "Persevere against all odds"; "There is strength in seeking help"; "Never lose sight of the beautiful"; "Never give up the fight"; and my personal favorite theme, "Live each day as if it's your first." Nothing should grow stale, routine, or boring or be taken for granted. Make your next life experience, whatever it may be, as full of wonder and excitement as the first time you experienced it. Living each day as if it's your last misses the mark. We should all be living each day as if it's our first.

Suddenly I was getting paid to share my story and experiences and impart the wisdom that I'd been lucky enough to discover. It is a perspective of experience but also of observation. I've seen dozens of amazing people locked in a struggle for their lives. I've witnessed and experienced heartache in its extreme. I know what total devastation looks and feels like. I have stared directly at death.

I've also seen the magnificence of human compassion. I've seen people at their absolute best in spite of circumstances that should push them to their absolute worst. I know what the complete and pure triumph of the human spirit looks and feels like. I know that there is a reserve of strength within each of us that can overcome anything.

As I spoke more about myself, I also learned more. My speaking became much more than just a means for me to give to others and share experiences. Within each given speech there was self-discovery taking place. I learned that life and how you live it is, in its simplest terms, a choice. How you handle something that happens to you—great or small, wonderful or terrible—is your choice.

There will always be something big and important and stressful going on in your life. It may not be as serious or debilitating as a battle with cancer, but if it's the thing most dominating your life, it's imposing. To you it is everything, and for that you need offer no apologies. But in spite of its presence, you can always choose to be happy. It is your choice to remain positive, upbeat, and focused on the good. Your attitude is entirely within your control.

The nature of my story is quite personal; the audience is left with a fairly intimate idea of who I am as a person and all of the good and bad I've experienced. And when I speak, a few people will almost always come up to me afterward and share the intimate details of their own struggles. The more this happened, the more I loved it. Those conversations always come with great personal meaning, and I've learned so much about myself through these moments shared with total strangers. Along with understanding that happiness is my choice, I've come to realize that survival is as well.

Survival comes with a number of definitions. For me, surviving means living my life. I don't quantify it with a number of years, places seen, or moments and memories filed away in photos. I have chosen to survive whatever comes my way, and that means I will continue to live my life in the best way I know how.

I choose to be happy. I choose to survive. And in 2002 I was gifted with the opportunity to build a second career on those two basic revelations.

In my primary career, as a writer for Fox Sports, I was getting the opportunity to write for a variety of different shows and a number of great sports figures, including NFL Hall of Famers Marv Levy, Jackie Slater, and Warren Moon. The baseball-analyst faces that were regularly camped out with us along writers' row featured former Dodgers Steve Sax and Eric Karros and my personal favorite, former Royals pitcher Mark Gubicza. Gubicza won a critical Game 6 against the Blue Jays in the American League Championship Series in 1985, keeping the Royals postseason alive in the year they wound up winning the World Series. If you are a Kansas City Royals fan, you are by extension a huge fan of Mark Gubicza. (It also helps that he's an incredibly nice guy.)

I was speaking for the Leukemia & Lymphoma Society on a regular basis and volunteering for them whenever their events and my free time connected. With their Team In Training program, I spoke to several hundred marathoners the night before the 2002 Los Angeles Marathon, and in June I flew up to Anchorage, Alaska, to speak to more than one thousand runners the night before their 26.2-mile Mayor's Marathon challenge. I was a long way away from being able to do a race myself, but it's hard not to be inspired when you see person after person take themselves from nonathlete to marathon finisher. It definitely planted seeds for the years to come.

Life was good and complete and only getting better, except for one rather important area—my dating life.

Anyone who finds him- or herself still swimming in the dating pool after turning thirty carries a certain amount of baggage. It's a reality appreciated by all, so for the most part the baggage remains unmentioned. But what's the "mention or not to mention" protocol if a particular over-thirty-year-old dater is carrying more baggage than an overseas flight on a Boeing 747? Miss Manners has yet to write the column on which date it's best to mention your four battles with cancer and current status on the heart transplant waiting list.

It was a serious problem for me. I was of course interested in dating, but I found myself avoiding anything resembling a traditional date that also might include a chance for a second. That conversation—the one you have to engage in with someone whom you like because you don't want her to feel down the road that she was conned into creating a relationship with a person who held such life-defining secrets—is a hard conversation to start. How do you break that piece of enormously thick ice?

It's heavy for a first date, but is it too late by the second or third? How do you tell someone you just met that you carry a pager in your pocket in the event that the hospital finds a new heart to transplant into your chest? But on the other hand, how do you not have that conversation?

I never figured out the answer to those questions. I once was on a first date with someone who I decided I'd wanted to ask out for a second, so I initiated the talk. She listened, was sympathetic, and then very honestly told me that it was too much for her to take on. It sucked for me, being rejected because of things beyond my control that I could never change. But if that's truly how she felt, as it clearly was, then I made the right decision to make it a first-date talk. Still, that truth didn't make it suck less.

I knew that love and a committed relationship were possible in the face of the grave and serious. I'd experienced it with Jessica. Of course, too much of the serious also ended up sending us on two very separate paths. Leukemia wasn't the only factor at play when the two of us parted ways. But it's hard to deny that the growing apart that had taken place was fueled by its stresses.

Surely the seriousness that comes with a heart transplant would have similar results. Maybe, I thought, I shouldn't be in the dating pool. My history is a weight that can only be carried by someone truly strong. Someone truly committed. But that history is hardly the half of it. It's the future, only defined at this point in the abstract, which will be the hardest to burden. And once that abstract becomes a reality, how can anyone know where the road will eventually lead? Was it fair to ask someone to make that commitment, when in truth she wouldn't really know what she was committing to? Was it even possible to find someone who met all of my needs and desires for a companion, someone who was both strong enough for that journey and willing enough to take it? I was almost sure that it wasn't.

On Halloween in 2002, I spoke at the prerace pasta party the night before the Santa Barbara half-marathon. I laid out my entire story from beginning to end and talked about the very real fears that surrounded a heart transplant. It was a good speech, and I got a great response from the crew of soon-to-be half-marathon finishers, some of whom came in costume. (It's a profound thing to have people come up to you and share their own connections to cancer, either through themselves or a loved one, while dressed as Wonder Woman.)

Also in the audience that night was a young woman named Carrie Riordan. A new Southern Californian transplanted from the Detroit area by way of graduate school at Georgia Tech, Carrie had shoulder-length brown hair, brown eyes, and the Irish features that her family surnames of Riordan and Durkin explained. She came dressed to the dinner that night as a nervous runner who'd never completed a race before. I'd actually met her earlier in the fall—she'd been training with the West Los Angeles team where I did my volunteering—but we hadn't exchanged more than a few sentences during any single training session. I worked the aid and water station on Sunday mornings when she was in training, but lingering was strictly forbidden by her watchful coaches.

I had, however, been able to learn a little bit about her. She worked as an environmental and planning consultant, had a recently acquired master's degree in city planning, liked college football (she was also a Michigan grad), and was quick with the sarcasm. She also appealed to the shallower side of my Y chromosome with a beautiful face and an athletic body. I wasn't convinced that she'd paid much attention to me, but I certainly had to her.

That night, we sat together for dinner and a much longer chat. We talked and connected on a fun and friendly level. The following day at the postrace victory party, I worked up the courage to ask for her phone number. She didn't dodge the request or give me the number for a North Hollywood sandwich shop, so I was starting to like my chances. She knew everything about me, my past, and my battered internal organs in all their vibrant and exciting technicolor detail, and that lifted the weight of the pressures and obligations that I normally felt.

Our relationship began with fun dinners and drinks and easy, relaxed conversations. One early date involved a thermos of hot chocolate, folding chairs placed on a darkened overlook along Mulholland Drive, and a 2 AM meteor shower. We laughed and found deeper connections, and soon I was spending as much of my free time with her as possible. My schedule with Fox still took my workdays deep into the night, but when I had an evening off, it was usually spent with Carrie.

I was amazed by her as a professional. She'd talk about her work and the projects she was tasked with, and I was enthralled. I was also completely lost. I've always prided myself on being smart enough to follow and participate in almost any conversation. When it comes to the intricacies that involve zoning, land use, growth management, and the city government agencies that regulate such things, I was relegated to silent yet enthralled listener.

She was smart; but beyond learned, she was perceptive. She understood my fears before I ever put voice to them. She not only "got me," she accepted me. She even preferred me. She didn't act as if there were any "yeah, buts" when evaluating my personal vitals. I was me, and that's not who I would be if any of my perceived deficiencies were less so.

She was kind. She volunteered at the Downtown Los Angeles Women's Shelter. She had no reason to do so other than it was right. She joined Team In Training and the Leukemia & Lymphoma Society with no personal connection to blood cancers. She wanted to meet people, and to do so while helping to find a cure made it an all the more desirable group to join.

And she was adventurous and brave. When I first mentioned the idea of going camping in the nowhere lands of Death Valley, she immediately said yes. I eventually got my aborted 1997 trip up the California coast with Carrie as lead navigator. Camping in Big Sur highlighted that trip. Perhaps her greatest moment of bravery came when she first introduced me to her mother. Less than twelve hours after I, the future heart transplant recipient dating her daughter, met Carrie's mom, Dale, Carrie left the two of us to spend the day in line together at *The Price Is Right*. It takes an incredibly fearless woman to trust her mother with her new boyfriend for multiple hours on end where there is nothing to do but sit and talk on a cold hard bench under a canopy at CBS Television City. It takes even more courage to trust her new boyfriend with the knowledge that her mom's greatest desire for her trip to Los Angeles is to see Bob Barker from a seat in his studio audience. We also went to the see Dr. Phil during that same visit.

Dale and I connected immediately.

By October 2003, eleven months after our first date, Carrie and I moved in together in Marina del Rey. Time was ticking by, and even though the heart transplant was expected to still take another three years, living decisions were made with it in mind. There would be days and weeks of convalescence as well as recovery and rehabilitation walks to take. I lived in a West L.A. neighborhood that provided very little of what I'd need, and Carrie lived in Hollywood. With the compromised immune system of a heart transplant recipient, future walks along Hollywood Boulevard seemed like a bad idea. The Marina was the perfect choice.

In January 2004 I realized that my education was woefully lacking in one imminently important and critical area—the four *c*'s of color, clarity, carat, and cut. We'd been together for fifteen months and living together for almost four, and for me the time was right. With my parents along to provide two extra sets of eyes, the ring searching and shopping began in earnest.

I'd commented to Carrie on quite a few occasions about the cop-out nature of giving a woman an engagement ring for Christmas or a birthday. Smart it may be, both in terms of saving money and eliminating the pressures of finding the appropriate gift (we really do care, but you're not the easiest people to shop for), I told her that I thought it showed a lack of imagination in planning a proposal. In reality, I was setting up my own version of the Rope-a-Dope. I had every intention of popping the big question to her on her birthday that March.

We went down to Mexico for her birthday weekend and stayed in one of the top floor suites of the Las Rocas Resort & Spa. My plan was that she would have a massage the next afternoon, and during it I would go down to my car and transfer the huge box of candles and champagne that

I'd smuggled across the Mexican border up to our room. I'd have an hour, but I'd have to work quickly to get everything set.

What I hadn't adequately planned for was the absence of an elevator and the six flights of stairs I had to contend with. They were tough enough for my heart and me to leisurely scale empty-handed. But add in a fifteen-pound box plus the pressure of a ticking clock, and I nearly didn't make it. Eventually I had to crack the box open and haul up the contents in smaller, more manageable portions. And after catch-my-breath breaks on each floor's landing, more than half of my preparation hour had been eaten away.

Rushing around like a chicken with its head cut off—or like a guy about to get down on one knee and propose marriage—I immediately went to work. I had planned for candles to line the in-suite stairs leading up from our room door to the living room above. I'd brought a different set of candles to chart a path from the living room, down a hall, and into a sitting room where the spectacular views of the Baja Coast and the Pacific Ocean made the perfect backdrop. Then there were the two special candles in their stands to place on the table, next to the ring and bottle of Dom.

I am not a pyromaniac with an unhealthy fire fascination. Too little practice and a decided deficiency in skill leave me as one of the world's worst match strikers. (I could never pull off the match-in-cupped-hand cigarette lighting that defined Hollywood cool in the 1930s and '40s.) While I do take pride in my history of campfires and lit barbecues, candles have never been my thing. But they were Carrie's, so I was game to make them work. Although I had no idea if the collection of wax and wick that I'd picked out were mood setters or mood killers. In truth, I'd settle for anything in between.

In the end, the only thing that really mattered was that she said yes. The stair climbing, box lugging, and normal set of nerves that follow any man about to become engaged left me a hot and sweaty mess. But since Carrie was returning to the room after an hour in the hotel spa, we looked much more like a matched pair. And our level of dehydration made the champagne taste that much better.

Carrie said yes that afternoon to so much more than just a marriage. Based on the doctor's timeline, we were counting down the final two and a half years until heart transplant. There was the uncertainty of that day, but also of the hundreds of days leading up to it. I was living a mostly normal life, relatively healthy when all things were considered. But that could, and most likely would, change as the months passed by. My condition was degenerating slowly, but there were no assurances that it wouldn't begin to degenerate rapidly.

In late 2001, a few months after I'd been listed for transplant, the electrical system of my heart began to fail. I was having moments of near blackout and extreme shortness of breath. I visited my doctor as soon as possible, and he told me that the connection between my upper and lower chambers was shorting out. I was going to need a pacemaker, and I was going to need it immediately. At any moment my heart was in danger of stopping.

I sat in the ER at UCLA that evening, waiting for the emergency surgery to implant a pacemaker and staring at the syringe of adrenaline that had been taped to the rail of my bed, just in case. It was an in-your-face reminder of just how quickly things could go south. I had a five and a half year wait for a heart, and most likely I would have that time to give. But there were no guarantees.

In 2003 my heart's electrical system continued to deteriorate, prompting my doctor to replace my regular pacemaker with an ICD (implantable cardioverter defibrillator). It had more leads than what was implanted in 2001, allowing it to control more heart chambers. And it had the ability to shock my heart with a defibrillator in the event that it detected an arrhythmia, something my first pacemaker could not do.

The ICD is an amazing piece of electronics. It's much more than just an engine that keeps your heart beating. It's a computer that can be set and customized to meet each individual's needs. Maximum and minimum heart rates can be changed with nothing more than a connection over a phone line and a small device that the patient holds over the ICD.

Doctors can also get full readouts from the ICD on how dependent you are on the device (how often your heart rate drops below the minimums or goes above the maximums) and if there have been any defibrillator firings since its last download.

But like all complicated electronic devices, there can be problems. For patients that are 100 percent dependent on their ICDs, as I was, those problems can come with very serious consequences.

In February 2005, I received a letter from the company that made my particular ICD; it was being recalled. Some of the devices were experiencing problems with leaking batteries. The leak wasn't so much the problem, but the sudden loss of power in the battery was. A battery that still had years of life left could suddenly go dead, and then so could the patient.

ICDs are not cell phones or snow tires. You can't take them to the store and get a rubber bumper to fix a faulty antenna. You can't throw the ICD up on the lift at your local Goodyear dealer and swap it out in twenty minutes. It requires surgery, anesthesia, and a full medical team to replace—not to mention the cutting, digging, and pushing that you, the consumer, also have to endure.

It's also not something you can get corrected the very next day. Everyone with the device—and there were many—got the same letter that I did. But with only one or two teams at each hospital capable of making the switch, it took time. For me the wait was three long weeks. Three weeks of worry that at any moment the very machine that your life required might go dead. Three weeks of sleepless nights, knowing that if your heart needed an electric shock to kick-start it back to life, it might not get it.

My medical team at UCLA did everything it could to make the wait short and livable and the extra surgery as painless as possible. They cared about the patient from the moment the recall was announced until the moment I was able to go home after the new device had been implanted. The manufacturer, however, was concerned with liability and their bottom line.

I won't relitigate anything within these pages, but there is a clear line of time between when they recognized the flaw in their design, realized it was serious enough to force a redesign, got FDA approval on that redesign, and then determined that financially the liability of not issuing a recall would cost them more than the expense of paying for new surgeries. Although they even figured out a way around that last point when they told me that my device was beyond its warranty. As far as they were concerned, they were not responsible for paying for the extra surgery. (This was only their tune after the procedure was complete and the bills became due; they never mentioned it beforehand.)

Lawyers became involved and depositions were taken, and unfortunately my doctor became stuck in the middle, even though as far as I could tell he had done everything right. It felt like absolute ridiculousness. I just wanted to have my surgery covered. Surely the cost of the four lawyers who sat across from me during my five-hour deposition cost more than that.

It was the second lawsuit that I'd been involved with because of my illnesses. In 1997, when I was diagnosed with the leukemia and forced to go on disability and move out of my apartment, the owner of my complex in Los Feliz (he owned many others throughout Southern California as well) sued me for breaking my lease. He called me personally to explain that he had no intention of letting me out of the lease, regardless of my reasons. He even went so far as to tell me that if I died from my leukemia, he'd make sure and sue my family for the money that he was owed.

I have since discovered that it is not a good idea to fill someone with a terrible resolve who also suddenly has hours of free time on his hands. I contacted a nonprofit group of attorneys who donated their time to help cancer patients wade through the legalities that many of them face, and they helped me countersue him for a variety of illegal practices, as well as punitive damages.

I had no interest in a lawsuit. I just wanted my deposit back so I could move on with my fight against leukemia. But when he suggested that even my death wouldn't be enough to make him go away, I hit back. It was some of the most rewarding money I've ever made.

THERE WERE NO guarantees when Carrie said yes to my proposal in 2004. Further dramas with my ICD were still to come. We knew that there would be, inescapably, days and nights of uncertainty. One of two ends was certain: I would make it to transplant, at which time I would undergo a complicated surgery that still had no guarantees on its back end, or I wouldn't. One option was far better than the other, but neither was optimal.

As months passed and we moved closer to our wedding date—October 8, 2005—I got a call one early March evening from a friend of mine at the Leukemia & Lymphoma Society. A television producer from ABC had called her that afternoon to ask if she knew of any engaged couples who had interesting and sympathetic stories. They were doing a reality-television wedding-show pilot, and they were looking for a legitimate couple to marry on it. It was going to be a spin-off from the popular Sunday night series *Extreme Makeover: Home Edition*. But this time, instead of quickly building a house for a deserving family, they were going to throw a wedding for a deserving couple.

I called the producer immediately after getting his number, and he asked the two of us to come in the next day for a face-to-face interview. We did, and the interview ended up lasting more than four hours. The more we talked to them, the more people gathered in the room, wanting to talk to us. They put us on camera, we talked some more, we met other producers, they brought in sandwiches, and we filled out lengthy questionnaires.

Over the next three weeks we submitted to drug tests and psychological evaluations. We handed in potential guest lists and answered more questions on camera so that network executives could see how we sounded and looked. Then, on March 29, with the help of Dr. Stein, who'd called me to ask if I would come out to City of Hope that Tuesday to speak with a newly diagnosed patient ("And, oh, please bring your fiancée, since this new patient also has a young wife"), we were surprised with a full camera setup and crew, announcing we were the selected couple. That Friday, with the help of "the I Do Crew"—the cast at the heart of *Extreme Makeover: Wedding Edition*—we would be married. (It was not lost on us that Friday also happened to be April Fool's Day.)

It was a week of the bizarre and the surreal. That Tuesday night we were whisked away in a limo and taken to the Sears in Pasadena for an all-expenses-paid shopping spree. You've never felt more out of your element than when cameras are in your face and executives from Sears are telling you, "Please take a second flat-screen TV. You need one for your bedroom."

After two hours of damage in the store that saw us load up on kitchen goodies, luggage, exercise equipment, surround-sound systems to go with our TVs, and new power tools and moments when we found the switch of a normal price-conscious shopper hard to turn off—we actually picked a sixty-nine-dollar toaster oven because we couldn't see the need of the one-hundred-twenty-nine-dollar model (some things are just too ingrained)—we met with a crew from *Access Hollywood* to do an interview that would air the next day.

On Wednesday I had a dance lesson with celebratory choreographer Cris Judd, while Carrie met with her bridesmaids to have dresses made. On Thursday it was time for my bachelor party at a pool hall with my dad, my groomsmen, Ted (who would be performing the ceremony), and Kansas City Chief's future Hall of Fame tight end Tony Gonzalez. After putting on the autographed jersey that Tony brought, our matching number 88s made us look like twins . . . of the Arnold Schwarzenegger and Danny DeVito *Twins* variety. Tony is six-foot-five, two hundred forty pounds, and has the olive skin tone to match his Mexican and Portuguese heritage. I am not any one of those things.

Friday was the main event, our wedding.

With a television wedding set to make its premiere on ABC, you hand over certain controls to the production team, and you go in knowing this. We weren't around for the building of our wedding and reception sets on the grounds of the City of Hope. We didn't put together the menu or pick out any flowers, and we had to trust that the guest list we submitted two weeks earlier was inclusive of everyone we'd want to be there. But based on our many interviews, the production team matched our desires and personalities as closely as they could.

It was wedding in the round, with the guest chairs making a perfect spiral leading to the center. Carrie did her bridal walk past every one of the more than one hundred fifty guests who had been flown in the day before. The colors and flowers were also matched to questions that we'd answered in the weeks leading up to the big day, as was the reception's menu. The favorites were macaroni and cheese served in martini glasses with meatballs standing in for the olives and a series of white, dark, and milk chocolate fountains.

But this was Hollywood's take on a nationally televised wedding, and food and flowers were not going to be its standouts. For that, we had a full New York City street set complete with a Rockefeller Center ice rink and matching giant Christmas tree. During one of my many interviews I was asked, if I could do anything for Carrie, what would it be? I wasn't quite sure how to answer such an open-ended fantasy, so I replied, "I'd take her to New York for Christmas."

And that became our theme.

There was a snow machine, the Christmas-themed storefronts of Fifth Avenue, and a wedding cake with Manhattan's skyline on top to complete the transformation from Southern California in April to New York City in December. And then there was Liza.

When asked about what kind of music we'd prefer to hear, Carrie picked Norah Jones. Our first dance—courtesy of the choreography I learned from Cris Judd—was to her song "The Nearness of You." But this was New York, and no one says Big Apple more than Liza Minnelli.

At first when she was introduced, both Carrie and I were struck with the same thought: *They hired a Liza Minnelli impersonator!*

But as she got closer and the song "New York, New York" got rolling from the live band, there was no doubt that this Liza was the real deal. By the time she was on stage and belting out her iconic number, it was close to 1:30 AM—or 4:30 AM in New York, where she'd just come from (she'd flown in specially for our wedding). Yet she was as fresh and as full of energy as if she was singing at home on any normal Tuesday.

Even when the night closed with the surprise gift of a car from Ford, all anyone could talk about was Liza.

MARRIED, AND NOW outfitted with my third device to keep my heart going, I forced my way, with Carrie, through the next several months. It was a cruel and arduous waiting game, but the rest of life rolled on without regard. There was nothing static about our wait.

I'd left my permanent position at Fox a couple of months before our wedding to write freelance. Work was sporadic at times and steady at others, but it was findable. I also began work on my first book in early 2006, discovering that there were a lot of rewards and freedom in being my own boss, creating my own project, and setting my own hours.

Carrie and I settled into a routine as a married couple. There were times, especially at night, when the oncoming transplant and the current failing state of my heart would penetrate the shine of our newlywed finish. Carrie revealed to me that on occasion she would wake up in the middle of the night and check to make sure I was still breathing. The thought of her doing that—knowing that she was in a position to even think to do that—broke my heart. I can't imagine the fear that adjoins such a total loss of control. Those nights and the weeks and months that passed after our wedding—weeks and months of my accruing time on the heart transplant waiting list—were especially hard on Carrie. But it was hard with no complaints. She was scared, but she always smiled. There was stress, but there was also fun.

A year passed, then more. By the end of August 2006, I got a call from my doctor at UCLA. "If you go any trips, please let us know. You're near the top of the list, and we don't want to lose time trying to locate you. Or, better yet, don't go on any trips."

My time on the waiting list was almost through.

13

OCTOBER 10, 2006

All of our biographies are shaped by just a few transitory moments in time. Single decisions or events—some controlled, many not—plot our charts for years and decades to follow. When we look backward, the significance is easy to see, even if at the time the path taken was shrouded or concealed. It's the reluctantly accepted date that turns into a life-long relationship—a missed job opportunity that ends up creating a new and more exciting career path; a case of insomnia, a late-night infomercial, the discovery of the amazing ShamWow and One Sweep, and a newfound love of housework that ends up saving the marriage. (The same phenomena have also been observed in the kitchen with EZ Peel Gloves and Ronco Rotisserie Ovens.)

There are, of course, the times when the weight of what's happening, both good and bad, becomes crystal clear. The ultimate destination may remain unknown, but the magnitude of the course change is as obvious as the day is memorable. Or as funny as watching Mr. T hawk his Flavorwave Oven Turbo. Set it to cook and you're off the hook. (It also deserves note that, according to the website, the oven "actually cleans up after itself. Simply place it in the dishwasher." Seriously.)

The day of October 10, 2006, was a palpable pivot point for me. It didn't take down-the-road reflection or wisdom gained from hindsight for its magnitude to register. That fall Tuesday was a game changer of the highest order; most of life as I knew it came to an end, and an undiscovered, foreign, and quite frightening path was forged. Just as I'm sure that my cat will never forget the first time I experimented with the as-seen-on-TV FURminator, I will never forget October 10.

At 3:30 that afternoon my wife, Carrie, got home from work, like she did on most days. She was an early bird to the office—not for worms, sunrises, or any other such nonsense that springs from the mouths of the annoying morning person (I recognize the redundancy), but for the necessity of missing the traffic that she would otherwise encounter on the two worst freeways in Southern California, the 405 and the 101. Therefore she was an early returnee home. And so, as I did most days, I put aside my afternoon's work so we could engage in the "how was your day" chitchat that dominates the early evenings in millions of married households across the country.

We'd been married eighteen months at this point and were still less than four years removed from our first date. I very much cared how her day was, even if I didn't understand 90 percent of what it was she did. What I did understand was the stress. There was always a project to manage. Always a client with lots of money tied up in a development that couldn't move forward until the appropriate permits were attained and filed with the corresponding city. As always, much of that responsibility rested on her shoulders. The wheels of the City of Los Angeles Department of Building and Safety never ran as smoothly or as quickly as the client wanted or sometimes demanded. She was tasked with trying to make them do that.

I, on the other hand, was writing a book about the worst referees in sports history. I spent my day doing baseball research and coming up with sarcastic comments to make about umpires.

As you might guess, my portion of this daily conversation was usually short and almost always lacking any dramatics. I wrote from home and typically spent most days uneventfully sitting with my laptop and adding to the noticeable butt dent in the couch. The day became mildly interesting when I would shift from one cushion to the other. It became downright exciting when I was actually forced to put pants on and venture outside our apartment. Since I was in the process of finishing up the edits on the manuscript for my first sports book, *The Worst Call Ever*, the 2.4-mile trips to the nearest post office were happening with more frequency, but they had hardly become more thrilling to describe to my wife.

At 3:49, however, that all changed.

My cell phone rang. I first ignored it, since the person who placed 75 percent of the incoming calls was sitting ten feet away and sipping a Diet Coke. But after the phone cycled through its four rings and took the unknown caller to my voice mail, it started to ring again. Clearly this wasn't someone willing to leave a message after the beep, so I got up and went into the other room to retrieve the phone and answer the call.

"Hello?"

"Is this Kyle?"

"It is, yes."

"This is Dorothy at UCLA. We need you to come to the hospital as soon as possible."

Then she said the five most important words in my English language: "We have your donor heart."

You know how in really bad eighties movies (again, I recognize the redundancy) or in TV shows with low budgets (and an even lower level of creativity) when something completely unexpected is said, there is this trifecta of cheesy double take, hard zoom of the camera, and poorly done sound effect of a record scratching? It turns out that doesn't happen in real life.

My jaw didn't gape open either. I didn't have a spontaneous muscle reaction that caused me to drop the phone. There was no rush of blood within my body that left me faint. And I was able to stay composed enough to keep from offending Dorothy, whom I didn't know at this point, with any excited utterances of profanity. I simply asked her, "What do I need to do?"

The instructions were simple enough. As I wrapped up my brief yet never-to-be-forgotten conversation with Dorothy, I walked back into the living room where Carrie sat patiently waiting for me to be done on the phone so she could fire up our TiVo.

"That was the call," I said, surprising myself with the banality of the statement.

"What call?" she responded quite sincerely, since she hadn't yet been thrust into the world that I now occupied.

"The call. The call we've been waiting for. It was UCLA. It's happening today."

With her reaction trailing recognition by just a split second, her face took on an odd mix of understanding and disbelief, followed very quickly by a distinct "Oh, shit!" quality. She might have even said it; I can't be sure because a few moments in there remained blurred. But I do remember the hug: very intense, reciprocated completely, and absolutely necessary to make the upcoming hours bearable.

We knew this day was coming. We'd anticipated the phone call. The emotions and reactions that it would create had been discussed ad nauseam months and years ago. Nothing came as a shock; yet surprisingly, it did. I actually even took a moment during the hug to contemplate the contradiction of the growing haze of astonishment that enveloped this scene when it had literally played itself out hundreds of times in our heads.

Then the freneticism hit. Time was wasting!

Quick, pack a bag. I have to call my parents, my friends. Say good-bye to the cat (he'll welcome the break). Dump the full Captain Morgan and Coke—nothing more to eat or drink. (You who haven't ever had a drink at 3:49 PM feel free to cast the first stone.) Wallet and insurance cards? Check. Car keys? Oh yeah, can't drive without keys. Check. *People* magazine? (For the wife, honest.) Check. One last kiss and hug before we hit the road? Check, check.

I am not a father, and I've never been a part of a frantic rush to the hospital because of an impending birth. My only knowledge of what that must be like comes from the very real portrayals I see on TV. Hollywood depicts the stereotypical dad-to-be as a man who trades in forty IQ points for the stimulus of forty cups of coffee at the utterance of the phrase "My water just broke." With those four words the male of the species goes from controlled and steady to spastic and panicked. When that switch is flipped, the job of ushering his pregnant wife to the car and getting her to the hospital safely takes on a 1950s sitcom quality, with the role of husband played by Lucille Ball.

Our rush-hour drive to UCLA didn't quite go that chaotically. There were no tragedies with conveyor belts of candy or fights in grape vats. And no one had any "'splainin' to do" at the end of the trip. But it did strike me as we drove to UCLA—me in the driver's seat and on the phone making calls to family and friends while Carrie did the exact same thing on the passenger's side—that at that very moment, while I was on a life-saving mission to the hospital, I was actually a pretty good candidate to take one.

This was in the days before California made it illegal to drive and talk on a cell phone without a hands-free device. I wasn't breaking any laws or subject to any fines. But if ever there was an example as to why the law is necessary and good and why dialing and driving is as dangerous as drinking and driving (or drinking and dialing for that matter), our weaving Ford Escape Hybrid heading north on the West Los Angeles artery of Sepulveda Boulevard was it.

Ten minutes away from the hospital and the uncertainties that would be met beyond its sliding glass doors, I glanced over at Carrie. For me, as her husband, the word "wife" is a very special designation. A ring and a piece of paper are meaningless when compared to the intensity and the intimacy of our relationship. Through our eighteen months of marriage, Carrie had sat willingly alongside me in the rickety lifeboat of time, unceasingly rowing toward today, the day when our boat would be found and we would finally be rescued.

We had survived the scary and stayed strong through the fear. The storm clouds of a declining heart that had engulfed me for eleven and a half years and hovered over our relationship for four years were showing signs of lifting. The rain that had been falling, that had been darkening the days, was showing signs of slowing. Eventually that rain—the storm of cancer that rolled in all those years ago—would stop. Maybe even by tonight. And then, as always happens after a rain, the grass would be green again, the flowers would fully bloom, the sky would be crisp and clear, and all that relied on the rain for life would be whole again.

My wife and I would be whole by the time this night was through.

Almost everyone has experienced the masterful efficiency of our nation's hospital admission system. You check in, only to be told to wait until someone calls you to . . . that's right, check in. Then finally it happens, followed by more waiting, until at last you are called into a tiny little room the size of the third-class lavatory on a nineteenth-century passenger ship. This room is so small that even an undersized Superman would have a hard time making the outfit transition from Clark Kent to a miniature Man of Steel, so small that the fire marshal of the Smurfs' village would cap its capacity at three (provided Hefty Smurf wasn't one of them)—but it somehow manages to fit a small table, two chairs, a computer terminal, and the admissions "specialist" (I can think of a few better descriptors for these soulless human beings who act as the Charon-inspired gatekeepers of Hospital Hades).

Then, no matter how many times you've gone through this process for the same medical condition, at the same hospital, and quite often with the same admission "expert," you have to answer the same list of eighty-five questions and hand over the same half-dozen cards that provide proof of insurance, proof of payment, and proof of illness—which really already should be in the computer that seems to be directing this person's every word and thought.

Eventually you are handed the deforested remains of what used to be a proud wildlife refuge and made to sign more autographs than Pete Rose at a two-dollar-a-signature baseball-card show. Predictably you get carpal tunnel syndrome and now need to be seen by a different doctor, which means more questions, more legal forms that cover everything from your familial relations to prominent malpractice attorneys to the middle name of your second-grade teacher, and then a final silent prayer of remembrance for the acre of felled trees that gave their lives to triplicate.

Well, the dirty little secret that health care legal eagles across the country have been trying to hide is out. None of it—not the strictly enforced waiting, not the insipid interrogation for the sake of dotting every "i" threefold, not the reams of wasted paper—is necessary. When I arrived at UCLA that day, I flew through admissions, no less the VIP than Angelina Jolie at an overseas orphanage.

Wait time: four minutes. Questions: "When did you last eat or drink?" Consumed paper: OK, still a lot. Even Angie and Brad have to sign a few forms before adding to their brood. But two out of three improvements ain't bad.

Within twenty minutes of my arrival, I was squirreled away in a private waiting room, fitted with my first of the night's fifteen IV lines, and visited by everyone with a series of fancy letters at the end of his or her name who got a paycheck from California's UC system and was not engaged with another patient. That moment for me may not have been an exact representation of the fifteen minutes that Andy Warhol had in mind, but there was little doubt that within those specific walls, on that particular night, I was famous. And like when my fellow celebrities Britney Spears, Lindsay Lohan, and Paris Hilton hit the clubs along the Sunset Strip, that night at UCLA I was wearing a skimpy little gown and meeting and greeting the masses sans underpants. Luckily there were no paparazzi to capture the moment and sell the photos to TMZ.

There are a few entries that everyone has on his list of things never to do with his spouse in front of his parents. Fighting, for one. The exact opposite of fighting, for another. And the lesser thought-about—but almost equally awkward—act of signing your last will and testament. In fact, parents or no parents, it's best to keep that particular legal document far away from hospital rooms. But sometimes you procrastinate, you hesitate, and then you suddenly get a phone call from a heart transplant coordinator that destroys your timeline and creates another. And since you also need witnesses to make a will legal, it goes into the overnight bag right along with clean underwear and a toothbrush.

My parents—as well as a few of the other voices that had been on the receiving end of those perilous drive-time phone calls—had already joined the room when I remembered the will. I pulled it out of the bag with my one yet-to-be-IV-tethered hand and watched everyone's faces. They revealed little—or as little as possible—but I knew what everyone was thinking. Along with "Really, you brought that with you to the hospital!" there was the obvious but unspoken elephant in the room that I just forced everyone to face.

There had been smiles and laughter, even if nervous, and there was a general upbeat mood in the room about the hours soon to begin. But with the introduction of the will, the unspoken dread of the day claimed its spot near the sunlit window, darkening it just a little. This was not a routine tonsillectomy that would have me out of the hospital later that evening. The required reading of all possible problems that could occur was not done merely to cover legal butts. In this case even the worst-case scenarios, usually dismissed as ridiculous, were very real.

So while my introducing the will to the room was probably bad form, it was responsible and necessary. With two of my friends standing in as witnesses (ironically one of the witnesses had also signed as a witness on our marriage license), it became legally binding. My wife would now forever be stuck with my baseball cards and decades-old collection of minihelmets that had at one time held hot fudge sundaes, like it or not. It's the law.

In the many months of anticipation leading up to this day, I often thought about how Carrie would handle the unsettled hours of waiting while I was locked away in the operating room. It worried me, not so much because I was afraid for how she'd manage—I knew her level of strength and I was confident that it wouldn't dip now—but because I was concerned for the overriding mood of the moment. Of course there would be worry. Nothing is certain in even the most ordinary of surgeries, and this was far from that. But to me, my parents, and Carrie, this night represented an exciting new beginning. The cracking of my sternum wasn't quite the carbon copy of a broken bottle of champagne to christen the maiden voyage of the SS *New Life*, but the adventure waiting on the path extended before me was very much the same. I wanted to make sure that happiness, not hesitancy, dominated the UCLA waiting-room atmosphere.

The presence of the will, with ink still wet, threatened the tenor of the room. But if my parents and Carrie found it difficult to rebound and refocus on the coming good, I knew the two friends that would wait with her would liven and reenergize everyone's spirits.

First was Inga, a fellow Team In Training marathoner who'd joined Carrie for multiple 26.2-mile adventures. She was a bridesmaid at our wedding and a frequent partner in laughing at life's absurdities. With her,

Carrie would be in good and light-hearted hands. But if things did get tough, it wouldn't hurt that Inga was also an officer with the LAPD.

The second friend that joined us that evening was Meghan. A former collegiate swimmer making her professional way as a success in sports marketing, Meghan first met Carrie in the laundry room of our apartment complex. It was a fortuitous meeting for a number of reasons. Meghan became a fast and faithful friend who would provide both support and welcome distractions during the hours of waiting to come. A year and a half later, in 2008, the fortunes changed faces when Meghan was diagnosed with Hodgkin's disease.

If I had been doing laundry that day instead of Carrie, we never would have met Meghan. I simply don't contain the same strike-up-a-conversation-with-anyone gene that Carrie does. If it had been me in the laundry room, then Meghan wouldn't have been there as a support for us during my transplant. And I wouldn't have been there, ready to reciprocate when Meghan was diagnosed with the one thing I'm most qualified to understand and assist with. (It should be noted that Meghan survived her battle with Hodgkin's and is thriving again both professionally and physically.) Still, despite my best efforts to illustrate this providential chain of events, I have not been relieved of all my laundry duties.

Four hours after my phone rang, breaking the comforting monotony of another evening of dinner and TiVo with my wife and our cat, the pre-game transplant preparations were complete. All the MDs who needed to be in the know had been alerted. My friends and family on the "call immediately" list were now firmly in the loop. And I, the main event of the evening, had been transported to the bowels of the hospital, where I was quickly surrounded by any machine within a three-building radius that beeped, blipped, or wheezed.

It was time.

First, there were hugs for my friends, who had been allowed into the normally off-limits waiting room—a fact that underscored the uniqueness of the night. Hospital rules and protocol that would normally be enforced with the zealousness of a 1980s East German athletic academy did not apply.

Then came my parents. Thankfully I do not belong to one of those families that find it necessary to assign the children cute nicknames like Bubby, Chip, or Junebug. I was never made to be a smaller version of them, and they never once tried to live vicariously through me. I had become my own man, and while my current position as a freelance writer and motivational speaker didn't provide me with the employment stability that their lives always enjoyed, I'd been allowed to just be me. With that still being true, on this night it was more important that I was their son.

This night had been seventeen years in the making. During that stretch, my parents had been broken and rebuilt countless times by my many health hurdles. There had been enough tears of fear, sadness, and anger to fill a swimming pool or two. But not this night. This night they were still, stoic, and solid for their son. It wasn't a hardening that had taken place. I sensed in them relief. The uncertain journey for which they had traveled alongside me for seventeen years was coming to a close.

Finally, it was time to say good-bye to Carrie. Married for such a short time, we'd known for the duration of our relationship that this day would come. This scene, playing out in a hallway just outside an operating room at UCLA Medical Center, was always a part of our future. It was one of the commitments that she'd said "I do" to.

There weren't really words to exchange. Or, I should say, new words. They'd all been said in the gathering months and weeks. We shared a long hug, an "I love you," a deep and intense eye lock, and a very hopeful "I'll see you soon." I could tell she was in a peacefully accepting place. She was more than willing to make a trade: accept the relative uncertainty of this night and give up the certain severing of our relationship without it. Tonight, though big and scary, was welcome and necessary.

Just like that, I was off on the rolling gurney, out of the hallway filled with loving faces and into a sterile operating room packed with more overhead lighting than Dodger Stadium. Perhaps the only tally that would rival my hospital bill for the duration of the stay would be the accompanying electric bill. Regardless of how the upcoming procedure played out, at least I'd be tan. And considering that one of the three masked figures who had greeted me upon entry was now shaving me in multiple places—some of them unmentionable—the tan would be even.

Lying there on the table, with both arms stretched out, strapped down, and now connected to new machines, I could only stare up at the ceiling and into the bright lights and think. I listened to the sounds of preparation that came from the already-present surgical team trio—a clanging here, a clatter there, and what I swear to this day was the sound of a four-stroke engine.

I'm not a doctor, so I concede it might have been something else.

AN HOUR LATER (it was almost 9 PM according to the clock on the far wall), the anesthesiologist's half-hidden face appeared above mine.

"We're going to get started now."

The strange combination of fear, anxiety, excitement, Valium, and Demerol that had been mushrooming within me over the previous sixty minutes had rendered me mute. I managed a blink and maybe a nod, and I was happy to be on with it. Inside your head can be a dangerous place to be unfettered for an hour.

He affixed an oxygen mask over my face and, with the push of a plunger, added the knockout blow to my already relaxant-clouded veins. "Kyle. Count backwards from one hundred."

"One hundred, ninety-nine, ninety-eight . . ."

My voice trailed off before I could drop the count to ninety-seven. I was leaving that room, leaving that life, and hoping to wake anew on the other side.

I remember thinking very briefly, right before everything finally went dark, about how it came to be that at age thirty-five, I was here, on this table, about to have a heart transplant.

There were no regrets about the course I'd traveled in the past seventeen years. There was nothing I wanted to undo, even though if it hadn't been for that very first diagnosis seventeen years ago, there wouldn't have been a bone marrow transplant and thus a need on this night for a heart transplant.

Without question, my life would have been easier and more predictable if I could undo that one event that changed so much in September 1989. I wouldn't have lost most of my twenties to disease and illness. I would have been on target to achieve my sportscasting goals with a broadcast journalism degree from the University of Missouri. Most immediately, I would not have a doctor looking down at me who would momentarily saw through my sternum and pull out my heart.

But undoing my original diagnosis would mean that most of my friends would have never entered my life. I wouldn't have moved to California where I'd managed to forge a future under the warm sun of the Pacific coast. And I would have never met Carrie, and we never would have been married.

On the ledger of pros and cons, there is no doubt that undoing any part of my past would have resulted in a different and darker present and future. I liked who I was, where I was, and the wonderful people around me that would be accompanying me into my future.

As I went to sleep on the operating table on the evening of October 10, 2006, I was at peace.

14

A HEART IN HARMONY

Heading into the transplant, I wasn't frightened by that many things about the surgery. UCLA was one of the most experienced transplant centers in the world. When I got my call that October, I became the 1,605th heart transplant to be performed there. If you had to have your heart in the hands of others, you'd be hard pressed to find any more capable.

I'd also been reading books about people who had gone on to live amazing lives on the other side of transplant. Kelly Perkins, who authored *The Climb of My Life* and has since become a friend of mine, had a heart transplant in 1995 at UCLA. Post-transplant, she's climbed Mount Fuji in Japan, Mount Kilimanjaro in Tanzania, and the Matterhorn in Switzerland, just to name a few. Clearly life can be active after a transplant.

The only thing that truly frightened me about the surgery was the first hour after I would wake. Throughout the many pacemaker surgeries, Hickman and Port-A-Cath procedures, plus the surgeries to replace my hip and shoulder, I learned one cold hard fact about myself—I do not do well with anesthesia. There are very few guarantees going into an operating room, but I can always make one: I will be sick and vomiting when I wake up.

The heart transplant was going to add an extra wrinkle to the post-op that had me even more trepidatious going in. I would wake up with a large tube down my throat to help me breathe. With my gag reflex already on full because of the anesthesia, the tube's presence truly had me nervous.

Waking with a start on the morning of October 11, 2006, I couldn't focus my eyes. There were people I could sense and machines and other noises that served as reminders of where I was. But the passage of time from when I was on the operating table and had reached the count of ninety-eight, when everything went dark, to that waking moment felt instantaneous. At night when you sleep, the subconscious betrays the passage of time. There are dreams and varying levels of sleep that allow for the recognition that hours have passed. I had none of that when I woke from the heart transplant. My consciousness made the seamless transition between pre- and postsurgery.

As I struggled for recognition, I immediately began to gag on the tube down my throat. My bottom lip was mashed and swollen from having been trapped between the tube and my teeth for so many hours. The inside of my throat felt raw. Then came the waves of nausea.

I threw up, then threw up again. I was having a hard time breathing with the tube still in, and I noticed for the first time that each arm had been tethered to the bed. I had lines coming out of each hand, wrist, and arm. My lines seemed to have lines. Since all of them were probably important, it made sense that I was strapped to the bed. That did not, however, make it any more comfortable.

About twenty minutes after I woke up, the nurses took out the breathing tube. I immediately felt better, minus the mess that I was laying in. But that was soon taken care of too, when a couple of very able-bodied members of the hospital lift team came to my aid.

It's not an easy thing to change the sheets and gown of someone who's immobilized following a heart transplant. What they did was first roll me on my left side, unhooking the old sheet on the right while starting to attach a clean one, and then they repeated the entire exercise the other way by rolling me on my right. What I hadn't really felt yet was the physical effect of the surgery on my chest. I'd been fixated on my stomach and the tube that was exacerbating its condition. But when I was rolled onto my side and onto the side of my rib cage, I felt the pain like a hot poker in the side of my pectorals.

When they crack your sternum to get to the heart, the rib cage is spread wide open. As you might imagine, this does quite a number on all the surrounding muscles. Also, the pectorals across the front of the chest have been cut to make it possible to reach the sternum. So when you go rolling around on that rib cage just hours after surgery ends, even with the help of very strong lifters, it hurts quite mightily.

The interesting thing in all this was that in spite of the nausea, the panic with the breathing tube, the obvious pain from surgery, my inability to move, and the sensation that an eight-hundred-pound man was sitting on my chest, I felt great.

I had energy, both in real terms and in my mental outlook, for the days that stretched ahead. I had normal blood pressure again. Prior to transplant, my blood pressure was regularly in the 80 over 50 ballpark. But now it was a boringly normal 125 over 80. And most dramatically, I could feel my beating heart.

When you haven't felt your heart beat in more than a decade because its strength is too weak to register within your senses, you forget that you haven't felt your heart beat. But then all of a sudden it's there. And loud. And fast. And strong.

There was also the noticeable lifting of the burden of heart transplant. For years there had been a storm cloud gathering; over the passage of time, things became noticeably darker and colder in its path. But that morning the cloud had passed. The sun was out, and the future was shining with possibilities.

During my months and years of chemotherapy, each treatment left my body more battered. During the eleven years that I'd been saddled with cardiomyopathy, I was becoming sicker and weaker with each passing day. It was a long, slow slide into a certain coffin.

Starting that morning, everything was different. With each new day I could expect to get stronger and healthier. The slide into my coffin had been arrested, and I was now engaged in an exciting and inspiring climb back into the physical. I couldn't move, but I felt like dancing.

TOLD BY HOSPITAL staff that I would still be in my anesthetic sleep for another couple of hours, Carrie left UCLA for the first time in eighteen hours to go home and grab a shower. She hadn't slept in more than twenty-eight hours and had only eaten vending-machine food since the previous day's lunch. She needed to go home and refresh after a long night of hoping, waiting, and ultimately celebrating. Twenty minutes after she left, I was awake and gagging on my breathing tube.

With Carrie on the road but frantically trying to get back to the hospital after my dad called to tell her that I had awoken, the first friendly faces I saw post-transplant were those of my parents. They were the same faces that I saw more than seventeen years earlier when I first heard the words "You have lymphoma." They were the faces of the people who cared for me during every one of my chemotherapy treatments in 1991. They were the faces behind the surgical masks that visited me in isolation during my bone marrow transplant in 1995. They were the faces that provided me comfort in July 1997 when I was convinced that a fourth cancer diagnosis was finally going to take my life. And they were the faces that looked on with pride and the gratitude of life when I was lucky enough to marry Carrie in 2005.

Those faces, worn by the passage of time and many a lifetime's worth of worry and burden, had witnessed every single one of my worst days. Now today, October 11, 2006, they were there to witness my greatest of days. It was the first day of the rest of my life, and their faces and smiles never looked more beautiful.

THE WEEK I was in the hospital was my transition back into the world of the truly living. After two days in the cardiac ICU, I'd been moved into my own room. I was eating normally, managing my own medications, and watching the baseball playoffs on television. Cards and letters from friends came pouring in, and I even received flowers from Chiefs tight end and TV-bachelor-party attendee Tony Gonzalez. Carrie and I had remained friends with a couple of the producers of our televised wedding, one of whom joined the vigil with my group of well-wishers in the UCLA waiting room the night of October 10, after I'd been taken into the operating room. She'd excitedly called Tony's people to let them know that the transplant was finally happening.

I began walking when I could, although my abilities failed to meet my high expectations. I was assured that even though the heart I'd been gifted had come from an "athlete"—my doctor's words—my progress, or lack thereof, was normal. I needed to keep in mind that I'd just come through a very physically traumatic surgery. After five and a half years of waiting for restoration, I'd have to keep my patience just a little longer.

One of the more daunting realities facing heart transplant patients is the prospect of being on medications for the rest of your life. There are many meds to keep straight and impressions by patients that you'll become a slave to watching the alarms that signal the next round of pill popping. In almost all cases, the power of the imagination greatly exaggerates the reality of the facts.

Before I was allowed to leave the hospital a week after transplant, I had to first take a class on medication management. My pill bottles were all assigned numbers, which were far easier to learn then the series of names that seemed to read like the New York City cab drivers' registry (although I can now recite without hesitation each of the medications that I take as well as their dose and frequency).

I also was given a handy guide to direct me on the time of day to take each medication and at what point in the cycle it would be best to order refills. Carrie took notes during class, and we both left the hospital that day feeling like the one last heavy-headed hurdle to a normal life after transplant had been reduced to a minor speed bump. With a weekly pill organizer and my trusty guide to consult, medication management would be a cinch.

Though I was home in a week, life was still about recovery. Because my sternum had been cracked, driving was strictly off limits for the first six weeks. An accident that could send me reeling into a steering wheel would be enough to cave in my healing bones. Even the front passenger seat, where the airbags might deploy, was considered a major hazard. So whenever I needed to go somewhere, I had to be chauffeured in the backseat like a big deal.

Not that there was any place to go that didn't contain the words "medical" or "center." I was on high doses of immunosuppressive drugs to prevent my body from attacking my new organ, and because of that I was highly susceptible to infections and viruses. Confined spaces with large groups of people—even when that space was my own home—were prohibited. The "welcome the new heart to the family" party would have to wait.

I couldn't eat out or have food that was prepared by hands I didn't know. What if someone working in the kitchen of the restaurant that night had a sniffle? Anyone else would never know or care. But even the weakest of germs could prove to be fatal to me. Eating in and thoroughly washing everything had to become our norm. We stocked every room in the apartment with Purell hand sanitizer just to be sure. (I also stopped touching doorknobs and elevator buttons when they could be avoided.)

I had a home-health-care nurse who visited me weekly. (Cytomegalovirus, or CMV, was the concern. It's a very common and largely symptom-free virus that infects most of the population. But since I was CMV negative and my donor was CMV positive, my compromised immune system needed a couple months of intravenous antibiotics as protection.) She was kind enough to call in sick a couple times because she didn't want to introduce new germs into my environment. If there was one thing I learned to take seriously during the three months that I was on house arrest—with exceptions made for visits to the hospital for heart biopsies—it was germs.

I'd been the kid who ate dirt when he was little. I was a firm believer in the ten-second rule, even when the wet side of food landed face down on the floor. As a frequent camper—Carrie and I made annual trips to go camping in the forests of Big Sur—I'd eaten my share of hand-to-mouth meals without a daily washing. Those times, at least in the interim, were over.

My physical recovery was aided by the therapist who came and visited me on a biweekly basis. We worked on strength exercises for my legs and stretches for my chest and shoulders. As the bones and muscles in my chest were healing, everything throughout that region was becoming excessively tight, and not in a "look how swole I am" kind of way. I felt more like Chris Farley wearing David Spade's tiny coat in *Tommy Boy*.

As work with my physical therapist progressed, my range of motion increased, the strength in my legs and arms improved dramatically, and I was able to walk short distances, and even some stairs, without getting short of breath. I wasn't becoming an athlete overnight, but the daily progress into normalcy was easy to chart. The positive feelings that had consumed me in the immediate days after the transplant continued to fuel my efforts. There would be no cheating on my home assignments away from the watchful eyes of my therapist. I wasn't going to cut any of the corners that my doctor had established for my aftercare. With so much at stake, I was completely committed to staying at full steam ahead.

As mentioned earlier, one of the most noticeable changes physiologically was the strong beating of my heart. It was a beautiful sound, but it was one I couldn't escape. At night when I would lay my head down to go to sleep, it was there. If my head lolled to either side and my ear pressed down against my pillow, it was really there. It was cheering to hear, that reminder of strength now inside me that had been gone for so long, but it made sleep next to impossible.

For the first few weeks, I struggled with sleep. Some of it was that I was back on steroids as part of my post-transplant care, and my entire system had its accelerator pressed to the floor. Much of it involved the rattling heartbeat that I simply could not get my brain to ignore when it was time for system shutdown. Part of it was the discomfort I still felt in my chest area. I like to be mobile when I sleep, going from side to side, onto my back, or even the occasional flip to my front. But with a chest cavity on recovery overdrive, I was forced into becoming a back-only sleeper.

As more days moved by, I recognized that the presence of something far greater than mere physical discomforts and the onset of steroid side effects had become the root of my sleeplessness. I was tormented by thoughts of my donor. A man lost his life so that I could live, and that knowledge had become an anchor of anxiety.

In the years leading up to my transplant, I'd thought a lot about the life and death exchange that was required to maintain my survival. It's a heavy thing to imagine that call from the hospital, which informs you that the long wait for a heart is over. It naturally sets off a mix of emotions in friends and family members that include both relief and elation. It's a formative day for every transplant recipient and one of the best moments of their lives.

But it will only come after another family has received the worst phone call imaginable. A loved one has gone to the grocery store, headed off to work, or done any number of everyday activities that they've completed without incident a hundred other times. But on this day, there was an accident. The family needs to get to the hospital as quickly as possible because the person they kissed good-bye that morning is in his or her final moments of life.

I'd rented the movie *Return to Me* shortly after landing on the heart transplant list. I'd heard that a transplant was central to the theme, and I'd had a thing for Minnie Driver since *Good Will Hunting*. Early in the film, David Duchovny's wife, played by Joely Richardson, is fatally injured in a car accident, and her organs are donated. Driver, in the hospital and waiting for a heart, is its recipient.

I think of myself as pretty stoic when it comes to fictional stories. I don't get too caught up emotionally in the lives of those who are make-believe. I love movies, but I never cry at them. (*E.T.* and *Field of Dreams* don't count.)

There is a scene in the film that occurs shortly after the decision is made to donate her organs: Duchovny, in a sling and bandaged up with his own injuries from the accident, comes home from the hospital. After feeding the dog and rereading a note that his now-deceased wife had left for him on the refrigerator, he collapses to the floor, curling up with the dog and sobbing.

I couldn't make it through that scene. Even now, just replaying it in my head and picturing the very authentic agony that Duchovny brought to life, the kind of scene that I'm sure plays itself out in homes and hospitals every night in America, I get emotional. It's the exact kind of agony that was required to infect a family before I could get my heart.

To think about that, and to think about the family that I had never met but who meant so much to me, I couldn't help but privately grieve for their loss. Their loved one was with me at every step. I felt his presence every moment of every day. Without him, there would be no me.

One night when I was having an extra hard time with sleep and struggling to shake the sensations of my donor's sacrifice, I began an Internet search to try and find him. I knew very few facts about this man—I knew his age, his profession, the hospital from where my heart had been transferred by helicopter, and of course I knew on what day his death occurred. There is a level of privacy that is maintained between donor family and recipient, and I wanted to respect that—that's why I'm not going to include the details here—but I was also desperate for a connection. I just wanted something to know him by.

After several hours of searching, I found a brief news story on a local television station's website about a man who fit all the facts. He was the right age and had the right profession, and he'd been taken to the right hospital with a head injury two days before my transplant.

I was immediately washed over with emotion. It was him.

The story was short, only a couple of paragraphs, and it didn't include his name or any details about his family. I didn't actually learn much more about him through my Internet search than what I'd already known. But suddenly he felt very real and very much a part of my life.

I cried for him that night. It was my first cry since the transplant. Until that moment, my outward emotions had flowed from the very positive feelings that were driving my post-transplant recovery. I hadn't cried because my future had providentially become the uncharted passage I'd spent years thirsting for.

But that night, alone on my couch, I mourned.

FROM THE MOMENT I was transplanted, I'd wanted to write the family to thank them for their gift. I'd read about the kind of letters that other transplant recipients were writing, and I'd received the instructions from my own transplant team as to what was allowed and what wasn't. Protecting the privacy of both parties, if it was privacy that they sought, was as important as the thanking.

Shortly after finding the Internet story on my donor, I wrote my letter, leaving out last names.

I confess that I'm not quite sure how to begin a letter like this. And certainly in these days and weeks following the sudden loss of your loved one, I don't pretend to know what is entirely appropriate to say. So let me just begin by telling you a little about myself.

My name is Kyle, and I'm a thirty-five-year-old writer living in Southern California. I've been married now for just over eighteen months. I like sports (it's usually what I write about), camping, travel, and on occasion some really bad television. I've also had quite a checkered health history beginning with an initial cancer diagnosis in 1989 (the first of four total cancer battles) when I was a senior in high school. I've been treated with radiation, chemotherapy, and ultimately and successfully a bone marrow transplant in 1995. It was successful in that it did destroy the disease that was working to destroy me, but it was costly in terms of the damage it did to my body. I was left with a scarred and weakened heart that has been slowly deteriorating ever since.

Or it had been deteriorating, until the miracle night of October 10, 2006.

Because of your gift that night, courageously given in the face of grief that I can't understand, I now wake up each morning with a strong and healthy heart and a future life with my wife. I am humbled in the shadow of your generosity, and I promise you that this is a gift that will forever be cherished. I will never take for granted the part of your family that now resides in me.

In fact, I would very much like to meet you, or at least know the name of the man who will be taking each step with me the rest of my life. But I also understand if that's not something you desire. Ever since I was placed on the heart transplant list more than five years ago, I have always been mindful that my family's future day of joy could only come on the heels of someone else's moment of loss. Please know that I will respect whatever decision you decide is best for you.

Words will never fully capture the gratitude that I feel toward you in this new strong heart—so unlike what I've experienced the last eleven years of my life in that it's actually keeping me up at night, knocking loudly in my ears—but I certainly wanted to begin with a heartfelt "thank you."

Because of you, I now have a second chance at life.

You have been, and will forever continue to be, in my daily thoughts and prayers.

At about 4 AM, I finished my letter. I was headed to the hospital in two days for another heart biopsy to make sure that I was remaining rejection free, and I'd give it to my coordinators then.

I went into our bedroom and fell instantly asleep. I was once again at peace.

15

NEW ENGINE, NEW LIFE

My love of and fascination with sports goes back to the earliest moments of my memory. In 1978 I played on my first Little League baseball team, and we took first place in the West Urban Little League's six-year-old division. That same summer, my Royals were beaten by the hated Yankees in the American League Championship Series.

Kansas has never been one of North America's hotbeds of hockey, but when the US Olympic hockey team shocked the Soviet Union at the 1980 Lake Placid Olympics, I and every other eight-year-old dreamed of lacing up skates and representing our country. It's also when I figured out that it was OK for grown men to cry. I still credit Jim Craig and Mike Eruzione—with an assist to Eric Heiden—for making me a lifetime fan of the Olympic Games.

A few years later, the extended arm of my father's family gathered in Los Angeles for the 1984 Summer Olympics. We were at the L.A. Coliseum when Carl Lewis won his gold medal in the long jump, and I've been moved by our national anthem ever since.

In 1985 it was the I-70 World Series between my two favorite teams, the Royals and the Cardinals. That same fall I remember watching a senior running back from Wichita North High School power himself more than thirteen hundred yards in the only seven games of his high school football career. Three years later, that undersized running back named Barry

Sanders won the Heisman Trophy. In 2004 he became a member of the Pro Football Hall of Fame.

In 1991, a week after my twentieth birthday and during my summer of chemotherapy, I was in the stadium when Kansas City's Bret Saberhagen no-hit the Chicago White Sox. For three hours that afternoon and for several more spent in euphoric celebration that evening, I wasn't sick. I was just a really happy baseball fan who couldn't stop smiling.

In 1994 I saw my second no-hitter in less than three years when the Braves' Kent Mercker threw one against the Dodgers.

I've seen Magic Johnson and Michael Jordan go head-to-head. I've witnessed in person a Joe Montana–led fourth-quarter comeback. And I was lucky enough once to meet legendary basketball coach John Wooden and listen to his wisdoms on life.

For me, the world of sports has always been more than just wins, losses, and a way to pass the entertainment hours with games and competitions. It's a metaphor for so much of life, and it inflames the passions and profits of achievement that are unique to the human experience.

Through my years of volunteering with the Leukemia & Lymphoma Society's Team In Training program, I watched person after person train, sweat, struggle, doubt, question, and hurt before ultimately changing their lives by crossing the finish line of a marathon. It's a powerful moment when you see people go from "can't" to "can" to "did" and have those medals of achievement hung on their necks. They stretched beyond the boundaries of their normal comfort zones, challenged the limits of what they thought was possible within them, and were rewarded for the risk.

It's only through the taking of that risk that the greatness of the reward is truly felt.

I wanted to be among those risk takers. It was a moment of pride of achievement that I wanted to have for myself. It was a challenge that I wanted to test myself against. But of course, as I sat on the sidelines for years because of my weakening heart, those dreams remained impossibilities.

Until the night of October 10, 2006, when everything became possible again.

Three days after transplant Carrie and I began looking at the triathlon schedule for the upcoming year. I'm not a fan of running. In every sport I have ever played, running was a punishment. Fumble the football; go run a lap. Bobble the baseball; go run a lap. Make a bad pass in soccer; go run a lap. I had been conditioned to think of running as a means of torture. And for me, who was once complimented by a football coach for my natural level of speed that ensured that I would never overrun the play (a fancy way of saying "You're really slow"), running was not filled with moments of grace.

But a triathlon, which only made you run a third of the time, I thought I could do.

In the hospital room surrounded by machines that monitored my heart rate and still attached to three chest tubes that were draining my chest cavity of excess blood from surgery, I made plans with Carrie. I wanted a local race in Southern California that I could do through Team In Training and, most important, that was far enough away to allow for adequate training. I had no illusions about the task at hand. It would be difficult.

Eventually we settled on the Nautica Malibu Triathlon to be held the following September. It fit all our requirements and had the added benefit of taking place on and around Zuma Beach—not the worst place in the world to have to race. It also had a celebrity element that would add an extra wrinkle of fun. Throughout the years, competing triathletes have included David Duchovny, Jon Cryer, Teri Hatcher, Matthew McConaughey, and Jennifer Lopez.

Initially the triathlon was just a plan. I was healing and rehabbing and doing nothing that could be considered training. My most important goal in those first few months was to not gain weight. I was an experienced steroid taker from my years as a cancer patient, and I knew the havoc that prednisone could wreak. Not only would weight gain make life more difficult for my new heart and waistline, but there was no reason to start carrying around extra poundage for the upcoming bike rides and runs.

In February my house confinement was over. The dosages of my rejection medications had been reduced to acceptable levels, and my immune system was considered strong enough to allow for my reentry into regular life. It will always be somewhat compromised; I will always have to be vigilant about germ management. I am especially susceptible to catching colds, and when they show up they act like the unemployed brother-in-law who thinks sleeping on your couch for the next six weeks is a perfectly acceptable visit.

With my freedom of movement finally restored, Carrie and I went about the task of bicycle shopping. The last time I'd purchased a bike it was a ten-speed Schwinn with cheap metal shifters attached to the down tube and a seat made of a molded plastic stretched over unforgiving steel mattress springs. I'd only just a couple of years earlier graduated to that ten-speed and away from the banana-seated Huffy that was purchased when I was seven.

Things had changed just a bit since 1982. Steel was out; aluminum or carbon fiber was in. Shifters had been integrated into the brakes, chain rings and derailleurs with as many as thirty gears had replaced the trusty ten-speed, and seats packed with gel cushioning pads were now the norm. (This last innovation has still failed to make the bicycle seat an anatomically comfortable place for a human rear end.)

Outfitted with new bikes by the middle of March 2007, Carrie and I went on our first ride—a six-mile round-trip spin to lunch at our favorite build-your-own-burrito joint, Chipotle. A mile in, I was taking my first break. At the two-mile mark we passed a bench in a park, and I stopped to sit down and catch my breath. By mile three we were eating burritos, and I was bushed. It had been five months since my transplant, and I had almost no strength or stamina for the shortest of rides.

I knew the running and swimming of the triathlon would be a challenge. Other than running the occasional errand, the word "run" and my name mixed about as well as the Brontë sisters do with Beavis and Butthead. And while at one time I was a good swimmer—I was Red Cross certified to be a lifeguard—that was a lifetime ago and long before my lungs had taken damage from Bleomycin.

I had high hopes for the cycling. When I was first placed on the heart transplant waiting list I made a proactive decision about my health.

Recovery from the transplant would be hard, even harder with an atrophied body. I had to do what I could, when I could, to stay in the best shape that my heart condition would allow. So I bought a stationary bike and rode it religiously.

I didn't ride with high resistance for hours on end or break any stationary bike speed records. And more than a few times I had to get off the bike just a couple of minutes into a workout. But nearly every single day I was on it, from as little as ten minutes to as much as an hour. My heart was weak, but it didn't mean that the rest of my body had to remain that way.

I was worried about the direction my fitness was headed after my first six-mile ride was complete. The race was six months away, more than enough time to train for a short-distance triathlon if you're equipped with the typical weapons of a healthy thirty-five-year-old. But in the five months since my transplant, while a lot of wonderful things happened, an increase in stamina was not one of them.

We forged ahead anyway. By the month of May we'd signed up with our Team In Training crew and began working with trained coaches. I was able to ride three or four miles without stopping, but I still had major problems on anything resembling a hill. I could run for a minute or longer before having to catch my breath with a short walk. In the pool I was making virtually no progress. I'd gone from being unable to swim twenty-five yards without stopping to finishing the twenty-five yards but sounding like a dying seal at the end of the swim lane, holding on for dear life and gasping for breath. There would not be walls and rope lines to hold onto during my half-mile swim in the Pacific Ocean. I had work to do.

By the time the race rolled around in September, I had done the work and was feeling confident . . . somewhat. A few weeks earlier in a moment of panic I'd confessed to a friend that I'd thought I was in over my head. I was still struggling in the pool, not getting much beyond two hundred yards without hitting my physical wall. I was frequently riding my bike along the race route of the Pacific Coast Highway (PCH), but it came with a series of hills including one at the beach at Leo Carrillo State Park that I had yet to ascend without walking. And the running—well, it was running. (If it had a Facebook page, I would not be clicking "Like.")

As a heart transplant, I was facing some very specific challenges. My new heart was strong and healthy and beating exactly the way it should. But during the transplant procedure the nerves that connect the heart to the brain are severed, forever ending all heart-brain communication. A typical person out for a bike ride gets the word from his or her brain: "We're almost to a hill. Heart, please beat faster." But my heart doesn't answer that call. As far as it knows, we're still sitting on the couch and watching reruns of *Family Guy*.

My obvious struggles come on hills, when I simply can't get my heart rate high enough to provide sufficient power. The de-nerved heart also presents other problems, like incredibly slow warm-up and cool-down periods. There's an issue with falling blood pressure when I go from an extended period of time lying horizontal, like a long swim, to vertical and running, like right after a long swim when I transition to the bike. Since I had no designs on winning in Malibu—my only goal was to finish—these didn't present insurmountable roadblocks. It simply meant I'd be slower than your average first timer. (I also have scarring in my lungs that limits my capacity there.)

The morning of the race, I was excited and nervous. A television crew covering the event took me aside for a quick interview before my wave of racers hit the water, and it helped provide a needed distraction. I could do this; I just had to actually get out and do it. It sounded simple enough in my head.

The cannon fired, and we were off and running into the crashing waves. Getting through the waves and past the break was the worst part of the swim. Your system is suddenly shocked by the cold water, and your respiration rate goes through the roof. It's all a matter of trying to keep that in check until you're past the break and into the normal rhythm of a swim stroke.

I'm a slow swimmer—I have limited lung capacity and a fake left shoulder that makes the smoothness of my stroke less than textbook. But I was able to get around the first buoy on the course before I heard the cannon fire again, which signaled the start of the next wave of swimmers.

I stayed steady and focused, thinking about control of form. Before a half hour was up, I was out of the water and on my way to the bike. A sub-thirty-minute half-mile swim is nothing for the record books, but considering how things had been going in the relative safety of the swimming pool, I was ecstatic. Really, anything that would rank above drowning on the scale of successful triathlon swims would have made me happy.

The bike ride along PCH was beautiful and pleasant, and I was having a great time. The stresses that led up to the start of the race had vanished in the waters of the Pacific. The previous September I couldn't walk up a single flight of stairs. Put a bag of groceries in my hand that contained more than a package of pretzels, and even flat walks became formidable. But here I was, just one year later, being directed by police to blow through stoplights because I was on my bike and riding in a competition sanctioned by USA Triathlon.

Out to the turnaround and on my way back, I saw the hill at Leo Carrillo looming large. It wouldn't be the end of the world if I had to stop and walk my bike up the last little bit of the hill. There would be no disqualification nor an end to my day. It was completely within the rules to walk your bike as long as you didn't get in the way of the other racers. But none of those other racers would be out of their saddles and walking. None of them would give in to the physical pain that forced feet from pedals and down to the ground. Damned if I was going to let it happen to me.

For the first time in more than a dozen rides up the hill, I didn't stop. I pushed, and I pushed, and I pushed. Before I knew it, the hill had crested and I was rolling down the other side. I wanted to stop and get off right there and give my heart a giant hug.

The rest of the bike ride was a breeze, and all that remained was an easy four-mile run. And truly, for the first time in my life, I enjoyed running. I wasn't any faster, and the run didn't require any less effort, but the meaning of that run was the official closing of the book on eighteen years of the unhealthy me.

I made the two-mile mark at the turnaround near the Sunset Restaurant and Beach Bar and was greeted with one the most spectacular vistas I've ever been graced to see. Turning back toward Zuma Beach, I was almost punched by the blueness of the ocean and the sky. The mountains dazzled in the sunshine, and the strip of sand between the competing blues and greens called me like a path to salvation.

Feelings of completeness came washing down my soul like waves of reclamation. The tunnel had been long, dark, and scary, but now I was standing squarely in its ending light. I didn't want those final two miles to end.

It was just about this time that Carrie caught me on the course. I'd started more than a half hour before her wave time, and she'd been working ever since to close the gap of my head start. With just over a mile and a half to go, she was with me and then past me, finishing out her race before coming back to run me in.

We closed the final four hundred yards together, hitting the finish line as the single unit that we'd been since Liza Minnelli treated us to song. We'd come through the heart transplant as a pair; I was the patient who took his medications, and Carrie was the chief caregiver who'd spent the week that I was in the hospital doing her best to make our apartment germ free. (That's no easy task when you also have a cat.)

We'd signed up for the triathlon together, taking on the challenges of a new sport as an equal pair of newbies—although Carrie had run a number of marathons prior to our bike purchases that March. We knew that if things were to take a turn for the worst at some point in the future— either with my heart, another cancer diagnosis, or, God forbid, something involving her—we'd climb that new mountain in tandem.

I cried at the finish line in Malibu. I hugged Carrie as hard as I could, and she cried too. I hugged my parents, and they started crying. I hugged both of the coaches, Todd and Tim, who'd worked so hard with me over the summer. Todd cried; Tim kept it together.

We all celebrated with champagne. Open-container laws did not matter on that September Sunday on Zuma Beach in Malibu. I had a new life to toast and new meaning to that life. I lost most of my twenties to one form of cancer or another. My body was beaten, battered, and now filled with titanium joints and titanium wires to hold my sternum together. I had multiple scars left by radiation, chemotherapy, and a surgeon's scalpel. But at thirty-six years old and less than a year removed from a heart transplant, my moment of achievement had arrived. My days of strength, health, and vitality had returned.

Since the days of Plato and Aristotle, and probably all the way back to the days of the Rubbles and the Flintstones, humankind has been seeking the meaning of life. Why are we here? What's it all for? What is our purpose? And if we can ever truly answer any of those questions, how do we then measure the quality in terms of life's meaning?

The ancient Egyptians simplified the quality of a life lived—and whether or not you fulfilled its meaning, thus earning your way into heaven—by the answer to two simple questions. Have you found joy in your life? And have you brought joy to others? If your answer to both is yes, heaven is yours. Your life was well lived.

I'd found my joy. It was in the people that surrounded me on the beach that morning, joining me in a champagne toast. It was in my wife, my partner in all things, my cofinisher that day, my confidant and best friend, the woman who gives of herself without concern or question or apprehension. It was in the new person that I was discovering within myself and the commitment that I made to him that day to promote organ donation and cancer research by celebrating my own physicality whenever and wherever possible. And it was in my heart donor, the man who gave me life, the man who walks with me at every step, the man who powers my physicality through his gift of total sacrifice.

I had my joy. Hopefully, through my speaking and writing, I could bring that joy to others.

A FEW MONTHS before I'd received my new heart, the city of Louisville played host to an event called the US Transplant Games. It's an Olympic-style competition held biannually that features both individual and team sports for any athlete who is an organ transplant survivor. The teams are broken into regions—I fall under the Team Southern California banner—and each individual can enter as many as four events. All ages and athletic abilities are welcome.

I'd heard about the Games in Louisville, and I made a decision then, before my transplant, that I wanted to participate. I wasn't sure what that participation would look like back in 2006 when I was making these promises to myself. Physically my future was an enormous unknown. But the Games offer sports like bowling and golf for transplants who aren't transformed into athletes, and I liked both of those plan B options.

By the time 2008 rolled around and Team Southern California was making its plans for that summer's Games in Pittsburgh, I had already completed the Malibu Triathlon and started training for another. Swimming and biking were now preferred to bowling and golf. I entered two cycling events, the 5K time trial and the 20K road race, and I'd also be swimming the 100-meter and 200-meter freestyles.

I'd love to tell you that I entered my four events with no desires or designs on winning a medal; I just wanted to compete. But that would of course be a big fat lie. I'd played for a first-place team in Little League baseball, and our freshman football team finished undefeated and won the City League championship. I still have my trophies from both seasons. Winning is more fun than not winning.

An appetite for a medal, however, does not equate to an assumption of one. The Games are competitive and filled with former collegiate athletes who've had a transplant in later life. Let's be honest: kidney transplants are not exactly forced to lean heavily on their new organ when trying to swim two hundred meters as quickly as possible. (I can kid them because each kidney transplant that I count among my friends agrees—the hearts and lungs have it toughest.)

I'd knuckled down on my swim work since I first started training for Malibu in May 2007. That next year leading up to the Transplant Games I began training with a new coach but an old friend, Paul Ruggiero. He was the Ironman coach for Team In Training, and he was giving me swim-specific lessons and workouts that would hopefully take me from a triathlon swimmer who just wanted to get out of the open water in one piece to someone who could swim competitively in a pool.

Mission accomplished.

Maybe it was a repeat of the 1960 Rome Olympics when the two favorites to compete for gold in the one-hundred-meter freestyle swim both missed the event—American Jeff Farrell because of appendicitis and Australian Jon Hendricks because of some bad Italian food that led to the euphemistic "Roman tummy." But the winner of the one hundred-meter freestyle in Pittsburgh, Pennsylvania, in 2008 was me. I then followed that up with a bronze medal in the two hundred meter to top off one of the most unexpected days in my life.

It was an incredible four days in Pittsburgh, and I really was happy to come away with a pair of medals. (I added two more swimming medals to my career total at the 2010 Transplant Games in Madison, Wisconsin.) But what really struck me about my time surrounded by transplant recipients was the amount of visible happiness that each person carried.

I knew what had been happening in me since October 10, 2006. It had been the best time in my life. But to see that joy on such public display in more than one thousand of the recently rescued left no doubt about the inherent strength and compassion of human beings. Those four days in Pittsburgh were magical.

The year 2008 also saw Carrie and me competing in our second triathlon. We were hooked on the sport and the friends we were making, and we both wanted to keep raising money for the Leukemia & Lymphoma Society. The decision was made to bump up our distance and take on an Olympic-distance race (1,500-meter swim, 40K bike, and 10K run). We signed up to do the Lavaman Triathlon on the Big Island of Hawaii the first week of April, making it the perfect anniversary trip as well. If we were going to race and raise money for cancer research, why not do it in style?

One of the most appealing elements of Lavaman is that its bike route runs along the Queen Kaahumanu Highway (known as the Queen K), the same highway that hosts the Ironman World Championship. For those of us who are huge fans of the Ironman but had absolutely zero thoughts of doing one, it was an ideal way to feel close to the greatness of that event. Lavaman also uses the numbered stamps that Ironman uses to mark each competitor as well as the same bike racks. For "tri" geeks, which we were becoming, that's cool.

The swim that day off Waikoloa Beach was fantastic. It was in the warm and protected waters of a bay that felt more suitable for snorkeling than competitive swimming. It's fifteen hundred meters of coral, fish, and sea turtles in crystal clear waters.

The bike ride along the Queen K is strikingly beautiful in its desolation. The highway cuts through endless fields of lava rock that run down the slopes of the volcano and into the blueness of ocean. It resembles a moonscape as pictured by the astronauts of Apollo popping out of the Pacific. It's a warm, rolling twenty-five miles, and it sets you up nicely for the six-mile run that finishes off the day.

For Carrie and me, that weekend was so much more than a race. We both had terrific times doing the event and enjoying the postrace beach party put on by the Kona Brewing Company. When you've spent more than a decade wearing the chains of compromise brought on by a busted heart, it never gets old to be physical and active and do the things that were once dreams of the ridiculous.

But that week on the Big Island was our anniversary. It was a chance for me to celebrate the three years since Carrie had signed on to the unknown.

We took a helicopter ride over the active volcano as a treat to ourselves, and we watched new earth being formed. It's clichéd to think of the newness of life as you witness our four-billion-year-old planet creating new crust, but it's clichéd for a reason. It's directed instinct. When you've stared straight into the frightening eyes of death, you're always searching the nearest horizon for obvious signs of life.

I saw signs of life in every direction I looked. The life-affirming places, people, and moments glow with distinction. It's the bounty of blessings that benefit the formerly condemned.

Our bounty was only beginning. We both said "I do" in 2005 with the very real fear that "till death do us part" might be just around the corner. Now all our corners were filled with discovery and adventure. Many couples find themselves tested by life's uncertainties early in their marriages. We'd been tested from the very moment that Carrie said yes to a first date. Like iron forged in the blacksmith's furnace, our relationship had been shaped, molded, and strengthened by the intensity of a heart transplant.

Neither one of us had played life safe. There were obvious pitfalls that could have taken down either one of us when we began our relationship in the closing months of 2002. But there, on the Big Island of Hawaii, together we celebrated our reward.

IT's A GREAT thing to see the world through the newness of eyes formerly clouded in fear. Moments are constantly recycling into something more beautiful, bright, and fresh. Where walls of difficulty once existed, you see windows of opportunity.

Down in Kona on one of our final days on the Big Island to buy gifts for our moms—Mother's Day was a month away—we stepped into a store that was filled with Ironman memorabilia. Old posters from classic Ironman moments of the past covered one wall, and calendars, hats, and race-course maps covered another. It's hard not to be impressed when you see the map that includes a 2.4-mile swim, a 112-mile bike ride, and a full 26.2-mile marathon to close the day.

The store that we were in was just a couple of blocks down the road from the race's finish line on Ali'i Drive, one of the most iconic finishes in all of endurance sports. If you've watched sports on television, you've most likely seen the images that many people associate with Ironman—athletes broken down and dehydrated, wobbling and sometimes crawling to the end. The images more closely resemble the zombie walk of a pack of masochists as opposed to the finishing chute that crowns the world's most complete athlete.

Looking at Ali'i Drive, seeing the pictures of past athletes, and remembering the moments I'd seen on television, I briefly thought to myself how cool it would be to cross that finish line as a heart transplant recipient. Of course it was a ridiculous idea. As my thought just highlighted, I had a heart transplant. I couldn't go 140.6 self-powered miles in one day (three days, maybe, if I could hitch a ride in a golf cart for the last half of the marathon). The real world allows for such fantasies, but it always slaps you with the reality that the fantasy has to stay in a separate mind-only delusion vault.

Then I focused in on the race calendars, noticing that the Ironman World Championship in 2008, which was six months from when we were there, was slated for October 11. I did the quick calculation in my head that told me the race in 2009 would be held on October 10, my exact three-year heart transplant anniversary.

It was a fantasy and nothing more, right? It wasn't something that could seriously be considered. I had a heart transplant. On October 10. They were holding the Ironman on October 10.

That would be really cool.

16

KONA

What are the limits of a heart transplant recipient? Can one even dare to begin the task of making his body capable of taking on one of the world's greatest physical tests?

According to my doctors when I asked them that question in 2008, the answer was yes. If I could train through the limitations of a de-nerved heart and scarred lungs, I could do an Ironman. I wouldn't be putting my health or life in any more jeopardy than anyone else. It would be hard, and I'd need to stay on top of certain things like hydration, because the medications I take tend to leech my body of fluids more readily. But as long as I knew where my potential pitfalls were, I'd be fine.

But being able to do it was one thing. Willingly putting your body through the pain of months of tortuous training was something entirely different. When I first contacted the people at Ironman about the process of trying to get into the race in Kona, they had a question for me. Why?

I stopped short when I first read their e-mail reply back to me. "Because I want to" seemed woefully inadequate. "It would be cool" didn't quite capture everything that I was feeling about the quest. I took a couple of days to really think about why I wanted to make my life more difficult by committing to such a monumental task. After two days of deep thought and introspection, I had my answer.

"Because I can."

There was more to it, sure. In my e-mail response to their question, I wrote, "There would be no better or bolder exclamation point on my recovery from multiple cancers and a heart transplant than to cross the finish line on Ali'i Drive. It's the place were Dick and Rick Hoyt became the faces of love and commitment. It's where Jon Blais became the enduring symbol of courage. And it's where I hope to redefine what it means to persevere and survive."

In truth, that was just a fancy way of saying "I can." It really was that simple.

For so long I couldn't—I couldn't even dream about it. The possibilities of taking on such a challenge were smaller than the likelihood that I'd be chosen for a mission to Mars. I couldn't carry a box more than ten feet. I couldn't stand up after sitting on my couch without having to hold onto something sturdy until the brief blackout spell passed. I couldn't walk on the beach with my wife because the sand made the task too difficult. I couldn't do any of the things that a healthy person does automatically.

But suddenly I could. I can. And what better reason did I need than that?

That "can," of course, doesn't need to be as extreme as an Ironman. Any challenge that felt previously beyond the reach of your capabilities but is now within them is a challenge worthy of effort. And there is no need to have greater reason or purpose behind the taking on of such a challenge than the very simple and direct explanation of "I can." Its simplicity is where its power and purity lie. And I think that makes it the best of reasons.

I could. Now it was time to do.

PAUL RUGGIERO, WHO'D worked his swim magic with me at the Transplant Games, became my full-time Ironman coach. He'd coached numerous Ironman novices across the finish line, and there was no doubt that he was exactly the kind of coach I needed. The jury remained out on whether or not I was the kind of athlete he was looking to coach. We both went into it understanding that in my case, we really did have to reinvent the wheel. His past experiences would provide a very rough blueprint at best.

I'd done as long as an Olympic-distance race—about one-fourth the total distance of the Ironman—so we weren't starting from a dead stop. But I needed to create a large experience base and get a multitude of miles under my belt. That meant a lot of long and boring workouts where we focused on nothing but distance. No speed, interval, or hill work, just mileage.

My body adjusted to the new strain I was putting it through, and my doctors continued to be amazed that my post-transplant life remained mostly side-effect free. They wouldn't come right out and say it, but it was clear that they were crediting my leap into exercise. Within a few short months after transplant, I was riding a bike and training for my first triathlon. As I prepared for the Ironman—still less than three years removed from transplant—short recovery rides were in the fifty-mile range, easy runs were often more than ten miles, and a light day in the pool consisted of a mile and a half or more. It was thrilling to see where I could push my capabilities, and it was rewarding to know that it was paying off in the place that mattered most, my health.

Ironman was my fixation. Every action I took had to be looked at in the context of "Will this help me get to Kona?" If the answer was no, I needed to rethink it.

I signed up to do Lavaman again in 2009 because of one simple reason: it was a race on the same bike course as the Ironman. I did rides in the hills of Westlake Village in the San Fernando Valley because the topography and the temperatures were a good representation of what I would find in Kona. I even started using words like *aloha*, *mahalo*, and *humuhumunukunukuapuaʻa*, just so I'd sound like I belonged.

Prior to my focus on Ironman, I'd done just two races, Malibu and Lavaman. I needed to do more races for my own preparation, including a half-Ironman or two, but also to validate my spot in Kona. Even if you are one of the lucky few who land a place in Kona without qualifying, you still have to work for your slot. You need to demonstrate a reasonable ability to complete an Ironman by doing a half-Ironman in the months leading up to the race. For me, that reasonableness would be put to the test at the Vineman 70.3 and the Utah Half.

The two races, a month apart, couldn't have been more different. At Vineman, which took place in Sonoma County, California's wine country, the temperatures that day easily topped one hundred. It's also a large race but with a very narrow swim course, so it's broken into numerous starting waves. My wave didn't go off until after 8:30 that morning, putting the end of my bike and meat of my run into the worst heat of the day.

In Utah we had only two wave start times for the field of just more than three hundred triathletes. But right before go time at 7 AM, a huge thunderstorm blew through the area. The swim start was delayed until a small crack in the weather opened. Once we were on our bikes, that crack quickly closed, resulting in one of the scariest and most oddly exhilarating fifty-six-mile bike rides I've ever taken. There was hail, rain, wind, and boiling black clouds that reminded me of the worst storms I'd ever experienced during my days in Tornado Alley. But by the end it was calm and serene, and the mountaintops that surrounded the run's course had all been dusted with a topping of snow. It made for a breathtaking finish.

Having done my second Lavaman that spring and the pair of half-Ironman races in the summer, I boasted a race total of five; my spot in the field at the Ironman World Championship had been validated. I would become the first heart transplant recipient ever to take to the famous waters in Kona—a tremendous honor for this painfully average athlete.

IT'S NO SMALL thing to take on an Ironman with another person's heart in your chest. (In truth, it's no small thing to live any average day being powered by a transplanted heart.) And it's even bigger when that Ironman comes with all of the pomp and circumstance of triathlon's biggest day, the World Championship.

I did interviews with every triathlon- and outdoor-specific magazine on the market. I was featured in *Men's Health*, and I made the front page of CNN.com. (For a two-hour stretch my CNN story appeared on the Google homepage, and in that two-hour span I received more than four hundred personal e-mails from people who'd read the story and found my website.)

Los Angeles stations KABC and KNBC did feature stories on my mission to the Ironman. I appeared on the syndicated show *The Doctors* with my surgeon and cardiologist. And a producer from *CBS Evening News with Katie Couric* came to our apartment to film a story on me that would air nationally the night before Ironman. The piece ended the night of October 9 with a shout-out from Katie herself.

It was wonderful to become the face of successful heart transplantation. But there was an underlying but overwhelming feeling to the label as well. There were no guarantees on how Ironman would go. I was training and putting in the necessary hours and miles, but there is a time limit on how long you can take to finish your race. The swim starts at 7 AM, and the run course closes at midnight. If you aren't across the finish line in seventeen hours, you won't end that evening as an Ironman.

I was slow. I was adding many layers of endurance through my training that would enable me to keep going and going for hours on end, but that going was still slow going. There was no doubt that I would be chasing the midnight cutoff.

What if I didn't make it? There were a lot of eyes following me to Kona. It would not be my failure alone, and I certainly wouldn't be doing it in the seclusion of anonymity. I was featured in the race program, and I was introduced to several thousand participants and their families at the welcome banquet two nights before the race. I was at the prerace press conference with the other incredibly inspiring people who had collected in Kona to take on the Ironman.

While I was on the island, I did a story with the Associated Press with a photo shoot to match. I was recognized by several of the competitors, and I overheard others talking about "the heart transplant" who was doing the race. Before the race got rolling on that Saturday morning in October, NBC Sports outfitted me with a GPS so that throughout the day they could chart my progress and have their cameras ready along the course.

It was the attention I knew I'd be getting when I first reached out to Ironman about competing in the event. With my dual purposes in life—

to help raise money for cancer research and to increase the visibility and awareness of organ donation—it was welcome attention. I was proudly wearing the logos of the City of Hope and the Leukemia & Lymphoma Society on my race kit as well as doing media and PR for both organizations. Through the Leukemia & Lymphoma Society's Team In Training and Light the Night programs, I had been an active fundraiser in the past and was now hoping to use my visibility to further aid the fundraising efforts of others.

The terrific heart transplant program at UCLA Medical Center was the reason I was healthy and strong enough to even think about Ironman, let alone toe the start line. Their logo was on my race kit as well, and I was actively engaged in publicity for the program and people who saved my life. For the larger cause of organ donation and transplantation, I became a volunteer and spokesperson for Donate Life, the nation's chief educator and advocate for organ and tissue donation. And as a fan of the Olympics—specifically an admirer of snowboarder Chris Klug, who became an Olympic medalist less than two years after a liver transplant—I began to advocate for his charity, the Chris Klug Foundation.

I'd asked for the attention, and it came running. And for the people, places, and causes that I supported, any and all attention was welcome.

I can't say that because of the wall-to-wall media coverage I was feeling any extra nerves that wouldn't normally be packaged with any athlete's Ironman preparation. I know lots of Ironman finishers, and short nerves and a disquieted stomach are part of the shared experienced. But I also knew that if things did go south for me on race day, I would not fade into the pages with the other failed finishers. Everyone would know my fate.

OCTOBER 10, 2009 (*Continued from Prologue*)

At the swim turnaround, I was feeling good. My pace was consistent, and I'd gone the first half of the 2.4 miles without ever breaking stroke. I was largely alone at this point—the rest of the field was phenomenal, and I knew that I had little hope of finishing near someone who wasn't pushing seventy. But I'd divorced myself from any time goals other than each sport's cutoff, the first of those being the swim's two-hour-twenty-minute requirement.

I wasn't a swift open-water swimmer—my gold medal at the Transplant Games notwithstanding—but I also wasn't concerned about getting out of the ocean and onto the bike. The bike cutoff at 5:30 PM, however, with its difficult course through hot lava fields known for unpredictable and intense crosswinds, was concerning. If the weather wasn't cooperating, even strong cyclists with a history of good health could have their troubles. So getting off my bike was worry number one.

My level of anticipation for the marathon portion of the Ironman was somewhere between paying taxes and going to the dentist. It would be done on legs of Jell-O trying to power a bruised and bike-battered body. The run would not be easy, but my worrying about it was less than the bike. My marathon would mostly be run in the dark, which meant the heat would drop and give me the cover of darkness for the grimaces and groans that were sure to accompany each painful stride. It would be slow and steady going; I would put one foot in front of the other, always moving forward. Just like the way I'd survived chemotherapy. Exactly how I made it through five-and-a-half years on the heart transplant waiting list. The way that any of us make it through a challenging time in our lives. Slow and steady, always moving forward, never becoming static.

The swim was my surest victory of the day. I'd spent the week swimming in this same bay each morning, and the waters felt sublime. They were warm and buoyant; the sensation of them surrounding your body forced a feeling of anticipation for the next hundred yards. For the entire 2.4-mile swim, there would be forty-two such hundred-yard sections.

Halfway out and now coming back in, I felt the swells getting to me. I started feeling a little seasick, and my head began to get fuzzy. I occasionally veered off my swim line when the next buoy along the course would become hidden behind a swell. But that was always fixed by a corrective command coming from the surfboard rider escorting me in.

Intermittently I noticed that my stroke was flattening out, but I'd fixate on its correction as soon as I spotted the flaw. My fatigue was minimal and my breath was still with me, and I began to allow myself to think ahead to the first transition—T1—and the first few miles on the bike. Most specifically I was mapping out my first hour of nutrition and reminding myself to keep ingesting fluids.

As I got close to the pier and into the final few hundred yards of the swim, it was obvious that not a lot of other swimmers were around me. Surfboards topped with supportive people shouting words of encouragement surrounded me. My internal clock had me coming in closer to the two-hour mark than I was hoping. Ideally I would be on my bike by 9 AM, but it felt like 9 AM was going to be the time for my swim finish. Not a huge worry. I could make up the lost ten minutes or so somewhere else.

At the pier and with less than one hundred yards to go, I heard the encouragement from the surfboards intensify. "Pull!" "Dig!" "You got this, Kyle!"

I could also hear the crowds on the shore cheering and calling my name. It felt good to have so much personal support as I was finishing the swim. If this was an indication of how it would be for me on the course the rest of the race, it was going to be a great day.

As I neared the end, I was a little surprised by the frenzy of the people around me. Yes, it was all very exciting. But I had a long day ahead of me and couldn't blow too much emotion with fourteen to fifteen hours still to come.

Standing up, I was immediately grabbed and dragged the final couple of feet to the steps signifying the swim's finish. "Touch the steps! Touch the steps!"

I will, I thought to myself. *Give me a moment. I've been lying horizontally for the last 2.4 miles, and it's going to take a second to get my bearings.*

A huge cheer went up as I touched the steps, and I heard the announcer shout, "He did it!" But as I turned to head up the steps to make my way into T1, an official stopped me and said, "I'm sorry, you're done. You didn't make it." My immediate thought was, "Yes, I'm done. Now move so I can get to my bike." But then the last half of his sentence registered, and I reflexively looked down at my watch for the first time since 7:00 AM. It read 9:20.

The reality hit like a punch to the stomach. I didn't make it. I'd had what I considered an easy-to-complete two-hour-twenty-minute swim, but for some reason it had taken me two hours, twenty minutes, and seven seconds. I was agonizingly close—but seven seconds too slow.

I think I shouted "No!" but I really don't remember. I know that I sunk to my hands and knees right there on the steps and started to sob. Months of training and years of dreaming had ended because of seven seconds. My worst-case scenario was playing itself out in reality. The day that I had prepared for was over, and it had barely even begun. I wouldn't get to ride along the Queen K, and there would be no magical night at the finish line on Ali'i Drive. I was crushed.

I was ushered up the steps and over to the medical tent so I'd have a place to sit down away from the cameras. Carrie met me there and joined the tears. My mom arrived, as did Coach Paul. Physically I felt terrific. I'd exited the water with energy and confidence, and I was confident in the plan that Paul and I put together for the bike. But there my bike sat in transition, loaded down with food and drink for the day's ride up to Hawi Town and back, but it wasn't going anywhere. I was destroyed.

SHORTLY AFTER MY near miss on the steps of the swim out, the Ironman officials, who I'd come to consider friends during the previous six months, informed me that they were inviting me back in 2010. My failure in the ocean was too close and too dramatic to remain my lasting legacy at Ironman. If it were a seven-minute miss, maybe they'd move on. But at seven seconds I made a good story even better for their television audience. I would have another shot in twelve months to fulfill the dream.

I cleaned up the best I could, changed clothes, and went to lunch at a restaurant called the Fish Hopper, overlooking the bay in which I'd just been swimming. I was coming back to Kona in a year, and that knowledge lessened the sting a bit, but most of my lunch was still spent in quiet contemplation. There are a thousand ways to make up seven seconds over the course of 2.4 miles. I'd started my race near the back and away from the chaos. Fifteen yards further forward could have made the difference.

The seasickness that I'd experienced seriously slowed the second half of my swim. A few less waves, maybe something different for breakfast, or more experience in the open water could have easily closed a seven-second gap. Or I could have just been faster, just a little bit. Or straighter.

Just better.

I finished up lunch, a meal I should have been taking on my bike. Ready to leave the restaurant, I was approached by our waitress. She knew me by name from having seen me at the end of the swim, and she handed me a handwritten card. Inside this token of kindness and concern were words of encouragement from every single member of the service staff. They'd heard my story and all stood on their patio to cheer me in. They were as disappointed as an old friend would have been at my disqualification.

It was one of the most touching gestures I've ever received or witnessed, and it was exactly what I needed. I still have that card, and I read it often.

The rest of the afternoon was spent back at our condominium. I took a nap, showered, and for the first time thought seriously about the next year of training that lay ahead. I'd said yes immediately to Ironman's offer of a return trip to Kona in 2010, but that did mean another year of sacrificed mornings, painful feet, and saddle sores. It meant another year of juggling bike nutrition and mixing bottles filled with electrolytes and carbohydrates. It meant another year of having to say no to late nights, long weekends, and beers with buddies over baseball. Was I prepared to make another such commitment for another twelve months?

Absolutely. It's what I'd become, the guy who doesn't give up. I get knocked down, but I always get back up. I try and I fail, but then I try again. I knew Ironman wasn't going to be easy. It just got a little harder, that's all. The reasons behind the dreams of crossing that finish line still remained. I still could.

That night I went down to Ali'i Drive for the final hour along the finish line. If you've never been to an Ironman, that last hour is pure magic. The pros who dominate the sport and cross the finish line in eight hours and change are impressive in their display of sheer athleticism. But it's the finishers who take more than sixteen hours to cover the 140.6 miles who have the true strength of heart and will. They earn their way to the finish by shutting out all natural human instincts to end suffering. They don't find their limits; they push beyond them. They chart previously unnavigated paths through unimaginable pain to the safety and pleasure of the dreamed-about end goal. When everything they instinctually listen to yells, "I can't," they instead focus on the one lone voice on their shoulder that quietly whispers, "I can." For these people there is no wall, there is no quit, and there are no limits.

I was down about the outcome of my day. I'd awoken that morning at 4 AM expecting to be among the ragged and limping heroes, but instead I was reduced to a spectator. I wanted the beckoning of the bright lights those final few miles and the thrill of the finishing chute. I wanted that moment and that medal. Instead I got a pat on the back and the unfulfilling consolation of "next year."

Then I saw the first late-night finisher cross the line; the crowd cheered as if he'd just been crowned the champion. The next finisher appeared in the distance, and a deafening roar brought him home. Thousands of people were dancing and smiling and rooting on total strangers in the final few yards of the best day of their lives. On several occasions I choked up, no longer because I'd wanted it to be me, but because you could see the rivers of joy in each finisher's tears. Why did I want to do Ironman? Because of these moments, these people, and that triumph.

October 10, 2009, was a great day. Disappointing, of course. It was not the dream that had put me to sleep so many previous nights. But there I was, three years to the day after my heart transplant and more than twenty years since I heard my first cancer diagnosis, healthy and happy and living the fantasy of everyone who competes in triathlon. I had friends who were willing to follow me thousands of miles to support my endeavors (although a trip to Hawaii has rarely been called a sacrifice) and a family and wife who stood by me without question, good swim or bad.

I would be back next year with a score to settle.

17

KONA, TAKE TWO

On December 3, 1967, in a nine-hour surgery performed with a team of more than thirty people, Dr. Christiaan Barnard successfully transplanted the first human heart. Its recipient was a fifty-four-year-old grocer from Cape Town, South Africa, who was suffering from diabetes and incurable heart disease.

When writing about the likelihood that Louis Washkansky would survive the surgery he'd been pioneering for several years, Barnard said, "For a dying man it's not a difficult decision because he knows he is at the end. If a lion chases you to a bank of a river filled with crocodiles, you will leap into the water, convinced you have a chance to swim to the other side." Washkansky was able to swim in that river for a total of eighteen days before succumbing to pneumonia brought on by his immunosuppressive drugs.

On December 2, 1967, twenty-four-year-old Denise Darvall was hit by a drunk driver. A day later, she became the world's first heart donor.

I don't know the name of my donor or much about his biography beyond a few basic facts. The family never contacted me after I sent my letter in 2006. But I don't need a name or a face to think of him daily. He walks with me every moment of every day. He runs, rides, and swims with me. I've worn a red reminder band on my right wrist since shortly after transplant, and with every stroke of my right arm, I see its color flash by my peripheral vision.

He's crossed every finish line that I have and made every early morning training ride without complaint. And he was sitting with me on the steps leading out of the water when my Ironman dream of 2009 ended seven seconds short of qualification to continue.

Following my near miss with the swim cutoff, I knew I wanted to grab the chance at redemption the moment the opportunity was offered. I'd lost too much sweat and too many hours of sleep to early morning alarms to let this opening slip away. There are no guarantees in life or in Ironman, but I was game for the challenge of another attempt.

I left Kona that year feeling very optimistic about the year of training and work that lay ahead. I'd only missed the cutoff by the smallest of margins, and there were hundreds of workout sets for me to swim in the coming year. I would conquer the 2.4 miles at my redo; that was a guarantee. Obviously there were still 138.2 other miles to train for, but as I was boarding my flight to leave the Big Island in 2009, I was feeling extremely upbeat. The positive energy of the place and the people of Ironman had replaced the momentary agony of the close call and subsequent early exit from the race.

A COUPLE OF months before my 2009 Kona attempt, my second sports book was released. Book one covered history's all-time worst umpiring and refereeing; with my second title, *What Were They Thinking?* I decided to alienate the rest of the sports world. It focused on the all-time biggest mistakes of coaches, general managers, players, fans, and the media. If you were guilty of history-making stupidity in sports, chances are I'd written about you in one of those two books.

Sportswriting is a lot of fun—who wouldn't want to write off DirecTV NFL Sunday Ticket on his or her taxes and actually have it be legal—but it was no longer my passion. Motivational and inspirational speaking had become my primary source of income and my primary source for professional gratification. It's very cool to walk into a Barnes & Noble or Borders and see something you created for sale on a special display table. It's incredibly rewarding to read a review from someone who likes your book and seems to have laughed at the places that you also thought were funny. But it can't compete with the feeling of reading an e-mail from someone who heard me speak or watched my story and is now ready to attack his own cancer. Or ready to embrace life after her organ transplant. Or now understands his loved one's struggle in an entirely new way. Or lost a loved one who went on to be an organ donor, which now gives her peace to see recipients flourishing because of the gift of transplant.

Heading into my second long year of Ironman training, I needed those e-mails. I set up a Facebook fan page to inspire those who needed it and to let people around the world follow my road back to Kona. But in truth, the majority of the inspiration flowed in my direction. That page, as well as the interaction with the people I spoke with during the course of my year, fueled my workouts. They got me out of bed in the morning for early rides and runs. When it was cold and rainy and a swim felt like the worst possible way to spend an evening, I read the notes I'd received from newly transplanted patients who just wanted to scale a staircase. Or newly listed future recipients just hoping for their miracle.

In November 2009 Carrie completed her own Ironman, crossing the finish line of Ironman Arizona in just under sixteen hours. It was a proud moment for the both of us, and it further deadened the sting of my Ironman failure the month before. But it also put her in a unique position to help me train for 2010. She was coaching triathlon for Team In Training at this point, and now she had an Ironman finish under her belt. She too became my inspiration, my Ironman mentor, and an extremely convenient workout partner.

We continued to live our normal lives throughout 2010. She changed firms, turning her brutal Los Angeles commute into an easy ten-minute walk to work. My speaking opportunities expanded beyond the borders of the United States; twice I traveled to Europe to speak to groups there. We remained active with Team In Training and continued to support the other causes that had been so instrumental in advancing the fields of discovery most responsible for my life and good fortune. And we made sure to find time for each other with weekend getaways, area restaurant explorations, and dinner parties with close friends.

The year 2010 for us was normal in every respect, except one. Every decision I made, every meal I ate, and every night out I took had to be reconciled with the most important question of my year: Will this help me reach the Ironman finish line?

From the moment I boarded the plane for my flight off the Big Island in 2009, my internal calendar was focused on the Ironman the following October.

As I ENTERED the water on the morning of October 9, 2010, I didn't give the previous year's swim a single thought. I was focused on form, on remaining confident, and on swimming with as much energy as I could create. I honestly did not flash back once to 2009. I'd done more than enough thinking about that day, that swim, and the seven-second margin that left me defeated on the steps. I had a 2.4-mile job to do that was unrelated to what did or didn't happen twelve months earlier.

The water was pretty rough that morning. Climbing down the stairs, I noticed that the ten-foot beach, which usually lies uncovered against the seawall at 6:30 in the morning, was instead hidden beneath a series of breaking swells. One large swell came in, broke on the steps, and nearly knocked over several swimmers, prompting one of my fellow racers to voice what all of us were thinking: "That's not good."

It wasn't the "good" and calm flat waters that we'd all been hoping for the night before. But there is only so much you can control in an Ironman, and the weather and water conditions have never been among them. So I noted the waves, mentally added five minutes to my expected time, and then moved on to my warm-up. I still had this.

My plan was to get in a solid fifteen or twenty minutes of warm-up swim. Swim hard, swim easy, and swim with stroke focus. Then I'd get into position for the start and float for a few minutes, waiting for the frenzy that would follow the crack of the cannon.

But warming up with eighteen hundred of your friends is a lot easier said than done. In each direction I went, I couldn't get more than ten strokes in before running into a wall of people. To the left and closer to shore was the only place where the crowds were breaking, but for good reason—that's where the waves were also breaking. So I did as much back-and-forth swimming as the growing mass would allow, then settled into a spot about forty feet behind the floating Ford Edge. (Ford is the title sponsor of the Ironman World Championship and always displays a vehicle on a floating island near the start.)

With the cannon shot, we were off. I was in moderate traffic, occasionally getting bumped and grabbed. But one of the advantages of swimming in the clear waters of Hawaii is the full vision you have. Contact, while fairly constant, is usually slight. You can see where you're going and who is already there, so you can avoid them. When you're close to the buoys, you can actually follow the cable all the way to the ocean floor. This allows you to navigate around the buoy and the gathering bodies more easily.

On occasion there was someone on my heels who repeatedly hit my feet with each stroke, and that got annoying. I could easily see the feet in front of me. Couldn't they see mine?

Thirty minutes in and the crowds were still consistent, which for me was only a positive thing. This race is filled almost entirely with qualifiers—that is, people who are great swimmers. The longer I could go without being dropped by everyone, the more my confidence grew. In fact I was feeling so good that when I would encounter the good swimmers passing me, I'd actually pick up my pace for two hundred yards or so and draft off their wake.

I was feeling strong, and that only made me feel stronger.

I hit the swim turnaround at what I would estimate was around the fifty-two-minute mark. I'd set my watch alarm to go off every fifteen minutes so I could keep track of the time in my head without having to kill the stroke to look at my watch. Since I don't swim with earplugs, I was able to hear each alarm.

At fifty-two minutes, exactly halfway into the race, I knew I was getting out of the water before the cutoff. Because of the currents and wave patterns, the second half of the Kona swim is a little longer than the out leg, but it's not enough to cause me problems. I was still with people—in fact passing a few that were taking a breather by hanging on to the turn-around boat's anchor—and I was feeling strong.

As I PREPARED for my Ironman attempt in 2009, I was still dealing with frequent ripples of self-doubt. There were the reflexive actions of the habitual, when my body's autopilot would kick in and force my physical self to pull back as if I was wearing the reins of a racehorse. I'd lived for so long having to be careful with my heart and making sure that nothing I did stressed it that any shortness of breath I experienced was treated like an automatic alarm. High heart rates and heavy breathing no longer carried the same risks, but the instinct that had been born in the eleven years of my cardiomyopathy was hard to switch off.

I also still had mental hurdles to get over. I thought of myself as a heart transplant patient first and athlete second, and I often allowed that status to dictate what I thought I could or couldn't do. I'd become a prisoner of my own modest expectations when I should have been reaching for the freedom and hope of endless promise that my new heart provided. I needed to become Kyle, the *blank*, with the *blank* being anything that wasn't patient related.

Changing my own self-perceptions was a large part of my 2010 training. Coach Paul, every bit as dedicated to my race-day triumph as I was, helped facilitate this growth as an athlete by asking me to do things that I'd avoided the year before. For example, I was a firm believer in my own inability to tackle any of the favored major canyon climbs in Southern California. I'd avoided one such climb, Latigo Canyon Road, like it was a Sarah Jessica Parker romantic comedy. It would end predictably: with my being very unhappy and needing a stiff drink. Same with the climb.

But in 2010 Paul and I tackled Latigo Canyon together. I was no king of the mountains that day, and if it wasn't for the decimal point on my speedometer, I might not have any actual evidence that I was moving forward. But he coached and I climbed, and I didn't collapse into a weeping pile of "I can't." It was a huge step forward.

We'd also made some of those same moments in the swimming pool during my countdown to Kona in 2010. Rest periods were shorter, efforts were more intense, and the expectations of me as an athlete kept pace with the physical growth that I'd gained by being another year out from transplant.

Mental hurdles can turn into impenetrable barriers if they are allowed to sit ominously unchallenged. So much of life is about effort—with enough of it, even the most modest of abilities can be enough to scale the previously insurmountable. What separates the doers from the dreamers is that effort. It's the belief that no hurdle, however big in your mind, will be too big in reality. The conquering of your mental hurdle is every bit as important in life as the accompanying physical preparation.

I went into the 2009 Ironman World Championship hoping that I could get my body across the finish line. By 2010, I knew I could.

WHEN YOU GO for a long swim, or long anything, you spend a lot of time in your head. Even when you're completely focused on the task at hand, as I was with my swim in Kona, your mind is still open and aware. While my brain was passing orders down the chain of command to my hands, arms, and legs, I noticed the fish below me. I took in the color of the surfboard that my main escort paddled on for the final mile of my swim. As for him, even though I only saw him through the foam of each breath to my right, I could easily pick him out of a lineup today.

Meanwhile I was having the usual conversations in my head about the swimmers around me, patting myself on the back when I was keeping up with or even passing others. I was counting the buoys and alarm beeps on my way back to dry land, tossing around the beginnings of my preparation for the bike, and giving myself a pep talk for the rest of the long day ahead.

When my alarm struck one hour and forty-five minutes into the swim, I glanced up at the pier that acts as the finish line for the swim and the transition area for the race. I could break two hours if I really hustled. So I did.

I spent the next fifteen minutes digging down as much as I could. I hadn't stopped to rest at all during the swim. All of my recoveries in the middle of those 2.4 miles were active recoveries. All swims, no treading.

There were several times in the water when my body wanted to take a break. It was asking me to stop and catch my breath. And there were a couple of moments when I nearly gave in, telling myself that just ten seconds of normal breathing and no swimming would have me back on the comfortable side of the anaerobic wall.

But I kept pushing, determined to break that two-hour mark.

Inside a couple of hundred yards left, I could begin to focus on the crowds cheering. I could hear people up on the pier on my left side— where Carrie turned out to be—shouting my name. I was getting the thumbs up from my surfboard-powered escort. It was a good start to a long day and hopefully a harbinger of things to come.

My watch alarm went off to signal two hours with me still twenty-five yards short of the swim finish. Oh well. All was still well. I was getting out of the water twenty minutes earlier than I had the year before, and I was confident. In the two weeks that I had been in Hawaii I'd done a series of rides along the course, and by race day I had ridden the entire thing. I knew what was ahead, I knew the conditions that I would face—I'd done a pretty hairy ride six days earlier in vicious crosswinds—and I knew that my body had been trained to ride 112 miles. And I'd have more than eight hours to get it done.

Out of the water and up the stairs, I shared a high five with the voice of Ironman, Mike Reilly. A year earlier he'd been on the steps calling the dramatic moment of my swim against the clock. This year he was there to announce to the crowd my triumph in the swim and to greet me with a big smile.

Quickly I went over to Andy Anderson, the timing judge who was forced to disqualify me in 2009. I'd seen him at the welcome dinner two nights before and promised that I wouldn't be putting him in that position a second time. That Saturday morning we exchanged a brief hug as I kept my promise.

Then on to the freshwater showers to rinse off some of the salt. My body was still shaking, a little from the rocking motion of the ocean, a little from the adrenaline, and a lot from the exertion. With calves that were sore from all the cramping I'd experienced while swimming, I wasn't exactly running through transition with any grace. But I eventually made it through the maze of swimmers, volunteers, and television cameras.

Into the tent, and two more volunteers immediately came to my aid. They took my bike gear bag and dumped it on the floor, grabbed me a towel, and even stopped to help massage my calves. Changing at an Ironman is like Jiffy Lube's full-service fourteen-point check.

My change from wet swim skin to dry cycle gear was complete in just a few minutes. I ran out of the tent and around the pier, finally reaching my bike after what felt like the first half of my marathon—my legs were sore and my head thought we were still swimming. Once at the bike, I stuffed some needed food into my bento box and quickly unracked it from slot 157. Wading through the cameras of NBC Sports, I stopped briefly to answer one quick question about how the swim felt, and I think I said something like "Good to get that monkey off my back." I really have no idea. I was focused on the mount line ahead and the very cool reality that I would shortly begin riding my bike at the Ironman World Championship. With the swim conquered and behind me and with the mental hurdle of Kailua-Kona Bay no longer my personal barrier, I was moving on.

That initial stretch up Palani Road and then left on Kuakini Highway is incredible. Throngs of cheering supporters line both sides of the road. When it's past the two-hour mark before you make it out of transition in Kona, you're pretty much alone. There were no other cyclists on the road with whom I had to share those cheers. It lasted for only a few seconds, but my heart swelled with pride.

Around the corner on Kuakini there is another PA system set up, and once again I heard the retelling of my story to the crowd: "Heart transplant . . . missed the swim cutoff in 2009 . . . now on the bike course. . . . Go, Kyle!"

The rest of Kuakini is pretty deserted, as is the turn north up Makala and onto the Queen K. And I was thankful for that. About halfway up the rise of Makala I became incredibly short of breath. I tried to slow my breathing, telling myself to relax, slow the adrenaline, and stay within myself. But the breathing issues remained, and the swirling clouds in my head were only getting worse.

I pulled over, stopping to catch my breath and take the break that I never really got in transition.

I still felt positive about things. I didn't feel that there was anything to panic about. After a moment or two my breathing slowed, and I got back on my bike.

But after I got to the top of Makala—a very modest rise—and made the right hand turn onto the Queen K, my head wasn't feeling any better. My breathing was once again becoming labored. I passed a couple of volunteers sitting along the side of the road—the rest of the road was nearly deserted—and after about one hundred more yards, I decided to pull over again.

Now there was panic. Now there was fear. I was only a few miles into a 112-mile bike ride, and these were some of the easiest miles on the course. Something was clearly happening to me, and for the first time that morning I thought about the possibility of not being able to finish.

I was by no means going to give in to that fear. I still was fairly confident that all I needed was another moment or two to rest and recover. Once things equalized I'd be set and ready to roll. I sat down, and that got the attention of the nearby volunteers. They came over and held my bike for me while I lay down and tried to get blood to my head.

A moment later I got back up, grabbed my bike, and thought about getting back on. But my head was still swirling, and I was just not feeling right. I sat back down.

Next to join me along the side of the road was a roving medical team. The volunteers had called them, and they'd been fairly quick to respond.

After getting a brief explanation of my not-so-brief medical history, they took my blood pressure. It was 80 over 60, which for me is incredibly low. I typically run around 135 over 80, and that's with medication to bring my blood pressure down. I don't naturally have high blood pressure, but it goes up as a side effect of the antirejection medications I take.

Because of my history, because of my blood pressure, and because my heart was racing, the medical team wanted to take me down to the main medical tent and put me through an EKG. Knowing that a trip in their van to the medical tent would end my day in disqualification, I politely declined. I asked for a few more minutes of feet-up time to see if that would solve the problem.

But as I lay there, looking up at a magnificent blue sky, I felt the Ironman slipping away. I was out of the water, but the clock was still ticking. My margin for error on a course as difficult as Kona is small. Time on my back was time lost. And a significant loss of time would be enough to steal my day.

I got up but stumbled as I did. My head was still fuzzy and light. I begged for five more minutes.

Back down in the grass with my feet up, staring at the empty sky, I felt helpless. I remembered back to the many ceilings I've stared at with that same feeling of complete incapacity. The ceiling in the bone marrow transplant ward at City of Hope. I would be sick, exhausted from vomiting what little food I'd felt like eating, and certain that I was dying. I would lie in bed, looking up at the ceiling and counting the tiles, then the holes in each tile, while waiting for the next nurse's visit, which would provide, if even for only a moment, enough human interaction to carry me through until the next nurse's visit.

I remembered lying on the table in the operating room at UCLA for almost an hour before they finally put me to sleep for my heart transplant. There were three or four people in the room—I couldn't be sure of the exact number, as I'd already been strapped in and all I could see were the lights hanging above me.

They added an IV line to this arm. Then to the other. Machines were moved into place. Trays of tools were opened and prepared. A few phone calls were taken. And all the while, all I could do was lie there on my back, staring up at the lights, powerless to affect the next several and most important hours of my life.

And that's how it felt in the grass along the Queen K Highway. The next several hours were supposed to be some of the most monumental in my life. In terms of shaping the perception of what a heart transplant patient can do, they were some of the most important. Yet I felt absolutely powerless to affect them.

We stood up one final time, but with no improvement. My day was done.

To be safe, the only option was to head to the medical tent and get an EKG. As I sat in the back on the medical team's van, hooked up to an oxygen tank and looking completely dejected and defeated, the television cameras arrived. For the second year in a row, one of my life's biggest disappointments would be captured on film and broadcast to the world.

Everything checked out as normal in the medical tent. In fact, the doctor commented on just how normal my EKG looked. I got a bag of fluid, stayed on oxygen for another hour, and, after proving that I could sit up without passing out, was released from medical and free for the day. Another day of being a spectator at the Ironman after beginning the morning as a participant.

I was admittedly angry. I was ready for this. I had trained hard for this. I'd improved my swim time by a full twenty minutes, slaying the dragon that had taken me down a year earlier. And yet here I was again, having lunch along Ali'i Drive on the afternoon of the Ironman when I should instead be eating out of my bento box somewhere along the 112-mile bike course.

But there was no one for me to be angry with. The medical team made the right call. They encountered an athlete with extremely low blood pressure and light-headedness who wasn't getting any better. Even if I hadn't been a heart transplant, I would totally understand their decision to take me to the medical tent. So was I angry with myself? Had I not put up enough of a fight? Was I at fault for what happened? Could I have done anything differently?

I could have done a few things differently. On long training days and race days, I don't typically take my morning medications until after I'm done. They tend not to mix well with Gatorade and the like, so I save them for later. But on this morning, because I was planning on going without my meds until late into the night, I did take my blood-pressure medication. So I didn't take the medications that drive my pressure up, but I did take the meds that bring my pressure down.

That probably wasn't the lone reason for what happened. I had also just been lying flat in the ocean for more than two hours, exerting myself quite extensively. I then hopped out of the water, ran up some steps, and never really took a moment to allow myself to recover. Throw in a de-nerved heart and my full dose of blood-pressure-lowering medication when most likely none was called for, and you get blood pressure that bottoms out.

The good news for me going forward was that those things were manageable. They didn't represent a structural problem with my heart or my permanent deficiency as an athlete. But the very bad news on that day was that the dream of the magical midnight moment at the finish line in Kona had been lost for a second time.

EPILOGUE

TODAY, TOMORROW, AND THE NEXT

I was never able to put a truly definable finger on a reason, but my miss at Kona in 2010 was much harder than it was in 2009. Perhaps it was the fatigue from another year of training, yet one without a finish line at the end. Maybe it's because I was far more confident in myself heading into 2010, so I was less prepared for failure. Perhaps it's because in 2009 I simply didn't swim fast enough. It was completely within my control. The nature of this second failure made me feel like the patient that I used to be, vulnerable to the whims of a body beyond my control.

I'd learned long ago not to live my life as a Monday morning quarterback. Your life's plan hardly ever lines up with life's reality. I could dissect to death the reasons for my failure and come up with another dozen or so explanations as to why it played out the way it did that morning in Kona, but none of it would change the result I ultimately had to live with. Other than education for a better foundation at my next go-around, the exercise was unnecessary pain. And the reasons behind the shifts in disappointment were ultimately unimportant as well. Moving on and accepting my new path was paramount.

A month after Kona I was able to squarely move beyond its letdown with a day of wonderful triumph along the coast of Wilmington, North

Carolina. Early in 2010 I was contacted by a heart transplant recipient named Brian Barndt. He'd heard of me and my Kona attempt in 2009 through the heart transplant grapevine, and he'd hatched an idea for an all–heart transplant Iron-distance relay team. He wanted to know if I was interested, and he wanted to make sure I knew that he would be taking the swim portion. (Apparently the image of me crumpled and sobbing on the steps of the Kona swim out didn't speak loudly to my future swimming glories.)

Not taking Brian's assertive swim declarations personally, I immediately said that I was interested and that I would be doing the bike. I just love the run so much that I figured I'd leave it for someone else to enjoy. That someone ended up being a Canadian named Mark Black, who'd also had a double lung transplant at the same time he'd received his new heart. (Show-off.) Brian and I had opened an Internet-wide search for the third member of our relay team, and we were just about to give up and settle for a transplanted kidney (does that even qualify as a transplant anymore?) when Mark found us.

Through the magic of Facebook and with the help of three great transplant teams from three different corners of the North American continent, our team, The Tin Men, was born. (Like the Tin Man of *Wizard of Oz* fame, we all needed hearts.)

We competed together at the Beach 2 Battleship Iron-Distance Triathlon in Wilmington, North Carolina, as the first-ever all–heart transplant relay team to cover 140.6 miles. It was an amazing testament to the power of transplantation and to the life that can be lived on this side of that dark and scary storm. The Tin Men will continue as a team, conquering more courses, winning more medals, and living more of the moments that we all thought were nothing more than figments of a fantastical future we would never see. It's never felt so good to be so wrong.

DURING ONE OF my television interviews before Kona, I was asked by a reporter, "With so many cancer diagnoses, and then a heart transplant, are you the luckiest man on Earth, or the unluckiest?"

I was taken aback by the angle of the question. I thought the answer was so obvious that someone who'd been fortunate enough to avoid anything truly catastrophic in his life would have to be the only one who could ask it. "The luckiest, of course," I responded without hesitation. "It's been more than two decades since I was first diagnosed with cancer. I had a heart transplant and surgeries to replace two joints. Yet yesterday I went for an eighty-mile bike ride. Tomorrow I'm going to swim a mile and a half with my wife, who loves me. And next week we leave for Hawaii where my parents, my mother-in-law, and a dozen other friends are going to join us for the greatest sporting event on the planet, and I get to participate. The word 'unlucky' doesn't enter into one facet of my life."

The simple fact is that people get diagnosed with cancer every day. I was one of them. People find themselves locked in battle with recurrent cancer. I was one of those. And people, every day, are being added to the organ transplant waiting list. I was one of those people as well.

Why should I have been exempt from any of these lists? Would it have been fairer if it had been someone else diagnosed with cancer instead of me? Would the balances of life be more equal if it was someone else who suffered the heart damage and then found him- or herself in need of a transplant? The answers, to me, are obvious. And hopefully by this point in the book, the answers are obvious to everyone.

The brightest minds and kindest hearts have worked tirelessly to keep me alive all of these years: from my very first oncologist, with his less-than-perfect bedside manner, to my current hematologist, Dr. Anthony Stein, a brilliant physician who doubles as my friend, to the men and women who make up my heart transplant team and work as the medical team for so many other lucky heart transplant recipients. Without these people and the loving and devoted nurses who have dedicated their lives to treating the sickest of the sick, I would not be here today.

For more than two decades, my parents, never wavering in their support, have walked the road with me, especially when it turned the most treacherous. Friends like Jessica, Ted, Inga, Meghan, Todd, Tim, Jim, Shawn, Chris, and Paul stood steadfast when I needed them most. And many of them today still work toward helping me achieve my life's goals and dreams.

Jessica and I remain close all these years and life experiences later. In 2005 she came to my wedding with her soon-to-be husband, and she will forever be someone whom I admire, trust, and respect. It's been said that adversity doesn't build character, it reveals it. I know no better example of that than my friend Jessica.

Carrie jumped headfirst into the fire with me, unsure of what she'd find. But with her trust, faith, and love to warm the coldest of possible future nights, I have little doubt as to our ability to handle whatever life's randomness has in store.

No doubt my survival and current life has been the result of an indefatigable team effort. Remove any one of these integral moving parts, and my place in today's world is anything but assured. But at the heart of it all, at the center of this success, was my own personal decision to survive. I made the decision to get up each morning and continue the fight for life. It was my choice to never give up, no matter the odds, no matter the pain, no matter the final price. It was my choice to find joy in life, however long of a life that may turn out to be.

It's a choice all of us have the innate power to make. We all have that same strength churning and swirling within us, just waiting to be tapped. Life can and should be great and wonderful and full of realized dreams. It should be filled with people who bring out your best. It should fill your soul to overflowing with the joy you have found and the knowledge that your life has also brought joy to others. You just have to make that choice.

In the coming years I will continue to have the joy of speaking to groups about my experiences and lessons learned. I hope to have more opportunities to write about those experiences, as well as to head out onto new life journeys yet to be taken. And you can be certain that one of the big joys that I continue to choose to pursue is the Ironman. It took four tries before I finally kicked cancer out of my life. My reality is that it's going to take at least three tries to finally get across that Ironman finish line. So be it. An adherence to life's formulated timelines has never fussed me much. Like with beating cancer, or receiving my new heart, or finally reclaiming my life, what mattered was the end and definitive result. And as with each of those challenges, eventually I will survive to the end of a 140.6-mile day.

These are the things I choose to do. These are the successes that I've chosen for myself. And they will, at some point, happen. I have made my choice.

What choices will you make?

INDEX

Gloucester County
Library System